Estranged Pioneers

Estranged Pioneers

Race, Faith, and Leadership in a Diverse World

KORIE LITTLE EDWARDS
AND
REBECCA Y. KIM

Oxford University Press is a department of the University of Oxford. It furthers
the University's objective of excellence in research, scholarship, and education
by publishing worldwide. Oxford is a registered trade mark of Oxford University
Press in the UK and certain other countries.

Published in the United States of America by Oxford University Press
198 Madison Avenue, New York, NY 10016, United States of America.

© Oxford University Press 2024

All rights reserved. No part of this publication may be reproduced, stored in
a retrieval system, or transmitted, in any form or by any means, without the
prior permission in writing of Oxford University Press, or as expressly permitted
by law, by license, or under terms agreed with the appropriate reproduction
rights organization. Inquiries concerning reproduction outside the scope of the
above should be sent to the Rights Department, Oxford University Press, at the
address above.

You must not circulate this work in any other form
and you must impose this same condition on any acquirer.

Library of Congress Cataloging-in-Publication Data
Names: Edwards, Korie L., author. | Kim, Rebecca Y., 1974– author.
Title: Estranged pioneers / [Korie L. Edwards, Rebecca Kim].
Description: New York, NY, United States of America : Oxford University Press, [2024] |
Includes bibliographical references.
Identifiers: LCCN 2023033890 (print) | LCCN 2023033891 (ebook) |
ISBN 9780197638309 (hardback) | ISBN 9780197638323 (epub)
Subjects: LCSH: African American clergy. | Multiethnic churches—United States. |
Leadership—United States.
Classification: LCC BR563.N4 E393 2024 (print) | LCC BR563.N4 (ebook) |
DDC 277.308/2908996073—dc23/eng/20231012
LC record available at https://lccn.loc.gov/2023033890
LC ebook record available at https://lccn.loc.gov/2023033891

DOI: 10.1093/oso/9780197638309.001.0001

Printed by Sheridan Books, Inc., United States of America

Contents

Preface	vii
Introduction: The Triumphs and Pitfalls of Diversity	1
1. The Road Less Traveled: Journeys to Leading Multiracial Churches	16
2. Estranged Pioneers: Pastors of Color Leading Multiracial Churches	42
3. Managing the Challenges of Leading Multiracial Churches	67
4. Advantages to Leading as Pastors of Color: "Why Would Anyone Want to Do This?"	95
5. White Pastor Privilege	116
Conclusion: Estranged Pioneers	150
Appendix: Methods	169
Notes	175
Bibliography	183
Index	197

Preface

Diversity is all the rage, at least at this moment in history. Organizations of all types, whether in business, education, or religion, claim to value diversity. When it comes to the United States there is good reason to pay attention to diversity, particularly racial diversity. With every decade since the Immigration and Nationality Act of 1965, the United States has become increasingly diverse racially. In 1960, the United States was 89% white.[1] In 2020, it was 62% white.[2] By 2060, it is predicted that the United States will be 44% white.[3]

Growth as an organization in this era means embracing, as least in our discourse, that we live in and ought to thus reflect our racially diverse society. With the expansion of the Black Lives Matter (BLM) movement across the United States and globally to the Netherlands, France, Japan, Australia, and South Korea, among many other countries, during the spring of 2020,[4] being attuned to matters of racial justice and diversity became all the more important for organizations. According to Marketwatch, "two-thirds of the largest companies came out in support of BLM after the [killings] of George Floyd and Breonna Taylor" in 2020.[5]

Over the past couple of decades, there has also been a burgeoning body of research on diversity in organizations. We have seen a marked increase in scholarship on religious, racial, ethnic, and cultural diversity as well.[6] While there are ecological factors, like changes in community demographics, that facilitate religious organizations becoming racially diverse as well as various strategies churches engage in to promote a racially diverse space, scholars consistently find leaders to be pivotal in developing and sustaining diversity. Leaders are central to making sure diversity happens and happens in a way that is effective for the organization. For religious organizations, it is often the case that the head clergy intentionally spearhead the move toward racial diversity in their congregations. Still, although leadership emerged as a consistent factor in making racially diverse organizations work, existing studies (ours included) were mainly about the organizations and not the leaders of these organizations. Leadership was presented as one of several factors that mattered in a process of doing diversity. So, I (Little Edwards) thought, if leaders are so important for racially diversifying their organizations, then it is important to understand that role, besides the list of activities and strategies they might employ to make diversity happen. For example, why do they choose to do this? What are the challenges they experience, personally and organizationally, in moving their organizations toward racial diversity? What resources are available for them to successfully foster cross-racial community in their organizations? What is their leadership capacity? How is their leadership capacity and experiences as leaders shaped by their social environments and structures in which they are situated?

On the subject of leaders, one might ask why we focus on leaders of racially diverse churches in the United States? There are several reasons. Religious organizations, especially in the U.S. contexts, are different from their secular counterparts. Religion is voluntary. People do not have to go to church if they do not want to. They can go where they want when they want and for whatever reasons they have. Religious space is also critical to building community. For sure, people gain community from work and school, but community and social support are not the primary aims of these places and what people are looking for when they join these organizations. Relatedly, groups draw upon religion as a way to create a sense of identity. Religious practices, symbols, and ideologies become part of groups' repertoires of cultural elements that are deployed to proclaim "This is who 'we' are." In fact, this is in many respects why religious organizations are overwhelmingly racially segregated. Yes, there has been an increase in racially diverse churches in the United States, but 85% of them are racially homogeneous. And this is being generous.

Being voluntary and a source for community and group identity for people in an environment that at almost every turn tells people they are to do life with people who are racially similar to them, these qualities work against religious organizations becoming and continuing to be diverse. So leaders of religious organizations, unlike their counterparts in businesses or schools, are trying to make something happen in a rather difficult context. They cannot rely on sticks or negative consequences to motivate compliance, as they can in the workplace or schools. They must rely almost solely on carrots, appealing to people's moral commitments and values and tapping into their sense of who they are and aspire to be. Given the role of religious organizations in the American context, a study of multiracial church head clergy can tell us a lot about race, diversity, and leadership in America.

* * *

We are grateful to the religious leaders who graciously and generously shared time and space with us to tell us their stories. As I (Little Edwards) have repeatedly noted, time and energy are in short supply considering all the demands that are placed on clergy. We hope we have treated these stories well, with respect, care, and authenticity.

We are also grateful for the generosity of Lilly Endowment Inc. for providing the grant that allowed the Religious Leadership and Diversity Project team to conduct the research for this book. We are truly grateful for the careful reviews, feedback, and comments of our colleagues who interacted with earlier iterations of this work. We want to acknowledge the anonymous journal and book reviewers whose input helped us greatly as we refined our arguments and writing. We are grateful to our editor Theo Calderara and the rest of the Oxford University Press team for their insights and guidance in the book development process. We also benefited from people in our personal lives who supported us throughout the years we were working on this book. Finally, we would like to give special thanks to our families for their patience, care, and support in the conducting and writing of this research, which took us away from family activities from time to time.

* * *

This book is dedicated to all estranged pioneers, those from times past, those who continue the work today, in quite often racially treacherous terrain, and those who will carry on the work in the future.

Introduction

The Triumphs and Pitfalls of Diversity

We are in a curious moment in American history. More than at any other time, racial diversity is celebrated. From the boardroom to the classroom, from Hollywood to the newsroom, people talk of wanting and valuing diversity. There are racial diversity rankings for schools, workplaces, places to live, and houses of worship. Saying that you care about diversity is nearly a must for all leaders of institutions and organizations. Yet right alongside America's professed love affair with diversity racial strife and injustice persist. We see racial discrimination, systemic police killings of Black people (many of them children), harassment and violence toward Asian Americans, and families being separated at the border. There is a resurgence of white supremacist groups across the globe and a rise in white Christian nationalism, as exhibited by the riots and violence at the U.S. Capitol on January 6, 2021. We are witnessing mounting challenges to educating people about the social, legal, and historical institutionalization of racism and racial discrimination. Christian organizations are not necessarily any different. The Southern Baptist Convention, a denomination created specifically to maintain Christian support of and investment in America's chattel slavery system, recently passed a resolution against critical race theory (CRT),[1] an academic theory that argues race is central to the historical, legal, and social structuring of society.[2]

At a recent graduation ceremony at one of the most racially diverse seminaries in the country, students of color held up signs that read "I did not come to be schooled in White Supremacy, I came to be schooled out of it." Meanwhile, white evangelical elites are branding evangelicals who call out systemic racism and pursue racial justice as "social gospel CRT fanatics" that have lost their way as Christians.[3] People have called out white supremacy and systemic racism, and people have lashed out against exactly such calls. There can be no doubt: race still matters, and it matters profoundly for people's sense of self, safety, freedom, and life chances.

A common response to all this racial division, strife, and injustice is to foster diversity. We see this in all sorts of organizational environments. This is sometimes framed as multiculturalism, or it is expanded to include not just diversity but inclusion and in some other cases equity as well. Though what this means on the ground is less clear. For people of color, evidence suggests that diversity doesn't eliminate barriers to inclusion and advancement. If anything, it can lead to increased unpaid labor and burnout, as it is often people of color who end up bearing disproportionate responsibility for creating and sustaining diversity.[4]

Indeed, creating empowering, diverse, equitable social environments, whether for businesses, voluntary organizations, or not-for-profit organizations, is critically important. This is true not just in the United States but across the globe. The wave of Black Lives Matter protests that erupted during the spring of 2020 revealed the reality that racial strife and oppression is not felt just in the United States. A review of the literature on organizational diversity finds that studies are being done in and by scholars from, for example, France,[5] India,[6] Australia,[7] and Brazil.[8] A general thrust of these studies is on the workplace, where diversity is seen as important.[9] Diversity, equity, and inclusion matter across organizational types and societies. Given the current racial climate in the United States in particular, this will continue to be increasingly critical for U.S. organizations in the foreseeable future.

In this contentious climate where diversity is both acclaimed and assaulted, our book examines what it means for people of color to lead in racially diverse spaces. Multiracial churches have steadily grown in their share of churches in the United States. Today they make up 16% of all congregations. Two decades ago, they made up only 6%.[10] We have also seen a fourfold increase in the proportion of people of color who head multiracial churches, from 4% to 16%. For sure this is considerable growth, but the percentages of multiracial churches and pastors of color heading them were at quite low levels to begin with, 6% and 4%, respectively. This was more than thirty years after civil rights legislation was passed, which included affirmative action, antidiscriminatory legislation, and an act that facilitated emigration to the United States from countries across the Global South. Now, fifty-plus years after the civil rights legislation of the 1960s, racial segregation in churches remains the norm. Five of six congregations in the country are racially homogeneous.

The data for this book come from the first nationally representative comparative study of multiracial congregations across the United States that examines race and pastoral leadership, the Religious Leadership and Diversity Project (RLDP, 2014–16). RLDP data include over 121 personal interviews with pastors and denominational leaders, over six hundred surveys of congregations and congregants, three dozen focus groups with 230 congregants, and several follow-up interviews. For this book, we rely primarily on the 121 in-depth face-to-face interviews conducted with the head clergy of multiracial congregations.

The RLDP sample of clergy is diverse along several lines. They head congregations from a variety of Christian religious affiliations: Catholic, mainline Protestant, and conservative Protestant. They represent congregations of varying sizes, from fewer than one hundred regular attendees to giga-churches with more than ten thousand attendees and anywhere in between. They head churches across the country in all four of the U.S. census regions. The head clergy in our sample are racially and ethnically diverse; about 40% are people of color. Ten percent are women.[11] (See the appendix for more on our data and methods.)

Our data show that heading a multiracial church is difficult for all pastors, regardless of their race, religious affiliation, or other identities. Indeed, white pastors who head congregations of people of different racial and ethnic backgrounds face an uphill battle, relative to their white peers who head largely white congregations. Like pastors of color, they report that there are relatively limited institutional resources available for them to head their congregations. Some discuss the stress that comes with trying to build community across racial lines and the cross-racial tensions that emerge in their racially and ethnically diverse religious communities, even as they demonstrate a commitment to challenging structural racism and discrimination.

Take, for instance, Father Mann. I (Little Edwards) interviewed Father Mann, a white Catholic priest of a mainly Black and Hispanic[12] bilingual parish in a large city out west. The congregation was at one point an ethnic white congregation that turned into a Black and white congregation and that is now mainly Black and Hispanic with some white members. I found Father Mann to be quite approachable and easygoing. Off the bat, we were joking around a bit. Before becoming the head priest of this congregation, he was engaged in social justice activism as an associate pastor, which he actually preferred. The neighborhood where the church was located experienced considerable socioeconomic disadvantages, including poverty and unsupervised children. He made it a habit to interact with young people and families in the neighborhood. Being connected to the community was something he valued. He also wanted to understand race in America. To improve his understanding, he turned to books. He was one of the few clergy in our study who reported reading scholarly books on race, titles like *The New Jim Crow* by Michelle Alexander and *Categorically Unequal* by Douglas Massey, among others. He also sought out mentorship from Black Protestant pastors. My overall impression of Father Mann was that he was genuinely interested in justice work and building a safe and healthy cross-racial Christian community in his parish.

Even so, Father Mann was perhaps not yet "woke." According to him, one of the longtime members of his parish, a white man who predated Father Mann's hiring, told him that Father Mann was "just totally ignorant about Black culture." Father Mann's commitment to understanding systemic racial inequality and attempts to foster racial unity in his congregation are notable, though I could also see how one could come to the conclusion of this member. Father Mann grew up in a largely white suburb. The first time he saw a Black person was in the fifth grade, and the first time he saw an Asian person was in college. Of his childhood he says, "We really had a childhood. We had fun. We played together. We felt safe." His background did not prepare him for a vocation where building authentic religious communities and engaging in justice work among urban African Americans and Hispanics was his primary responsibility.

Over the course of the interview, we began to delve into the challenges he experienced heading the congregation. One that gave him considerable stress was figuring out how to build a bridge between the newer Hispanic immigrant congregants and the older Black congregants. Strategist that he was, he had devised a plan to do so and felt good about it, though it was difficult, in part because some of the Hispanic immigrant congregants were prejudiced against the Black congregants. He recounted one instance when a young Hispanic child in the church hurled a racial epithet at an older Black woman in the congregation. Some of the Black congregants were feeling disrespected and were concerned about displacement from a space that had been central to their sense of community and safety in a racially hostile urban environment.

For sure this would be a challenge for any leader to navigate. As a pastor of a multiracial church, Father Mann experienced quite a lot of stress associated with his position. However, he did not have to stay there. And in fact, he did not. He had an escape hatch and he took it. He was slated to go on sabbatical in the coming year and afterward was headed to a largely white, "affluent" (his word) parish in another part of the state. Pursuing racial diversity and engaging in justice work was a choice for him. He was able to opt out of racial diversity and justice and return to the comfort of affluent white homogeneity.

In this book, we focus on pastors of color for several reasons. Father Mann's story provides some insight into why. One reason is that, unlike white pastors, they do not have an escape hatch available to them to easily vacate multiracial church ministry, even if they want to take it (and our interviews suggest they just might if they easily could). Like Father Mann, white head clergy of multiracial churches have greater opportunities to do pastoral work elsewhere, that is, in predominantly white congregations, if they decide they are no longer interested in leading racially diverse churches. This is not the case for pastors of color. It is more difficult for pastors of color to go back to their ethnoracial[13] home religious communities once they are on the road of multiracialism in the church.

Pastors of color are consuming an increasing proportion of multiracial church head clergy positions in the United States. These are pastoral positions that come with considerable stress and strain. Moreover, the journey is especially hard on them personally. It is already a rough road being a pastor. Multiracial church pastors have an even harder time as head clergy. They are leading people to build community—and by "community" we mean equitable, just spaces of mutuality—across racial lines in a society that works against racially diverse communities. But the pastor of color of the multiracial church has the hardest of roads to traverse. The broader sociohistorical context as well as their immediate Christian community privilege whiteness and erect barriers for them along the way. Their ethnoracial religious home communities are no longer reliable social and cultural resources for them. Still, even despite this, the pastor of color has the potential to be the best equipped to do this kind of work.

We make three primary arguments in this book. First, we argue that pastors of color who head multiracial congregations are what we call *estranged pioneers*. They are leaders of color who leave their familiar ethnoracial home churches to explore a new way of doing church by leading multiracial congregations. However, their endeavors are not valued by their home religious communities, and they are left to navigate a racialized space, including in the multiracial religious communities they head, where they are consistently perceived and treated as inferior to their white peers. Their home religious communities do not see the goals and aims of multiracial churches as aligning with those of their churches, which centralize the cultures and experiences of their ethnoracial group. Multiracial church pastors of color do not experience the same power and privileges as their white counterparts in multiracial congregations.

Despite the additional personal costs that pastors of color bear in their role as head clergy, our second argument is that pastors of color may have certain advantages that make them particularly well suited to lead in multiracial spaces. This is mainly due to their standpoint. Pastors of color have had to navigate life in a white supremacist world as a racial and cultural "other." This affords them a capacity for what we refer to as *racialized multicultural competency*. All of them are sufficiently and minimally bicultural and able to traverse at least two cultures, their own ethnoracial culture as well as the majority white culture. As a result of their experiences with individual and/or collective racism, they are likely better able to see and understand how the U.S. racialized system works when compared to their white counterparts. While the contours and levels of this proficiency for sure vary, we propose that leaders of color often have a racialized multicultural competency that can make them more suited to lead in multiracial spaces.

With their unique standpoint and competency, we argue that these leaders of color can function as indispensable brokers who can bridge segregated racial networks. We live in a society that is becoming increasingly racially diverse. A report by the U.S. Census Bureau says that between 2010 and 2020, "nearly all groups saw population gains. . . . The white alone population declined by 8.6% since 2010."[14] Today, the United States is 58% white, 19% Hispanic, 12% Black, and 6% Asian. It seems this broader diversity is having an impact on some of our institutions. We already mentioned we are seeing an increase in multiracial churches. The Black/white neighborhood divide, though still high, is on a slow decline. We have also seen a decline in the federal prison population since 2008, and this decline is evident across racial groups.[15] Yet, with all this diversity around us, racial segregation and racial inequality persist on multiple fronts. The neighborhood racial segregation of Hispanics and Asians, while it has not increased, has pretty much stayed the same since 2000, despite or perhaps because of their growing proportion in the American population. Neighborhoods are predicted to continue to be racially segregated for some time.[16] Racial integration of schools was on the rise in the 1970s and 1980s; however, there has been a retrenchment of racial segregation of schools since then.[17] The incarceration of Blacks and Hispanics remains very high. They still make up 33% and 23%, respectively, of the prison population. And while we have seen an increase in multiracial congregations in the United States, these churches remain overwhelmingly segregated. People who can broker relationships between disparate networks and communities are therefore needed.

In this context of persistent racial segregation and inequality, we have the multiracial church pastor of color. They do not necessarily have the capacity nor the insight to address all these issues. Such an expectation would be unrealistic. However, they are unique leaders in the U.S. landscape because they occupy structural holes that exist between largely segregated racial communities. In this strategic location, pastors of color with racialized multicultural competency are uniquely situated to function as brokers that connect otherwise segregated communities. As such, pastors of color are among a minority of formal leaders in the United States who may hold the keys to a more united multiracial future.

The Meaning of Diversity

Theoretically, racial diversity is important because it has the potential to minimize social inequality. Studies show that diverse spaces can lead to integrated intimate relationships[18] and potentially reduce racial prejudice and oppression.[19] In contrast, social and physical segregation limits the flow of ideas and resources, culture, and a sense of commonality.[20] It isolates the already disadvantaged and limits access to people who have the kinds of resources that facilitate socioeconomic mobility.[21] Examining the pervasive social and physical racial segregation in the South, Du Bois[22] famously showed how this can also cause sociopsychological damage and harm the very souls of Black people.

What does diversity really look like in the United States? What does it mean? The United States has always been racially diverse at some level. The first U.S. census in 1790 showed that people of color made up 20% of the country. The country was the least diverse in 1940, when people of color made up 10% of the country. Of course, these percentages vary by region. Black people have been and continue to be heavily concentrated in the South. Hispanics are heavily concentrated in the Southwest.[23] These are also regions where we have seen the most resistance to racial integration and equality. Think of chattel slavery, Jim Crow, campaigns of mass deportation of Hispanics, and the building of walls at the Mexico-U.S. border. Segregation in the midst of diversity is a long-standing practice in the United States. Social inequality and racial oppression persist right alongside diversity. Diversity alone does not mean there is equality and justice. Indeed, to have a racially oppressive society, that society needs to be racially diverse.

Over recent decades, scholars have begun to pay greater attention to this dynamic in a variety of settings, schools, neighborhoods, businesses, and religious organizations. The overall consensus is that modern-day diversity and affirmations of diversity in the United States are by and large social mechanisms that sustain structural racial inequality. This happens in a variety of ways. One is when diversity acts as a good, one that white people can use to feel morally superior to other whites, presumably "racist" whites. White people, in this case, intentionally live in integrated neighborhoods,[24] are engaged in racially diverse activist organizations,[25] or pursue interactions and relationships with people of color[26] to bolster their sense of who they are or aspire to be as white people. This is not limited to liberal whites. We also see evidence of whites who are members of white supremacist and nationalist organizations using their diverse social networks and appreciation of Black culture to protect themselves against claims of racism and assert that their racial attitudes are benign.[27] In short, people of color generally, and Black people more commonly, are seen as objects to serve white people's purposes. One is being antiracist when one is simply kind and civil to people of color.[28] Being a part of diverse spaces is a way for white people to project to themselves and others that they are better than other white people.[29] It is argued that they can do this without having any compunction because of socialization and lack of knowledge about the social reality and history of racism and racial injustice.[30] This allows them to assume an idealized white racial self.[31] Ultimately, white people draw upon a variety of cognitive mechanisms and frames to construct themselves as nonracists.

Another common pattern is that racial diversity cannot disrupt white comfort.[32] To disrupt white comfort is to disrupt the status quo, a world where white people, their culture, and status are still the norm. When your group's culture or status is normalized, other groups have to regularly address and respond to it, even if they don't want to. White comfort rests on maintaining white hegemony[33] and white habitus.[34] Edwards's[35] study of multiracial churches argues that racial diversity can be maintained to the extent that white congregants are comfortable. Multiracial congregations sustain white comfort by reproducing white hegemony, where "white hegemony is a form of rule where whites dominate society with the consent of [people of color]."[36] This manifests through the normalization of white people's culture in the space and structures that facilitate this arrangement. Burke (2012), in her study of a racially diverse urban neighborhood, similarly finds that well-intentioned residents reproduce white habitus, which Bonilla-Silva[37] defines as "a racialized, uninterrupted socialization process that conditions and creates whites' racial taste, perceptions, feelings, and emotions and their views on racial matters." Residents across racial identities express affirmations of diversity. Their actions, though, show that they are really invested in contexts that reproduce white middle-class values and norms. As Bonilla-Silva and Embrick[38] note, a persistent paradox exists between whites' stated affirmation of diversity and their persistent investment in white homophilous associations.

This aligns with other work that examines how people talk about diversity. Diversity discourse is what Bell and Hartmann[39] call "happy talk." It is void of any discussion of concrete racial inequalities and injustices, resides in the abstract rather than the concrete, and is limited to matters of diverse demographics. And it treats dominant American values as neutral, never problematizing their rootedness in whiteness and racism. Color-blindness is also threaded throughout diversity discourse as people call for diversity but do not see or acknowledge what is behind the racial segregation in the first place.[40] Diversity discourse focuses on mere demographic diversity, which subverts any real assessment and destabilization of the deeply structural and historical realities of racial inequality and injustice.

None of these processes, however, is about individuals. These are parts of a system where whiteness is rewarded and where challenges to whiteness are negatively sanctioned. It is tempting to boil racial injustice and inequality down to white people versus people of color. But white people can be antiracists in both their thoughts and their actions. And not all people of color are antiracists. People of color can intentionally or unintentionally participate in reproducing contexts that are oppressive to themselves. This ought to be expected. Everyone is socialized to affirm whiteness. People of color do not have automatic immunity to the messages we regularly receive in the media, at work, in school, and at church that say white culture and structural dominance are right. Scholars show that people of color reproduce white hegemony,[41] and racially diverse churches are no different.[42] We even see evidence of this at historically Black colleges and universities.[43] Whiteness is powerful.

Some people, and perhaps especially the people who lead, may hope that racially diverse religious organizations could be the one place where the commodification of people of color and happy talk would be limited. Given the history of the relationship between race and religion in the United States, this is truly a hopeful exercise. It has been repeatedly shown that religious space may in fact exacerbate racial division and oppression. This should not be surprising. As Emerson, Korver-Glenn, and Douds[44] have noted, in the United States "religion is racialized, and race is spiritualized."

More than a couple of decades ago Emerson and Smith[45] showed that Black and white conservative Protestants think about race in fundamentally different ways. Black conservative Protestants are more structural in their view, pointing to discrimination, for example, as a reason for racial inequality. White conservative Protestants are individualistic, boiling racial inequality down to personal immoral behaviors or failings. Other scholars suggest that this is not merely individualistic thinking but evidence of racist attitudes among white conservative Protestants.[46] Other work shows that diversity in congregations is managed in such a way that people of color are largely regulated to visible but powerless roles as a way to attract attendees.[47] Multiracial congregations draw upon color-blind frames that sanitize racial discourse. This happens through appealing to notions of shared humanity[48] or minimizing racial differences and emphasizing a Christian identity.[49] Religious leaders of multiracial churches similarly downplay racial inequality, drawing on a racial reconciliation frame that "suppresses" discourse and actions highlighting racial injustice and redirects the focus to maintaining unity and affirming people's Christian identity.[50] Racism is framed as a spiritual matter and thus insulated from secular solutions.[51] Similar to work on other organizations, matters of racial injustice can be solved by creating more diverse religious spaces that are devoid of structures that challenge and undo racism, both within and outside organizations. Multiracial churches are places, then, where white Christians evoke what Metha and her colleagues[52] call a "divinized colorblindness" to ignore their white privilege and maintain the white cultural and structural center.

Why Study Leaders of Multiracial Churches?

We have seen an increasing proportion of diverse churches in the United States over recent decades. This change may be due to a variety of reasons.

The country has become increasingly diverse since the passage of the 1965 Hart-Cellar Immigration and Nationality Act, which opened up immigration after having been severely limited for over fifty years. Greater diversity in the population increases the likelihood of diverse communities. Over the past couple of decades, we have also seen Christian leaders in some circles promoting the formation of multiethnic churches across religious traditions. We are seeing an emphasis on multiethnicity and racial diversity among evangelicals and mainline Protestants. The parish structure of the Catholic church along with high levels of immigration of Hispanic Catholics to the United States has facilitated an increase in diversity in Catholic parishes. Racially diverse parishes were seen as the norm among Catholic priests we spoke with in cities where we recruited participants. When asked if they could recommend diverse parishes in the area to us, a common response was "They are all diverse." Knowing the ethnoracial numbers for Catholic churches, we know they are not all diverse, but we suspect a good many are, especially in cities.

The racial compositions of the country more broadly, and religious space specifically, have changed over the past couple of decades. Given this, it is valuable to understand how people are leading multiracial churches, particularly in a broader field where, as noted previously, racial segregation remains the norm. Moreover, racial diversity is often touted as desirable. Yet what we consistently see is that, whether in churches, neighborhoods, schools, or businesses, diversity centers on whiteness and has little to do with undoing racial injustice or inequality.

Looking at head clergy of multiracial churches, who are shown to be central to how diversity works in churches, can therefore tell us how leaders navigate structures that on many sides work against what they are aiming to do. It can also show the extent to which they reproduce the very structures they may purport to want to undo.

Additionally, head clergy are similar to others who are leading diverse organizations. Like their peers in business or education, for instance, they too have to establish and meet the goals of their organization, maintain budgets, secure financial and human resources, manage other leaders and staff, and foster a positive work environment. Racially diverse churches are not exempt from the structural barriers that other racially diverse organizations face just because they are religious. Multiracial churches are under the stress of the forces of homophily, that process by which people "flock together" with others they perceive to be like them. They also have to deal with in-group bias where people favor those they perceive as being a part of their group, which in a highly racialized society like the United States means that people generally flock along racial lines.[53] In diverse spaces of business and education, this can work against creating a space of equity and fairness and can reproduce, whether intentionally or inadvertently, systems of institutional discrimination and bias. In churches, these processes have been shown to exclude people of color from power and influence and reproduce organizational structures and cultures that support white hegemony.[54]

While the experiences of leaders of multiracial churches are similar to those of other organizations in important ways, they are rather different in other ways. These differences matter for how leaders can cultivate racially diverse communities. Religion serves a unique function in society and for people. It provides a transcendent moral frame that anchors the ideas that inform the structures of other institutions. Religion also integrates people into society, providing a place where people can connect and build community. It is where people go for comfort and counsel when facing life's difficult events. Still, that which makes religious organizations distinct from, for instance, the workplace, neighborhoods, and schools in the United States—being wholly voluntary—can actually exacerbate tendencies toward homophily and in-group bias. Attendees can leave or switch their congregations whenever they want for whatever reason. People are free to switch workplaces, neighborhoods, and schools. Critical resources like money and educational credentials as well as market forces operate as barriers to accessing or switching among many of these spaces for many people. Leaders of organizations in other institutions can rely on both carrots (incentives) and sticks (negative sanctions) to compel people to be a part of their organization and behave in ways that support a diversity and justice mission. Multiracial church leaders, however, must rely almost exclusively on carrots (incentives).

Thus, a focus on multiracial church leaders allows us to understand how leaders can motivate organizational racial and ethnic diversity and inclusion without requiring it of people or relying upon "sticks" to make it happen. At the end of the day, people have to choose to follow their leaders and be part of a racially diverse community to make any kind of meaningful progress in interracial relations. Whether it is how people vote or whom they choose to befriend, studying multiracial church leaders enables us to see how leaders can compel people to voluntarily make decisions and act in ways that support building racially inclusive and just community.

Multiracial Churches and Their Leaders

Multiracial churches are embedded in white-male-dominated Christian traditions, whether those are Catholic, mainline Protestant, or conservative Protestant. This is true of the multiracial churches headed by white pastors as well as those headed by pastors of color. Multiracial church pastors, then, regardless of race, are embedded in organizations and networks that are largely white and that are organized and structured around the cultural norms of white people. Thus, white pastors in these contexts can more easily sustain and develop social ties with people who are like them, racially. And they are already proficient in the culture of the context because it is generally their "native" or first culture. Furthermore, white head clergy who choose to head racially diverse congregations actually gain prestige in their networks. This means that if a white head clergy of a multiracial church, like Father Mann, decides they want to move to a largely white congregation, they can do so without losing the support of their white peers in their network. They can even draw on this network to exit. That is because they are still in their structural and cultural context. By leaving, they don't risk losing their social networks or cultural capital. Doing diversity is in fact perceived as a noble cause, even if it is not a practical one.

Head clergy are charged with building community and connectedness—to the divine and other people—among groups of people who have different ideas about what is important for achieving these goals and how to go about achieving them. Although this can be difficult for any clergy, ethnic and racial diversity in the congregation adds layers of complexity to the challenge. Moreover, leaders of multiracial churches are charged with this difficult task of building community and connectedness in a societal context that is highly racialized.[55] Thus, what we have is leaders heading their diverse communities in a broader context that espouses and celebrates diversity and justice but does not support this socially or structurally. Religious leaders who aim to foster a racially diverse religious community, particularly in an egalitarian setting, are therefore swimming against the tide, if not a tsunami.

A good deal of scholarship, particularly the work of researchers between 2000 and 2010, focused on multiracial congregations.[56] There was a real growth in this work. As discussed elsewhere,[57] scholars arrived at rather consistent conclusions. One of the main conclusions is that it was the head clergy who were particularly consequential for churches becoming racially diverse and sustaining that diversity once obtained.[58] We learned that fostering racial diversity hinged, in no small part, on their own theology or philosophy about diversity.[59] The path they took toward becoming pastors along with their own racial background and experiences impacted how they led their congregations.[60] We also see that head clergy have had to be intentional and strategic in their efforts to racially diversify their congregations.[61]

Existing scholarship on multiracial churches also suggests that the path to starting a multiracial church or transitioning a church to becoming multiracial puts leaders in a challenging and precarious situation. The journey, not surprisingly, is not an easy one. For instance, a longitudinal study of congregational diversity in one denomination shows that racial diversity is related to a decline in church attendance, which likely also means a decline in resources available to these churches and their pastors.[62] Studies also show that congregants of multiracial churches may put on a happy face in public all the while feeling they do not get what they want from their church experiences, feeling less than satisfied with the direction in which their head clergy is taking the church, and even contemplating leaving the congregation.[63] "On the surface, multiracial churches, simply because they are numerically diverse, may look like successes, but a peek below the surface reveals they are not necessarily spaces that foster equality, justice, or belonging."[64] There is abundant evidence of this problem.[65]

There are considerable barriers in place that suggest that leadership for pastors of multiracial churches is far more complicated than simply choosing what to do and doing it. This is truer for religious leaders in the United States than elsewhere because they cannot compel people to attend their churches. They must appeal to them. Additionally, religious organizations are primarily places where people gain a sense of connection and identity.[66] Due to the principle of homophily, this is more easily achieved in homogeneous than in heterogeneous contexts. Encouraging diversity rather than homogeneity, then, invites tension.

Despite the tremendous task ahead of them, scholarship at the time of our study did not address these and other constraints on head clergy of multiracial religious organizations. What was missing and is still lacking today is attention to the structural context that head clergy are working with, where racial diversity and justice are celebrated but not structurally supported. These clergy have to make diversity happen in a racialized, segregated society where "birds of a feather flock together" when given any kind of opportunity to do so. Moreover, the aim of much of the scholarship on multiracial church leadership is to understand the congregations, not the leaders.

The Study

This book builds on the existing literature on multiracial churches by focusing specifically on the leaders and paying attention to how structural constraints impact their job as leaders of multiracial spaces. We do this by interweaving multiple theoretical frames and perspectives. We apply C. Wright Mills's "sociological imagination" to consider how the leaders' individual experiences of leading are connected to broader social structural and historical contexts. We incorporate social identities and social networks theories as well as race theory and pay attention to the "social facts" that govern the role of head clergy who lead multiracial congregations.[67] We bring to light the social matrix that the leaders are working in as heads of multiracial congregations.

In contrast to most studies on multiracial church leadership, which tend to be limited to a few case studies of pastors, this book is based on a comparative nationwide study of a racially diverse sample of head clergy who lead multiracial congregations. Moreover, unlike the majority of publications on leadership, which spotlights white leaders and only marginally, if at all, provides the perspectives of leaders of color, this book centers the experiences of pastors of color.

* * *

Pastors of multiracial churches are not miracle workers. They are people who for one reason or another ended up occupying a role in society that holds considerable promise but that is particularly challenging. Multiracial church pastors of color are situated in social locations in the American landscape that affords them a unique opportunity to take people beyond happy talk and lead in matters of racial equality and justice. Yet we are all too aware that potential and practice are not synonymous. These pastors will have to choose a hard road ahead if they want to lead others toward a more equal and just, racially diverse America.

In the pages that follow, we share who they are, the joys and challenges that come with being pastors of multiracial churches, and the implications of being a pastor of color of a multiracial church, for them and the broader American racial landscape.

1
The Road Less Traveled

Journeys to Leading Multiracial Churches

How did they get here? It is a reasonable question considering that most churches are racially segregated and most of the people in this study grew up in homogeneous churches made up of people from their ethnoracial group. Even now about 85% of churches are racially homogeneous. But nearly twenty-five years ago, that rate was close to 95%. We don't have representative, reliable data on the racial composition of churches prior to 1998, but we can imagine that churches were even more likely to be racially homogeneous then, when the pastors in our study were coming up. When you consider this level of racial segregation among churches, it is quite an unlikely path to end up heading a racially diverse congregation in the United States.

There are several common themes across the experiences of pastors that help us understand why they took this difficult path to head multiracial churches. Their paths are guided by the everyday, what we might think of as serendipitous interactions and experiences. Put another way, they did not plan on heading a multiracial church per se. For sure, several planted churches with the intention of creating a racially diverse religious community. This idea came well into their pastoral career. On the whole, their paths unfolded before them and now here they are, heading a racially diverse church. The factors that guided them are structural in nature. For instance, pastors and priests affiliated with denominations that have an episcopal polity are assigned by their denominations to their congregations. The racial compositions of the neighborhoods around their churches changed. They decided to accommodate the new populations. Pastors of color go to colleges or seminaries that are predominantly white Anglo or largely led and embedded in white Anglo Western Christianity. Experiencing sustained exposure to white Anglo Christianity and largely white Christian social networks impacted them and worked to diversify their social networks in the process.

There are other, though less common patterns that warrant noting as well. We touch upon these secondary patterns briefly here to provide a broader picture of the biographies of the pastors in our study. For instance, several pastors come from families where a parent or older adult relative was a pastor or missionary. Another common theme is that several pastors of color have racially diverse families; that is, their spouses or their children are of a race different from theirs. For several of the Catholic priests, Vatican II (when Catholicism opened up to diverse cultural expression and language in their masses) and the civil rights movement impacted how they understood the priesthood and how they would live out their ministry as priests. These priests came of age during an era when there was a strong focus on social justice, especially in the urban context. As this happened in the 1960s, it also means most of the priests in our study are older.

There is, of course, variation across pastors' biographical stories. Each pastor has their unique story and journey that led them to where they are now, heads of multiracial churches. They have their own experiences with family and friends. They come from different parts of the United States and even from around the world. They go to this or that college or seminary. They have their own childhood church experiences. Yet all this happens within a broader context where they make choices about their lives. Those choices are out of an array of opportunities available to them. Their experiences—where they grew up, where they went to school, where they go to college or seminary, whom they befriend and marry—are happening within a broader structure that guides them in ways beyond them. We highlight these common patterns across their varied stories.[1]

Telling Stories

The broader RLDP team wrote a series of articles on pastors of multiracial churches that touched upon a variety of issues, including worship, resources, and reconciliation frames. Oneya Okuwobi[2] wrote one piece for this series called "'Everything That I've Done Has Always Been Multiethnic': Biographical Work among Leaders of Multiracial Churches." It is about how pastors in the RLDP selectively draw upon and reflect on their biographies to make sense of why they ended up heading multiracial churches. She finds there are two types of stories pastors commonly tell about themselves and their journeys to becoming pastors of multiracial churches. One story is about past experiences with racial injustice and how these influenced their path. White pastors in the study talk of witnessing racial injustice in their towns or families. Pastors of color talk of racial injustice they or their family experienced. The other common story is how exposure to racial diversity during their formative years prepared them for their current role as a multiracial church pastor.

To elaborate on Okuwobi's[3] work on the pastors in the RLDP, we note that she looks at how pastors use stories to make sense of their lives—how they do the biographical work to explain themselves as leaders of diverse churches. They connect the dots for themselves and others, drawing the lines between life moments that might appear random and scattered. We are looking at their life journeys to see if there are similar "dots" across pastors' journeys. We are less interested here in how they make sense of how they got to where they are and more interested in what is common across pastors' biographies that might help us understand how people get to a place where they pastor multiracial churches in a society where this is uncommon.

There are multiple "dots" along their life journeys that we think matter. One is the polity of their religious affiliation. Whether their religious affiliation is episcopal, presbyterian, or congregational matters for how they end up heading a multiracial church. Another dot is exposure to and embeddedness in white Western Christianity. This is the water white pastors swim in, but it was not originally meant (and often still isn't) for pastors of color. College or seminary is a critical space where nearly all of the pastors of color first experience sustained exposure to white Western Christianity and white Anglo Christians. This is important because of their racially homogeneous religious socialization, particularly while growing up. Black pastors in our study, with one exception, were generally raised in predominantly Black churches. Asian American pastors similarly came from ethnoracial Asian churches, whether an Asian immigrant church (e.g., a Chinese immigrant church), an Asian American church, or an Asian ethnic church in Asia (e.g., a church in the Philippines). And Hispanic American pastors came from Hispanic immigrant churches, Hispanic American churches, or Hispanic churches in Latin America (e.g., a church in Colombia). White pastors generally grew up in largely white churches. These "dots" or life experiences or events begin to help us unravel how these pastors ended up heading racially diverse churches in a society where religious racial segregation is the norm.

Options

At times, the spiritual nature of the job of being a pastor can lead one to mystify the role. Because the people occupying this role focus on spiritual matters, the work itself, one might gather, is somehow otherworldly. Truth is, much of the work of a pastor is quite ordinary and mundane. They engage in the work that any director of a nonprofit would be engaged in: raising money, managing staff and serving the needs of people, among others. As Okuwobi[4] notes, it was uncommon for the pastors in the RLDP to see their story as mystical. Many spoke of having a calling, but only one pastor explicitly "relied on divine inspiration" for how they came to head a multiracial church. This one pastor said, "The whole thing [becoming a multiracial church pastor] started because I actually had a spiritual encounter where basically God said, 'I'm going to make your church a diverse church and when I'm done there won't be a majority group.'" Still, whether directly inspired by the divine or not, the role of a pastor is a profession or vocation.[5] Like other professions or vocations, most pastors cannot just choose whatever congregation they want to head. They are looking for a job, and they take what jobs are open to them. There are factors that seem to guide their paths and provide them with a particular set of options.

Polity affects pastors' options.[6] Mainline Protestant congregations and Catholic parishes, which have episcopal or presbyterian polities, operate differently from conservative Protestant congregations. Some church buildings are owned by individual congregations, but denominations with episcopal polities often own the church buildings and the land they sit on. These denominations are thus motivated to make sure their churches stay open, and they need pastors who are qualified to help ensure this happens. Final decisions about pastoral leadership and property are made at the denominational level.

Consequently, mainline Protestant pastors and Catholic priests are assigned to their congregations by denominational leaders, superintendents, directors, or bishops. As would be the case with any organization, denominational leaders assign these pastors or priests to churches based, in part, on their perception that the person they select can serve that church well, which typically means that they will be able to revive or maintain its growth. Pastors and priests have some input into where they go, but those who are members of denominations with episcopal polities know that this is all part of the calculus.

One Black priest, Father George, who was previously serving a parish in a different state, explained how he ended up at the church he was heading at the time of the interview: "We're now pulling out of parishes, because our numbers are small and we're a [state] foundation. So they're pulling everybody back into [the state]."

An Asian American priest explained, "[W]hen I came back [from sabbatical] . . . my superior asked me to take responsibility here in [this city], and then under obedience I had to do that."

The wife of a white mainline Protestant pastor in our study was also a pastor. She was assigned an appointment in another city, and he followed her there. He was heading a largely white congregation before his move. He matter-of-factly said, "Part of the deal with [my denomination] is a guaranteed appointment, so I said, 'If she's coming, then you've got to find an appointment for me too.' . . . And this [position] opened up. And here I am."

Pastors and priests who are a part of denominations with episcopal polities end up where they end up because their superiors in their denominations place them in their congregations. It is that simple. They do not get the final say on what church they go to and what the racial composition of that congregation will be. Their superior does.

This doesn't mean they have no say in their appointments. They do at times. Father George, for instance, was moved to a parish where the number of parishioners was dwindling. He was actively involved in matters of race within Catholicism and even authored a book on race and Christianity. He said about his assignment, "I wanted to do urban ministries. They [the bishops] said, 'We have a place in [this city], you can do that!'" He was assigned to a largely Anglo and Hispanic parish in the city, which also happened to have a good deal of internal conflict between Anglos and Hispanic immigrants. Father George seemed up to the task, given his knowledge and experience. Similarly, Father Mann, whom you met in the introduction, shared that his past involvement and interest in urban ministry and "justice issues" as an associate priest likely influenced his assignment to a parish in the city as a senior pastor. Another white Catholic priest who expressed considerable commitment to matters related to race, the LGBTQ+ community, and immigrants was committed to urban ministry and was able to stay in the city where he grew up for his work as a priest.

Like the priests just discussed, the other pastors in our study who are affiliated with episcopal polities struck us as generally willing to be assigned to racially diverse congregations. And many impressed us as genuinely invested in religious racial diversity and justice. With that in mind, however, the bottom line is that pastors affiliated with denominations with episcopal polities are heading racially diverse churches because their bishops or superintendents assigned them there. The process is pretty similar, regardless of the racial identity of the pastor. Some are looking to pastor urban or diverse congregations. Their interests might be taken into account when their superiors are considering their posts. Bishops and superintendents are, we imagine, assigning people to posts based on their capabilities and capacities. However, it could also be that the people who are assigned to these less popular posts are those who are willing to take them without much fuss. Multiracial congregations in episcopal polities are perceived as less desirable; at least that is the impression we get from people in our study. They are often located in urban areas that have fewer material resources compared to their suburban counterparts; they are churches that are dwindling and need someone to turn the tide and cause growth. It doesn't sound like there is much competition to lead in these urban areas where congregations generally tend to have a sizable proportion of racial minorities. In short, pastors and priests who are a part of episcopal polities may have some say in where they are assigned, but ultimately their denominational leader has the final say in where they actually land.

Polity: Congregational Denominations

This is not the case for pastors who are part of religious traditions that are based on a congregational polity, who, in our study, are almost exclusively conservative Protestant or evangelical. There are two usual ways these pastors become head clergy. One is that the congregation hires them. Pastoral candidates submit their applications. They are considered by a team of people at the church. A candidate rises to the top and then, often, the church membership or lay leadership votes on whether to offer the candidate the position as their pastor. The other way is to start a church from scratch, otherwise known as "planting" a church.

These two patterns among conservative Protestant pastors in congregational polities were to some extent racialized. Conservative Protestant pastors of color often came to head multiracial churches by planting churches. These pastors start their organization from scratch with the aim of developing a multiracial church. They have to seek financial support and recruit people to help them in the process. Richard Pitt[7] argues that these people are entrepreneurs, as are other people who start organizations. Similar to other entrepreneurs, religious entrepreneurs have to manage the risks that come along with such an endeavor: financial risk, career risk, social risk, and psychic risk.[8] There were very few conservative Protestant white pastors, however, who had planted churches. Moreover, when they did, it was not with the specific intent to plant a multiracial church. They planted a church that happened to be or become diverse.

White Conservative Protestant Pastors

In most cases, conservative Protestant or evangelical white pastors had been hired by their churches. One pastor explained the process in his denomination: "The church sort of puts out some feelers when they're looking for a pastor.... The church seeks their own pastor, and they put out, you know, through relationships and through, 'Do you know someone?' That kind of thing." This is how he got his position as senior pastor. He went on: "And so, we were pastoring in [another state] and I got the call and came up here [to interview for the position]."

One white conservative Protestant pastor actually ended up resigning from the congregation he headed because of difficult, ongoing conflict between him and certain church members and lay leaders. As he recalls, he was soon afterward hired by another church as senior pastor. He says, "So, uh, we [i.e., he and his wife] resigned and they gave me severance pay for six months and I started looking at that point. Well, that's when this church hooked up with me. I came down here." It all seems matter-of-fact. He resigned from a pastoral job. He got another pastoral job rather quickly. He was even courted by another church to become their senior pastor before taking his current position, but he had already moved residences and gotten "settled," so he chose not to pursue the offer. Plus, it was out of the country.

Regardless of whether the church was planted by the pastor or the pastor was hired by the church, the churches of both of these pastors started out predominantly white and over time became diverse. The pastor who "got the call" to interview with the church explained that when he was hired the church was "ninety-eight percent white," but the outside community was only "twenty-seven percent white." In other words, the church was located in a town that was largely populated by people of color. He explained, "My heart has always been to work to bring in multiculturalism, you know, that's just a passion I have." So before he took the job, he told the church, "Listen, when I come, this is what I hope to do. I hope that we'll begin to reflect our community." The church officials agreed to his plan, and they hired him.

The pastor who resigned and was back in a job as senior pastor soon after also shared that everyone in his current church was Anglo at the time of his hire. But over time the congregation became increasingly Hispanic. He explains, "We are the community. I'm trying to reflect the community. The community has changed drastically. We're now roughly, as a community, adult-wise, we're probably forty percent Hispanic and other ethnicities. Maybe forty-five percent." To a question about whether the church does anything to foster diversity, he responds, "The only thing that we do is . . . [teach] ESL, English as a Second Language. We are also doing Spanish as a Second Language. . . . And we do everything in Spanish and English. We sing in Spanish and English. We preach in Spanish and English. We announce in Spanish, and we pray, etcetera." Addressing language differences helped the church to become diverse.

Another white conservative Protestant pastor was on the pastoral staff of his church for well over a decade when he began to develop a passion for diversity in the church. He went from being hired at the associate pastor level to being promoted to executive pastor. We see that he was promoted internally with seeming ease. He explains why his church became diverse:

> I started thinking about race and the local church. I started thinking about race and our city. In 1998, I helped start an intentional, cross-racial pastors group and discussion in our city. I began sharing with leadership at our church. What was growing inside of me was the need for racial reconciling [of] churches, if we're going to begin to see healing of the racial divide and racial inequities of our city. So we began a transition that included an election. The church decides through a vote who their next senior pastor is going to be. Our senior pastor stepped down at sixty-five to make room for this vision and has been a part of my team ever since as our biggest cheerleader.

This church too was "ninety-eight percent white" when he was voted in as senior pastor. His passion for diversity is what sold this pastor to the church. The older, white senior pastor was apparently not up for the job or no longer wanted it. At the time of the interview, this pastor had been head of the church for sixteen years.

White evangelical and conservative Protestant pastors of multiracial churches, out of all the pastors in the study, have the greatest agency and support when it comes to if and how they will head a multiracial church. They do it because they want to, because they believe it is right. They don't have to work as hard as the rest of their peers to move in that direction or get permission to do it from a superior by way of getting assigned to a congregation. Moreover, white evangelical and conservative Protestant pastors have the greatest freedom to guide their congregation in the way they want to take it. We discuss this in greater depth in Chapter 5.

Conservative Protestant Pastors of Color

Unlike their white counterparts, conservative Protestant and evangelical pastors of color, particularly Black and Asian American pastors, do not have such an easy path to becoming head pastor of a multiracial church. About 85% of Black and Asian American pastors in our study planted their congregations. As noted, that is a high-risk investment. These pastors come from churches that are made up of their ethnoracial groups. That is, African American pastors generally grew up in "traditional" Black churches, and Asian American pastors, by and large, grew up in Asian immigrant churches. Over time, they end up choosing to start a church with the explicit intent of heading a multiracial church out of a sense of a "calling." Sometimes they go straight from pastoring at some capacity in a church primarily or completely made up of people of their own ethnoracial group to planting a multiracial church. Others make a stop along the way and work on the pastoral staff of predominantly white, usually large churches.

One African American pastor worked as the executive pastor at his father's church for a few years, which he described as "a traditional African American church." He explains, "I started realizing that my life experiences, my business know-how, and everything, it started really meeting in my divine design, and it was like, 'Okay. Time for me to make some decisions here.' And so we made the decision to do ministry full time." He goes on, "When we started this ministry, we did everything possible to make sure that we were intentional to embrace and welcome diversity." This pastor's experience in the world of business and his father's church brought him to a place where he thought he should start a racially diverse church. In many ways, this affirms how Pitt[9] talks about church planters as entrepreneurs. While this pastor doesn't say so directly, heading a racially diverse church is a good business decision, likely leading to a more diverse portfolio of resources, human and financial. He also made it clear that heading an intentionally racially diverse church meant letting go of traditional Black church cultural elements. He went from being squarely embedded in a Black church, led by his father in fact, to starting a multiracial church that had little in common with that tradition.

Nearly all other Black pastors in our sample also grew up in a Black church tradition. Take Pastor Carter. He had grown up in the Black holiness tradition. He was even the senior pastor of a small "all-Black church" in the South, which is where he was originally from, before moving out west, where he was on the pastoral staff of a "predominantly white" but "multi-ethnic kind of" megachurch. It was while he was in this church that he "got the call to plant this church [out in the west]." Yet another Black pastor, this one originally from the Midwest, grew up in Black Pentecostalism and says, "I love the roots of [his home church]." Along his pastoral journey, he joined a religious association that promotes church planting and also received a "calling" to plant a racially diverse church.

There was an exception to this pattern. Pastor Rowe, a Black-white biracial pastor, didn't grow up going to church with his family. Members of a large, predominantly white church would come to his predominantly Black urban neighborhood and pick children up and take them to church:

> It is a ninety-nine-point-nine percent [white] church.... That was in the sixties, seventies, eighties. They had the bus ministry. All churches had what they call the bus ministry. And so I came to Christ and came to the church through that ministry and then just kind of grew up in the church. And ... I was at youth camp and I felt a call into the ministry. And then just a series of doors ... were opened for me. I started working [part time] at the church when I was seventeen.... Then I received a scholarship for one year at ... a small little college and seminary. And then finished and then came home to be the associate pastor

He was an associate pastor for seven years at this nearly all-white church before choosing to plant a church. While he didn't have the "traditional Black church experience," as he put it, he did grow up in a Black neighborhood, went to Black elementary and middle schools, and attended a "multicultural" high school, all of them public schools in the city.

Over time, though, he began to notice some uncomfortable things about the church:

> There were some inconsistencies there and I came to realize, in my mind, I could be wrong, but it was fostering a certain culture.... Meaning they were making their culture into doctrine and dogma.... Meaning that you would think, from attending that church, and I attended it for my whole life, that God was a white Republican ... Baptist.

He believed the church was too conservative in other ways as well, particularly in music and preaching styles. In short, he was no longer feeling this was the best fit for him. It came time for him to act on what he was feeling: "So I went into my pastor's office and said, 'Hey, God's calling us out, you know, and I want your blessing.' And, of course, there were hurt feelings. And he said, 'Well, where are you going?'"

The plan was to plant an intentionally racially diverse church in another city about two hours away. Pastor Rowe received $200 a month for two years from his church. Just before our interview, the church sent him a letter telling him, "We've fulfilled our commitment, we're going to support you another six months at half" —that is, $100 a month for another six months. Pastor Rowe's childhood church was "nice," he says, about his departure. But they showed no love or support for him after he left to plant a multiracial church where more upbeat music was being played and where he didn't just teach but also preached. "No call to say, 'How are you doing? How is the church going?' ... Essentially [our relationship] was over once I left."

Pastor Rowe had been at that church since he was a child. Once he chose to do something on his own, the relationship was broken. I (Little Edwards) interviewed him. He was the kind of person who never met a stranger. He was an open, easy-to-know kind of person. I found him to be likable. But it was clear to me that Pastor Rowe was deeply hurt. You could hear in his voice and see in his countenance the pain he felt from the rejection of his childhood church.

Similar to the African American evangelical pastors in our study, Asian American pastors who planted churches grew up in an Asian ethnic church (e.g., a Korean immigrant church), but after working in ministry, usually with Asian Americans or in a predominantly white church, they moved to start a multiracial church.

One Asian American pastor we spoke with, Pastor Park, didn't grow up Christian. He became a Christian while in college through a Korean American Christian organization on his campus. In time, he moved into ministry himself, and at the beginning he had "always been a part of very small [immigrant] Korean Churches . . . always like the youth pastor or in college ministry." He was recruited by a white head pastor of a large, predominantly white church located in a predominantly Asian suburb to be the church's youth minister. This pastor continued to figure quite prominently in Pastor Park's career. This same pastor, he says, asked him to "start up this young adult ministry and plant this church."

> And I said, 'You are absolutely insane.' You know, I had just come from a church planting experience and, honestly, I kind of thought I really don't ever want to go back into planting. . . . I don't know. I just didn't want to go back into church planting after that. I just wanted a more stable experience, honestly.

The head pastor didn't give up, though.

> So really what kind of triggered everything was that John [his boss at the time and senior pastor] really wanted to plant this new church and I wanted nothing to do with it, and so for the thirty-ninth anniversary at our church he wanted me to team-teach with him about the vision of the church for the next thirty-nine years. . . . I don't know if this was a part of his sinister plan or not. But he wanted me to teach on the apologetics of church planting, and why it was important for us to go and plant a new church.

From his sermon preparation, Pastor Park came to the conclusion that "the most effective way to get an unchurched person to come to Christ is the planting of new churches." Europe and the United States were not doing well in this area. After he and his wife discussed the matter, they decided to take the plunge and accepted the offer to plant a church. Although his former church offered financial support for several years, Pastor Park declined the offer because he didn't want to be "nickel-and-dimed" by the head pastor of the sending church. That was seven years prior to the interview. Today his church plant is bigger than the church that he left.

Another Asian American pastor, Pastor Hurh, has similar "dots" along his path. He moved from the Korean immigrant church experience, in which he was raised, to the Korean American church experience later in life and on to the multiracial church experience. Unlike Pastor Park, though, he was never in a predominantly white church. He had a professional secular job initially, but he ultimately left it for pastoral work. He explained, "I went through a process of transitioning from law into ministry.... I was at my church [a large Korean American church] ... going on their staff, and the first responsibility that I had, as a kind of pastoral person, was to oversee their urban ministries." He felt good about this work. "It was there," he says, "that I learned how to preach on skid row, outdoor preaching."

One day, he had a serendipitous moment that started him on the path toward planting a church:

> I was sitting in the office of the church one day and somehow a call from some guy got routed to my phone and he basically said, "You guys are a big church near downtown, right, and I'm only, like, a couple miles away." And he said, "What are you guys doing to reach out to all these new people in downtown?" So I had no idea why he was calling a Korean church about this.... But for some reason that question resonated and I began to do some research.

After what he calls a "discernment process," which involved seeking advice from several others and "praying about it" with his wife, they decided three years later to plant the church with the full enthusiastic support of their Korean American home church. The church "wrote me a check for one hundred thousand dollars and gave it to me and told me to go for it." (This makes the $5,400 total stipend Pastor Rowe received seem like a childhood allowance in comparison.) The church also offered human resources, saying they could send "fifty to a hundred" people to help Pastor Hurh with the church plant. However, he did not accept this offer.

> I said, "You know, no ... give me the freedom to invite whoever I wanted to invite. Don't talk about this on the pulpit. Don't encourage people to go with us." I mean, I don't want to have fifty to a hundred Korean Americans to plant a neighborhood church here in downtown. It doesn't make any sense. And so, for some reason the one thing I got right, right from the beginning, was that I knew that this was going to be a neighborhood church in downtown and that I wanted it to look like downtown, and so I was recruiting people who are from downtown or people who looked like they were from downtown.

Looking like downtown meant having Blacks and Hispanics on the church planting team because that is who the people in downtown were, the ones on "skid row" in his city.

There was one Hispanic American conservative Protestant pastor, Luis Montoya, who participated in planting a church. You learn more about him in the next chapter. He was a missionary in his denomination in Latin American countries and had been a senior pastor of a congregation in Latin America. He explains, "While we were waiting for our next assignment, the church came to us and asked if we would be interested in helping them to find somebody to plant the church. . . . We couldn't really find anybody, so then they asked me . . . if I would be willing to lead the team." He was. The church was planted, with him as the lead, out of another church in the denomination in the local area with the specific intent of being a diverse congregation, "a church," he says "that welcomes anybody who comes through the door . . . whether it be ethnic, whether it be racial." He did make a point to say that he is one of several elders of the church. While he is the main pastor, he doesn't have full authority. Plus, the church does not have sufficient resources to financially support him, or others on staff. He and others on the pastoral team at his church are "bivocational." He explains, "My full-time job is still a missionary. I'm an area leader for our mission agency for Latin America and the Caribbean."

On the whole, pastors of color of multiracial evangelical churches are passionate about intentionally racially diverse religious communities. So passionate, they make some risky moves to make it happen: they start a church from scratch. Unlike their white counterparts, they did not talk about being approached by churches to be a senior pastor. They don't apply for pastoral jobs at homogeneous churches and let the church know they want to make it diverse. They are not applying for jobs at churches that are already diverse. Frankly, it doesn't sound like these options are available to them, though we cannot say for sure. Churches of their own ethnoracial home religious community may have approached them. It seems if we read between the lines that this could have been an option for many of them. This is evident with Pastor Hurh, who experienced a lot of support from his Korean American sending church. Others have indicated that they could have gone this route, if they wanted. But they chose otherwise.

The one Hispanic American pastor in our study who started a church was not particularly passionate about diversity in the church. He was asked to take the lead on a church planting team, but not until after no one else was willing to do it. It was not his idea. He went along. He was waiting for his next assignment. In some ways, the arrangement was more akin to the experience of the mainline Protestant pastors. He had some cross-racial and cross-cultural experience. He is bilingual. The denomination wanted to plant a multiracial church and he was a good candidate (or at least good enough since he wasn't the first candidate) for the job.

Hispanic American Pastors: The Immigrant Experience

The experience of Hispanic American pastors in our study differs from those of Black and Asian American pastors in one distinctive way: their biographical trajectories are more profoundly impacted by the immigrant experience. While several of the Asian American pastors in our study were born outside the United States, with few exceptions, they came to the United States when they were children. These pastors were 1.5-generation immigrants. But most Asian American pastors in our study were at least second generation. Among the Black pastors, only one was an immigrant. All but one Hispanic American pastor in our study grew up in predominantly Hispanic, Spanish-speaking contexts. And most were born in Latin American, Spanish-speaking countries and maintained active connections to those countries. We focus on two Hispanic American pastors with biographies that differ in important ways to reveal the factors that guided their path to heading multiracial churches. We continue with Pastor Luis Montoya, whom you met already, first.

Pastor Montoya was 1.5-generation Hispanic, having come to the United States with his family when he was seven. He did not grow up Catholic, as is common among Hispanic people. He grew up in a conservative Protestant Hispanic, Spanish-speaking congregation. In fact, he was among the fourth generation in his denomination. That made him an outsider in some ways, he thought, among Hispanic youth growing up in the States.

Pastor Montoya says he didn't fit in when he was in middle and high school. . So he is not really "in" with whites. But he does not feel really "in" with many Hispanics either.

> And so it didn't matter which setting I was in, I was the odd duck out. So, if I was with, around, with a bunch of Chicanos my label was a *coconut* because I acted, like, different than they do. It wasn't because I was white, because I didn't have anybody around me who was white. I was a Christian.

That was my identity, and so that's how I carried myself. But, to them, I was a *coconut*.

Portes and Zhou,[10] in their study of immigrant youth of color, talk about the experiences of second-generation Mexican Americans. It is similar to that of Pastor Montoya. He attributes it to being a Christian. Their research suggests that it might be because he was not sufficiently acculturated in speech, dress, and other cultural signifiers. Pastor Montoya spent most of his time with people who were not white. Still, he was labeled a "coconut," that is, brown on the outside but white on the inside. For those not familiar with these labels, they are not compliments. They are ways people of color police the boundaries of their group and communicate acceptable norms and values. "Coconut" is one such label that communicates that you are not authentically Hispanic, that you look Hispanic but you are really white culturally. For that reason, you are considered suspect by the in-group, perhaps not to be trusted. For Black people, the label is "Oreo"; for Asian Americans, it is "Twinkie" or "banana"; and for American Indians, it is "apple." Each of these labels does the same work for the in-group; they communicate that you are perhaps Black, brown, Asian, or American Indian on the outside, but your allegiances, cultural preferences, and embodiments are white.

While navigating who he was racially and ethnically, Pastor Montoya went to seminary. This was an eye-opening experience for him:

> So, I'm navigating through these minority statuses and learning to figure out who I am, and then I end up going to my last two and a half years [of seminary] . . . and that is all-white basically and super conservative. As a matter of fact, my roommate—this is a great story. . . . I arrived [at seminary] a week before everybody else, and so I'm, you know, doing my orientation stuff and he's not there. And I get there and he's there one night and it's this huge six-foot-five, six-foot-six guy, huge guy, and he's standing there in his underwear and he reaches out his hand and he says, "Hi, my name is—. I'm from Indiana." [Interviewer: White guy?] Yeah. "Are you Mexican? Do you speak Spanish?" . . . That was his—that was his greeting to me.

The interviewer (Kim) followed up by asking if the roommate assumed Pastor Montoya was Hispanic because of his surname or because of his physical appearance. Pastor Montoya says, "No. Just by looking at me."

Pastor Montoya was embedded in white Christianity when he went to seminary. That was the first time he was not connected to a Hispanic Christian community. From there he went to Latin America to be a missionary. But he can sympathize with other Hispanics who, once they go to seminary, are not particularly excited about going back to a Hispanic-centered congregation. Speaking of young Hispanic adults, he says:

> I had the same experience where you come out of an all-Spanish church where it's not just the language but more the culture, and so you are now in a master's program and you don't want to go back to deal with the immigration issue. You don't want to go back and deal with the level of teaching that goes on. You don't want to go back to the discussions about the soccer team from Mexico. You don't want to go back to the, um, the head pastor who is God and king over the congregation. You don't want to go back to, um, the mom calling you "my little boy," so you have deliberately said, "I'm done. I'll go back home for Christmas and the holidays, but essentially my world is now over here." Their kids don't even speak Spanish.

Pastor Montoya clearly outlines how college can be a strong assimilating force for first- and second-generation Hispanic Americans. Of course, this may not be typical, but it is common in his world. And he "had the same experience" as they did. What is striking is how specific Pastor Montoya is. The younger adults—and he too, it seems—learn to eschew all kinds of cultural elements that are "Hispanic," the language, the sports they prefer, the "level of teaching," suggesting it is subpar relative to whites, the hierarchical, community-centered nature of relationships. They say, "I'm done!" And it is in seminary where this turn happened.

Father Ricardo Rodriguez's experiences contrast with Pastor Montoya's in some critical ways. Father Rodriguez is the head priest of a large urban Catholic parish. Before coming to the priesthood, he worked outside the church professionally for nine years. Now he has been a priest for a couple of decades. He has served as a priest in parishes across the country. They have all been diverse. He was appointed to his current parish by the archdiocese and has been there for nine years. His congregation is racially diverse but majority white and young, mostly people in their twenties and thirties. The church has a sizable Spanish-speaking community within the parish and holds a mass in Spanish. But the Spanish-speaking community in the congregation is diverse. "Puerto Rican, Dominican, Mexican, other South American and other Central American, so there is no one dominant group," he explains. Blacks make up about 5% of the congregation. It is also diverse across class, citizenship status, and sexuality. A self-identified "big Barack supporter," Father Rodriguez is socially progressive. This is evident in the sorts of social action he supports and teaches about, including the Sanctuary Movement, LGBTQ+ inclusion, and Black Lives Matter.

Father Rodriguez was born in the United States and grew up in the Southwest and West. He had many stories to share about experiences with racism while growing up. People are most familiar with the state-sanctioned Jim Crow segregation of the South. However, out west, where there were concentrations of Mexicans, institutionalized racial segregation was also normative, but it was at the local rather than the state level.[11] The institutionalization of racial segregation, therefore, varied within states across the Southwest and West. Father Rodriguez experienced strict racial segregation growing up. There were clear and severe consequences for challenging white Anglo hegemony. He says:

> I'm from a large Mexican Indian family from [the Southwest].... And things were very segregated in those days. It was very difficult.... We learned very early on not to speak Spanish at all because you'd get spanked in school for that.... If you were Spanish-speaking in any way ... if something slipped out, even on the playground we used to get ... they'd spank us.... The town I grew up in ... the white people lived on one side, the Mexicans lived on the other side. We went to school together like ... in elementary school but high school we were segregated and then ... and the expectations were low. You went to high school ... there was really no expectation if you were Latino to do anything but work in the fields.

In fact, he says, he was bused past three schools to get to the high school for Mexicans.

Father Rodriguez was "quiet" and a good student, by his own account. But it didn't matter. Teachers accused him of cheating. They could not see him or other Hispanics as anything but field workers. He recounts one teacher saying to him, "Why are you studying? You're supposed to go to the ... we need your help in the fields. That's how you support society blah, blah, blah. So ... at least it was some reasoned argument but that was always ... it was always in your face."

Father Rodriguez ended up being accepted to a prestigious university in his state. At the time, the university had all the Mexican American students live in the same dorm, as a way to foster support. Back then, according to him, they made up just 1% of the university. So, he says, "I didn't have that many interactions with whites until after I moved out of that dorm."

Race was ever present for Father Rodriguez growing up. He experienced considerable racism and racial discrimination. This may be why he sees himself as different from many other Hispanic American priests in his order. "There's a handful of Mexican American priests in our order . . . four or five," he says, "but I guess with the exception of me, the rest have said, 'I joined this order so I would not have to do . . . you know . . . Spanish-speaking ministry.' They don't want to." It may also be why Father Rodriguez is attuned to matters of social justice related to race, immigration, and sexuality.

Pastors of Color and Exposure to White Christianity

Multiracial churches, as we understand them today, are a phenomenon of white Christian traditions. They are not something you are going to hear discussed in the Black church or Asian immigrant church traditions. White pastors in our study not only grew up within white Christian traditions, but they continue to work and serve within white Christian traditions, even as they move to become head clergy of multiracial churches. In contrast, as pastors of color grew up in religious communities predominantly made up of people who share their ethnoracial identity, their journeys to leading multiracial churches are longer, socially that is. By virtue of where multiracial churches are situated, their journeys included becoming increasingly embedded in predominantly white, Anglo Christian circles. This meant a move away from their ethnoracial religious home communities.

As we already mentioned, pastors who went to church as youth, save very few exceptions, were raised in religious contexts made up of their ethnoracial group, but they were exposed at some point to white Western Christianity and embedded in this network. The pastors of color in our study rarely moved straight from their ethnoracial churches to heading a multiracial church. There was an intermediary stage where they were exposed to and experienced sustained socialization in white Western Christian spaces. Going to college or seminary was a critical moment when this happened. In many ways, this moment on their journey was consequential for where they ended up as pastors. Before this, they were usually not thinking of being a multiracial church pastor. The colleges or seminaries they went to were simply proximate, accessible, or recommended by people they trusted. While there, their paths led them to where they are today.

Take Pastor Carter. He made significant shifts into largely white evangelical spaces or ones that were racially diverse and heavily influenced by white evangelicalism. Looking at his life trajectory, we suspect that the transition out of Black Christianity into white evangelical circles started with his college education. Pastor Carter went to a Bible college for undergraduates. When asked why, he answered, "That Bible college was in my neighborhood." It was that simple. The college was proximate to where he lived when he wanted to go to college. At some point afterward, as we mentioned, he pastored a small Black congregation in the South where he grew up before moving west. It is unclear from the interview when and why he moved. The interviewer noted that his responses were "efficient," but he was not as forthcoming with details as other respondents. We know he was working on a master's degree at an evangelical seminary in the West at the time of the interview, which "came highly recommended by friends. So I came and checked it out and liked it." From there, he became increasingly embedded in other evangelical communities that are either largely white or diverse.

Pastor Bradley, who grew up in a Black Pentecostal church, went to a predominantly white, wealthy university. College, it seems, was fun for him, maybe a little too fun. He says, "When I first got to college, I was spiritually hanging on by a thread. I was in a [Black] fraternity and on a football team." Then he learned about a Bible study:

> It was through a guy ... that would come to our team and he would do Bible studies with guys on the team, and I would show up every so often. It started getting too close to the fire. And I could just remember going to a conference my sophomore year—and seeing people as passionate for God as I was about football. And, just saying, "Man, I've prayed prayers in the past, but I'm not going after God." And they [people at the conference] happen to be predominantly white.

Pastor Bradley stopped going to church in college but became involved in a campus ministry, one that was predominantly white. And the reason he got involved in this largely white, conservative Protestant campus ministry was because it was available and easily accessible. He was not looking for it, but a white guy was evangelizing his team and he connected with what this ministry was doing at a moment when he needed a spiritual reconnection. From there, Pastor Bradley became involved in a religious network that was racially diverse and that promoted church planting. He eventually planted a church with the intention of building a multiracial congregation. That first step away from the Black church happened when he got involved in a largely white college campus ministry.

There are a variety of conservative Protestant and evangelical ministries on college campuses across the United States: Intervarsity, Campus Crusade for Christ (now called Cru), and the Navigators, to name a few. They are diverse. There will be a general group for everyone, which is in practice organized around white religious culture. These campus ministries also often have subgroups within them that are organized around ethnoracial groups, such as a Black campus ministry, a Hispanic campus ministry, or an Asian campus ministry.[12] These organizations are providing spaces for students of color who want to be involved in an easily accessible Christian community. Still, they are rooted in and remain largely organized around white Western Christianity, even as they aim to adapt to students of color. Moreover, even the campus ministries that are started by people of color for people of color, like the growing numbers of Asian American campus evangelical organizations, are heavily influenced by white evangelical Christian traditions.[13] This is even the case for international campus ministries that are started by people of color to reach a broader campus demographic.[14]

One wonders what would have happened if a predominantly Black campus ministry affiliated with a Black network was holding Bible studies on campus when Pastor Bradley was in college. Would he have moved away from being embedded in the Black Christian community if such a campus ministry reached out to him? We cannot say for sure. What we can say is that a predominantly white campus Bible study drew him back into his Christian identity. From there, he didn't turn back.

Pastoring is a second career for Pastor Leon. He was a part of the Black community within a mainline Protestant tradition. He worked in the business world for twenty-five years before going to seminary. He went to his home church, a Black church, until he was in his late thirties. He explains when his pastoring journey started:

> I went to the Black [denominational annual meeting], and our current bishop was a [seminary name] grad. And he introduced me to two people

from [that seminary], and I said, "Okay." I applied, and they gave me a scholarship. So I went. And it was wonderful, because it was very different politically, geographically, seasonally. It was just a different place, and it was stepping out in faith. I quit working after twenty-five years to go to seminary. So that was life-changing.

His bishop was Black and, it appears, a prominent person in the denomination. Following his bishop's advice, he went to the predominantly white seminary in his mainline Protestant tradition. After seminary, he was assigned to a predominantly white church as an associate pastor. From there, he was repeatedly reassigned to racially and ethnically diverse churches, none of which had a substantial representation of Black members.

Another Black pastor, Pastor Wilson, who lived on the West Coast, talked about his southern roots with great appreciation. He too grew up in the Black mainline Protestant tradition. Both sides of his family had been in this denomination for generations. When he eventually wanted to become a pastor, he was told that a seminary education was required. So he went to seminary in his denomination. But when he was done, he was not assigned to a Black congregation. The point along his journey where he moved from Black congregations to multiracial congregations began with seminary. Pastor Wilson's first congregation had fewer than ten people, all of them white. He explains: "Well, this is my fourth appointment, and I would say I probably go to churches where there is some kind of struggle or serious issues. And they sent me there to address it."

Similar to Pastor Wilson, Pastor Cho comes from a long line of mainline Protestants, but his denomination followed a Presbyterian polity. Pastor Cho was born in Korea but went back and forth between Korea and the United States growing up. While in the United States, he lived in predominantly white areas and went to predominantly white schools. His home "was an immigrant home, so, you know, one bedroom, nine people." He is a fourth-generation Korean Christian. His grandfather was a pastor in the denomination in Korea. Pastor Cho grew up in Korean churches in Korea and in Korean immigrant churches in the United States. He finished high school in Korea and went to university there. After working professionally for a few years, he felt a "call" to ministry. So he moved back to the United States for seminary. He first got a master's degree in divinity and then another master's related to religion. At the time of the interview, he was pursuing a PhD at a theology school in the United States. His pastoral experience prior to becoming a senior pastor was as a youth/young adult pastor in mostly Korean churches. His current position is the first one in which he is a senior pastor. He had been in it for four years. He explains how he got the position:

> In [my denomination], they have a pastoral search site that allows you to contact the churches that are seeking pastors. . . . I made a direct contact and met with the nominating committee and went through the process of a pastoral call, which are too many [steps] to go through. . . . But, that's how I came to this church.

The process sounds similar to that for any job. Once candidates get their credentials, they look for a job. After going through an interview process of some kind (what he calls a pastoral call), if everyone is agreeable, they get the position.

Pastor Cho's experience is different from that of most other Asian American Protestant pastors in our study in that he spent many of his formative years in Asia. He even went to college there. Still, the arc is similar. Like most other Asian American pastors in our study, he is 1.5- or second-generation American and grew up in Asian immigrant churches. He served in an Asian American church prior to becoming a head pastor. Like both Pastor Leon and Pastor Wilson, his exit from predominately Asian American churches occurred after going to seminary and searching for a job.

* * *

When we look for similar "dots"—common moments or experiences—across the lives of pastors of multiracial churches we see some patterns that help us understand how they came to head diverse congregations in a society that is largely racially divided and where a large majority of congregations are racially homogeneous.

Nearly all of the pastors in our study grew up in churches where most if not all of the people in their congregations shared their ethnoracial identity. Not surprisingly, considering that the only other ethnoracial group besides whites that control denominations in the United States are African Americans, nearly everyone grew up in congregations that were embedded in largely white-controlled denominations. Several of the pastors of color, Black pastors included, noted that their families were in these denominations for generations. Still, many Black pastors grew up in traditional Black churches and ones affiliated with Black denominations. And Asian American and

Hispanic American pastors were largely raised in immigrant-oriented churches. Church was a place where their ethnoracial identity and sense of community were created and reproduced.

Then many go off to college or seminary. Roger Finke and Kevin Dougherty[15] examined how seminary education affects a clergy person's social networks and religious practice. Specifically, they propose that clergy develop new kinds of social networks in seminaries, which expand their social resources and opportunities as well as bringing them new religious capital, which "consists of the degree of mastery of and attachment to a particular religious culture."[16] Mastery of a religious culture includes learning the rituals, skills, and knowledge of a particular religion as well as developing a certain emotional attachment to that religious culture.[17] Others too find that seminary really matters for clergy, for how their careers as pastors will unfold.[18]

There are a handful of Bible colleges, seminaries, or divinity schools that are largely made up of and controlled by people of color, such as the Payne Theological Seminary and the Interdenominational Theological Center. But the vast majority of colleges, Christian or otherwise, and seminaries in the United States are either majority white or controlled by whites. These are the ones the people in our study went to. Structurally speaking, as soon as a person of color enters college or goes to seminary they will begin to develop the social capital, those important, resourced social networks, and the religious capital valued in these largely white Western Christian spaces. They will be socialized into the cultural norms and values that emerge out of the experiences, ideas, and theologies of white Western Christendom. They will gain greater emotional attachment to the religious rituals and beliefs and cultural practices of the same. Their social networks will expand to include white Christian leaders. And they will gain job opportunities after Bible college or seminary that are generated from the social and religious capital they gain while there. As a result of all this, they will be increasingly "at risk" of leaving Christian spaces that are made up largely of people who share their ethnoracial background. This can even include emotionally leaving these spaces and rejecting the Christianity of their home ethnoracial Christian community, as some do. Unless pastors of color intentionally and actively work to maintain and cultivate the social and religious capital of their ethnoracial home church, the structure of most colleges, seminaries, and divinity schools will make it challenging for them to sustain a robust connection to their ethnoracial Christian roots.

Once done with seminary or college, the graduates aim to get a job as a clergyperson. The polity of the pastors' religious affiliations affects what clergy job they get and where. Pastors and priests who are a part of episcopal polities, such as Methodists and Catholics, are simply assigned to their congregations. Their superiors in their denominations choose where they will go. This does not vary much by the race of the pastor. Whether they are white or people of color, they speak of being assigned to their congregations in similar ways. Bishops and superintendents may or may not take into account the desires of the pastor or priest, though based on how the people in our study talk about their appointments, it seems they do to some extent. A calculus that these denominational leaders are surely considering is what pastor or priest will be able to sustain and promote growth in a given congregation. Urban congregations, because of migration patterns and changing demographics, are much more likely to be located in communities with people of color. Our data cannot test this, but pastors of color may be more likely than white clergy to get these posts. Still, both whites and people of color are assigned to multiracial churches. While we argue in subsequent pages that pastors of color are likely better suited to head racially diverse churches, several white pastors and priests in our study affiliated with episcopal polities were genuinely invested in racial diversity and justice.

Pastors who are a part of congregational polities have greater agency when choosing the type of congregations they want to lead. These pastors are affiliated with evangelicalism or conservative Protestantism. White evangelical pastors, in fact, demonstrate the greatest agency of all the pastors of multiracial churches in our study.

The vast majority of these were hired by congregations, which often started off as predominantly white and became racially diverse over time, in part because the neighborhood surrounding the congregation changed, in part because of their leadership.

The clear majority of evangelical pastors of color choose to start churches with the intent of cultivating a racially diverse religious community. They have a commitment to religious racial diversity, a "call" to the work. The growth of multiracial churches over the past twenty years may be due in part to their initiative. Still, this pattern stands out because, as Pitt[19] reveals, planting churches is risky business and requires a high level of investment, as would be the case when starting any organization. The journeys of these pastors suggest that they are not as readily recruited by congregations to be the senior pastors of their churches, especially those that are largely white or racially diverse, compared to their white counterparts. They don't talk of these sorts of opportunities being available to them. While they may have been pursued by congregations of their own ethnoracial group, if they felt "called" to develop a racially diverse church, then perhaps they wouldn't have accepted offers to pastor these churches. Multiracial churches generally either start off racially diverse or move from predominantly white to racially diverse. Rarely do churches move from predominantly Black or Asian or Hispanic to racially diverse. This puts pastors of color at a distinct disadvantage in the multiracial church world.

2
Estranged Pioneers
Pastors of Color Leading Multiracial Churches

Being a pastor of a multiracial church often comes at considerable personal costs, causing much added stress to what is already a stressful role in our society. In this chapter, we address the personal costs that pastors of color pay heading racially and ethnically diverse churches. With few exceptions, pastors of color come from religious communities (e.g., congregations, religious networks, denominations) primarily made up of people from their ethnoracial group. Yet, as discussed in the previous chapter, along their path to becoming head clergy, they moved away from serving in churches like their home religious communities and came to head multiracial congregations. These pastors are in many respects pioneers. They embarked on new territory, doing something that a large majority (about 86%) of their peers in the United States have not done, and along the way, they are providing a blueprint for how to do religious racial diversity.[1] As the United States becomes increasingly diverse, knowing how to foster a racially and ethnically diverse religious community will likely be a necessity for more religious leaders in the country.

Congregants' expectations about church life, what they should get out of it, and how they ought to experience it are informed in no small way by the religious experiences of their ethnoracial group. When pastors of multiracial churches are deciding what music to play at worship services, which statues to place in the narthex, or what foods to serve at the church potluck, for example, they are negotiating racial and ethnic identity and belonging. In the U.S. context, where racial identity, in particular, is highly salient to people's sense of who they are and how they connect in society, as well as their access to power, pastoring becomes all the more challenging. For sure, all pastors of multiracial churches, regardless of their racial and ethnic identity, have to deal with these sorts of issues that come with the territory of pastoring generally and pastoring a racially diverse church specifically. White pastors of multiracial churches, however, do not experience alienation as they navigate the multiracial church terrain. They do not have to leave the familiar, as do their counterparts of color, to lead racially and ethnically diverse churches. They can remain connected to the predominantly white religious communities they come from and continue to receive the cultural, emotional, relational, and material benefits embedded in them.

All pastors of multiracial churches, at least at this moment in U.S. history, can be considered pioneers. Pioneers venture into the unknown, hoping to forge a new path forward. The unspoken bargain is that the knowledge and resources gained on their journeys could be beneficial for the communities they leave. However, we argue that pastors of color of multiracial churches are *estranged pioneers*. They leave the familiar to explore a new way of doing church, but their ventures are not valued or celebrated as something that will potentially benefit the communities they come from. What's more, their sense of identity is challenged or destabilized in the process. Alienation characterizes their journey.

The ways in which African American, Asian American, and Hispanic American pastors experience alienation vary. African American pastors face challenges to their authenticity for leading multiracial congregations. Asian American pastors experience a sense of ambiguity that stems from a lack of clarity about what it means for them to lead churches that are not oriented around Asian ethnics. Hispanic American pastors experience tensions stemming from the mixed paths of assimilation within their congregations and the Hispanic community at large.

Despite these differences in how they experience alienation from their home religious communities, they are left to navigate a racialized society where they are othered and perceived as inferior to their white peers. African American and Asian American pastors especially but Hispanic American pastors too are first dismissed and then are "dissed." They are dismissed because being a multiracial church pastor is not compatible with the goals and functions of their home religious communities. They are dissed because they are not given the same power and privileges as their white counterparts in multiracial congregations. This has profound implications for them. It can lead to a loss of support and relationships, including mentorship; limited opportunities for material and social resources; the devaluing of their cultural capital (such as ways of preaching and teaching or norms governing how leaders and congregants should interact); limited possession of valued cultural capital in their new contexts; racialization as the other; and emotional and psychological stress and low self-esteem.

Authenticity, Ambiguity, and Assimilation

Racial Authenticity and the African American Multiracial Church Pastor

Philosophers have long contemplated what it means to be authentic.[2] Originally, philosophers focused on the individual as the source of authenticity. A person was understood to be authentic when they chose to act in accordance with their own understanding of what it means to be true to themselves. Contemporary philosophers, however, have generally abandoned this egocentric conceptualization of an authentic self for a more socially situated one.[3] As Charles Taylor[4] argues, "I can define my identity only against a background of things that matter. But to bracket out history, nature, society, the demands of solidarity, everything but what I find in myself, would be to eliminate all candidates for what matters." Put another way, authenticity must be measured against a standard that is external to the individual.

For this reason, we are drawn to Andrew Pierce's[5] conceptualization of racial authenticity. Pierce's perspective on racial authenticity emphasizes collective identity. He defines racial authenticity as "an ethical ideal governing the relations among group members committed to a common project . . . of collective identity construction."[6] As a collective identity process, racial authenticity is about establishing group boundaries.[7] And group boundaries are identified and reinforced by symbolic boundaries[8] such as unspoken traditions, institutional arrangements, customs and routines.[9] They also include physical symbols, values, tastes, preferences, styles, beliefs, behaviors, and so on.[10]

Pierre Bourdieu[11] refers to these symbolic boundaries as cultural capital. And among cultural capital, only what Bourdieu refers to as "legitimate culture" can be used as capital. Legitimate culture, which dominant groups control, can be utilized to exclude subordinate classes from accessing desirable resources.[12] Implicit in the concept of legitimate culture is that groups have certain ways of thinking, doing, and being that legitimate or *authenticate* who is "in" and who is not and that govern who gets access to the resources that groups control. Whereas legitimate culture is used by dominant groups to signal who is "in" and who is "out," we propose that racial authenticity is used by subordinate racial groups to signal who is "in" and who is "out."[13] Its purpose is to protect, conserve, and distribute subordinate racial groups' resources. While members of a subordinate racial group can claim a collective identity, their access to those resources controlled by the group will depend upon their racial authenticity.

The experiences of African American pastors in the RLDP suggest that one marker of racial authenticity for Black religious leaders is supporting and leading predominantly Black congregations.[14] Conversely, a marker of inauthenticity for Black religious leaders is heading congregations that are not predominantly Black, especially those that have a sizable proportion of whites. This becomes apparent in the challenges that the African American pastors experience to their identity as Black religious leaders. These challenges can be subtle, but sometimes they can be quite direct. They communicate how African American pastors are expected to believe and behave, and they police the boundaries designating authentic Black religious leadership. This has implications for the access that African American pastors of multiracial churches have to resources that Black religious leaders control.

Racial Ambiguity and the Asian American Multiracial Church Pastor

Contemporary Asian Americans are primarily part of the post-1965 immigration wave. And no matter their place of birth and length of stay in the United States, Asian Americans are perceived as "perpetual foreigners" who are never fully accepted as "Americans."[15]

Robert E. Park's[16] classic marginal man theory helps to frame the experiences of Asian immigrants and their descendants in the United States. Park recognized the impact that migration can have on the "personality" of the immigrant who is caught between cultures and peoples in their new country. The marginal man personality emerges in response to the necessity to "[live] and [share] intimately in the cultural life and traditions of two distinct peoples; never quite willing to break, even if he were permitted to do so, with his past and his traditions, and not quite accepted, because of racial prejudice, in the new society in which he now sought to find a place."[17] Managing these two social worlds produces internal conflict and a crisis of identity, although the internal conflict varies in intensity, depending on various contextual factors and people's character traits.[18]

The image of the marginal man struggling to find their way between two conflicting cultures captures the experiences of the Asian American pastors in the RLDP. They too are either immigrants or the children of immigrants and come from predominantly immigrant Asian ethnic congregations. Like other Asian Americans, the Asian American pastors in the RLDP traverse their ethnic home community and the broader mainstream society while feeling at home in neither. They are perpetually "betwixt and between," caught between two worlds and incompletely home in both.[19]

Stuck between these two different worlds, Asian American pastors who leave ethnic home churches to lead multiracial congregations embark on a journey that is not only alienating but ambiguous. This reality reflects the fact that most Asian American churches are immigrant ethnic congregations that function much like ethnic enclaves.[20] They are primary spaces where immigrants can worship in the language and culture of their home country and find comfort and support as they struggle to adjust and "make it" in the new land.[21] As such, these ethnic churches are marginal communities. What's more, the Asian pastor in America is more often than not an immigrant who is expected to function as a central leader of a particular ethnic religious community (e.g., Chinese Christian). Thus, a clear conception of an "Asian American" pastor in a broader context is lacking. Coming out of these marginalized ethnic spaces oriented toward the old country and survival in the new, Asian American pastors who head racially and ethnically diverse congregations are uncertain how they should lead.

Assimilation Tensions and the Hispanic American Multiracial Church Pastor

Similar to Asian Americans, Hispanic Americans are quite ethnically diverse.[22] They or their ancestors migrated to the United States from Central America and South America (16%) as well as the Commonwealth of Puerto Rico (10%), among other Latin American countries. By far, though, most come from Mexico (61%).[23] Their immigration experience differs, however, in important ways from their Asian American counterparts.

There was a time when people from Latin American countries were categorized as Anglo by the U.S. Census Bureau. But since the 1960s, there has been a steady move toward the institutionalization of the panethnic Hispanic category that we are familiar with today,[24] distinguishing them from Anglo whites. For many contemporary Hispanics in America, their paths toward assimilation are complicated by undocumented status, real[25] or perceived,[26] their color (or race),[27] and the relatively low socioeconomic status of second-generation and later Hispanics in America.[28] They also experience considerable residential segregation, which has continued to increase over time.[29] Consistent with the institutionalization of the Hispanic category, a large majority of children of unions between Hispanics and non-Hispanics (who are largely Anglo) identify as Hispanic, which suggests that Hispanic is a salient identity.[30] This may have a good deal to do with the discrimination Hispanics experience in the United States.[31]

We see some indications that Hispanics are assimilating into dominant society. But in other ways they are not. For instance, while neighborhood white/Hispanic segregation has declined over time, it still remains high,[32] and Hispanics in the United States are more likely to live in neighborhoods with Blacks than with whites. Hispanics are perhaps seeing their fate more aligned with whites, but their socioeconomic opportunities are constrained similarly to those of Blacks in America. Another measure of assimilation is intermarriage with whites. There was a time when it looked like Hispanics were assimilating through marriage as rates of interracial marriage with whites among Hispanics was on the rise, but there has been a reversal in recent decades as intermarriage with whites has declined since 2000.[33]

It might be assumed that assimilation into the dominant society is a good thing. But this is not always the case. We see this in the health-related outcomes of Hispanic Americans. U.S.-born Hispanics experience poorer health outcomes than first-generation Hispanics.[34] U.S.-born Hispanic youth are more likely than whites and first-generation Hispanics to engage in drug and alcohol use.[35] One particularly dire outcome is suicide: U.S.-born Hispanics are more likely than their immigrant counterparts to commit suicide.[36]

Hispanic Americans may also need to navigate authenticity within their community. We see this among the youth of the largest group of ethnic Hispanics in the United States, Mexicans. Those who align with behaviors and values seen as affirming of whiteness experience some exclusion from second- and third-generation Mexican youth.[37]

The experiences of Hispanics in America, then, is a story of tension. It's a mixed bag. Consistent with the theory of segmented assimilation, the assimilation path is not by any means straightforward. Hispanics in America have been systematically othered and racialized as different from whites. Assimilation is possible under particular conditions but is not available to a large majority of Hispanics because of racial (or color) discrimination and barriers to citizenship and economic advancement. Even after assimilation is underway, it does not necessarily yield positive outcomes. The negative impacts of assimilation on the mental and physical health of Hispanics are a poignant example of this.

Most Hispanic American pastors in our study head congregations affiliated with episcopal polities, the modal congregation being Catholic. While there is a community of Hispanic peers in these pastors' denominations, their peers often head Hispanic congregations that are mainly Spanish-speaking and cater to the specific needs and cultural desires of Hispanic people. Hispanic American pastors in our study do not express a sense of welcome from or similarity with this pastoral community. In this respect, their path is characterized by questions of their authenticity. This is not necessarily perceived as a problem, as it can be for Black pastors. Many of their close ties are with whites, whether their spouses, pastor peers, or friends. And they talk about heading congregations with at least a subset of Hispanic congregants who are actively eschewing signs of "Hispanicness," including the Spanish language and Hispanic culture, even aiming to separate themselves from less affluent and less assimilated Hispanics in their own congregations. They are on a path toward assimilation, and so are many of their Hispanic congregants. This path, however, seems to be available only to certain Hispanic American pastors, particularly those who can speak without a noticeable accent. Those who have a noticeable accent express a stronger connection to their Hispanic pastor peers who head predominantly Hispanic churches, as well as expressing a stronger sense of being othered by white people in their religious communities. In this regard, the experiences of Hispanic American pastors are dichotomous, driven by their immigrant generation status along with how much they can and have assimilated into the dominant culture.

The stories of African American pastors in the RLDP suggest that they are perceived as having strayed from their prescribed role as Black religious leaders, making their identities as Black religious leaders questionable and less trustworthy. Challenges to their authenticity characterize how they experience alienation from their home religious communities. Asian American religious leaders generally have an assimilationist orientation toward the mainstream. As a result, Asian American pastors can perceive heading a racially diverse congregation (particularly one with whites) as desirable, even more so than heading an Asian congregation. And much like the children of immigrants who cannot rely on their immigrant parents to help them navigate American society at large, Asian American pastors from ethnic congregations cannot expect their home churches to provide them with much guidance on leading multiracial churches. Hispanic American multiracial church pastors' paths are characterized by tensions revolving around assimilation. Those who have begun a path toward assimilation—culturally, linguistically, and socially—do not find community with Hispanic American peers who head Hispanic congregations. Instead they have or seek connection with whites. Hispanic American peers who remain connected to the Hispanic community have been assigned to congregations because of their multicultural characteristics, one being that they are a person of color, specifically a Spanish-speaking Hispanic. They are othered by their religious communities as specialists who can lead congregations that are diverse and/or have Hispanic congregants. Yet, even though African American, Asian American, and Hispanic American pastors of racially and ethnically diverse churches experience estrangement from their home religious communities differently, they all embark on their journeys alone, uncertain of how to find their place as heads of multiracial religious communities.

Estrangement

At the beginning of each of the following subsections, we highlight the biography and experiences of one pastor to provide contextualization for pastors' alienation. Afterward, we expand our analysis to the experiences of other pastors in the study.

African American Pastors

Émile Durkheim argues that individuals become aware of the existence of social structure once they deviate from it.[38] This is how African American pastors learn that heading multiracial churches, especially those with white congregants, is not the most acceptable path for Black religious leaders. Pastor Dennis Mills's story highlights this discovery.

Pastor Mills is an African American pastor of a mainline church. The two largest groups in his 175-person congregation are whites and Asians. Mills grew up in a predominantly Black community and remained involved in his predominantly Black "home church" (his description) well into adulthood. Similar to several other African American and Asian American pastors in the study, he developed a commitment to diversity in the church. Although his religious heritage is in the Black church, he never pastored a predominantly Black congregation. He became an associate pastor of a predominantly white congregation after finishing his Doctor of Ministry degree. He was then hired as head pastor of a multiracial church and has led only diverse churches since then.

Knowing that he grew up in a predominantly Black community and attended a Black church for most of his life, the interviewer was curious if he missed being in a Black church. He responded:

> I miss worshiping in the Black tradition. There's something about the Black tradition—the singing, the Spirit, the movement—and I miss that. Every other year, I go to a convocation of pastors of Black churches. I'm not in a Black church, but I go. . . . My soul is set on fire and I get fed. And I come back, and I'm ready to go. I'm just rejuvenated.

A good deal of scholarship describes the Black church worship tradition. It is characterized as structured yet free, effusive, and participatory.[39] Mills describes it as "the singing, the Spirit, the movement," and he misses it. Pastor Barnes, the Black head pastor featured in Edwards's[40] case study of Crosstown, a multiracial church in the Midwest, similarly expressed missing Black worship. Mills misses it so much that he makes it a point to attend a large meeting for pastors of Black churches, where, he says, "My soul is set on fire and I get fed." These metaphors communicate that this environment does more than allow him to experience something he misses; it reignites a passion and purpose in him, fuels him to continue doing his work as a pastor of a diverse congregation.[41]

However, what is particularly striking about Mills's comment is what he does not say. Given that pastors serve many people and regularly give of themselves while receiving relatively little care and nurturing in return, it makes sense that Mills would seek out places where he can be supported and affirmed. Especially telling, though, is that he does not go to conferences for pastors of multiracial churches to get "rejuvenated." Mills looks for affirmation, support, and replenishment at an assembly for pastors of Black churches, knowing that his particular pastoral experiences are different from those of his peers in this context. Mills is committed to diversity in the church, but those spaces are not home for him. Being a multiracial church pastor is what he does, not who he is. He is a lonely nomad of sorts, moving from one multiracial church to the next. But unlike typical nomads, who move from place to place in community, he moves alone, never able to settle into a community where he feels he fully belongs, where important parts of his identity are embraced.

Still, Mills experiences sanctions from other Black pastors and Black Christians for heading congregations that are not predominantly African American:

> I realized when I started pastoring my first church, I was in the in-between. There were Black folks—some Black pastors, Black church members—that seemed like they had an issue because I was in a white church. . . . "Oh. He's making more money. He thinks he's all of that." . . . But the white church didn't see me as . . . white. They saw me as Black. So I didn't fit in. Right? So when I went back to my home church, I felt out of place, and it took me several years until I felt like I was in the in-both. . . . Where I felt, "Now, I feel I'm comfortable being in the white church. I understand some of these expectations about leadership style, differences around preaching, differences about visitation, what it means to do outreach."

When Mills began heading diverse churches, he experienced sanctions from Black people in his close circle, including other Black pastors and Black church members, who challenged his commitment and authenticity as a member of their Black community. At the same time, white people did not accept him as one of them either. This experience was so destabilizing that he began to feel like an outsider even at his "home church." Simply put, he "didn't fit in." Pastor Mills did come to regain some stability and a sense of where he stood, but, as he explained, it took "several years."

Authenticity Checkpoints

Pastor Mills's story highlights the marginalization that African American pastors can face from their home religious communities for leading multiracial churches. Barring a few notable exceptions,[42] the Black pastors in the RLDP find themselves having to traverse authenticity checkpoints where the boundary of the Black religious leader identity is policed.

Take, for example, the experience of another mainline pastor. In response to a question about the advantages associated with being a multiracial church pastor, he tells of his experience participating in an invitation-only meeting of about a dozen pastors and leaders in his denomination. The main organizer of the meeting was a Black pastor of a predominantly Black congregation:

> About the *only* [emphasis added] advantage I would say is that . . . when I'm in a context amongst my peers, my voice can be a bit more . . . versatile because I'm not speaking for one ethnicity. [For example,] . . . a lot of times when there's an issue—like, for instance, when recently some colleagues [in my denomination] wanted to get together to talk about Ferguson[43] . . ., it was very apparent that I needed to be present.

When the interviewer follows up and asks why these pastors of Black churches were so insistent that he "needed to be" at the meeting, he explains, "Because . . . well, I'm familiar with white and Black. I'm familiar with what whites and Blacks are thinking about, not just what Black people are thinking about. The bridge, for lack of a better word."

This pastor's Black peers who head Black congregations believed he had special important knowledge: he understood what it was to be Black, but he was also familiar with white people. Given the topic of the meeting and how important it was that he was present, it seems the main organizer hoped he knew something about white people that would help them understand how Black people could safely navigate potentially life-threatening interactions with white police officers. In some ways, it might appear that this pastor is being included as one of the group as an expert among his peers. But this was not the case. He was, in fact, being singled out as having special knowledge, but being singled out also meant he was seen as different.

He is more explicit about this when asked if he experiences any disadvantages heading a multiracial church:

> Now, the same reason for why I thought I was invited could also backfire on me. Because some of my colleagues who look like me think that, uh, I don't understand. . . . Therefore, sometimes I'm not invited to some things because they don't think that I can relate to what's going on in the Black community.

Ultimately, this pastor is perceived as an outsider. When his Black peers needed intel on whites, they called on him. But when they got together to be Black together, he was not included. Not only was this because he was not perceived as being authentically Black; it was also because they perceived him as being more invested in and aligned with white people. It did not matter that this pastor grew up in a Black neighborhood and a Black church or that his primary mentor and accountability group are Black. What made him an outsider among some of his Black peers was heading a congregation that was not predominantly Black but instead comprised of mostly white congregants.

This policing can occur in more subtle ways as well. Take, for example, a young conservative Protestant pastor who had intentionally started a multiracial church within the past few years. As he was considering this path, an African American pastor counseled him on the challenges he would experience heading a multiracial church:

> He is, like, "You, as a Black man, will never lead a multiethnic church because Black people will follow white people, but white people will not follow Black people on a large scale." And I don't think he meant that maliciously. I thought he was being honest. And I've heard that . . . in different ways . . . on several occasions.

That white people would not follow his leadership was communicated to him not just once but on "several occasions," presumably by other Black people, if not other Black pastors. Even before this pastor took any concrete steps toward starting a multiracial church, he was told repeatedly that this was an endeavor that would likely not end well. He was warned of imminent failure because white people would not follow him. But concern for his well-being was not only what was going on here. More than simply warning him so that he avoided failure, he was being schooled on what it meant to be a Black religious leader. By telling him that his plan wouldn't work, the African American pastor and others who counseled him were, under the guise of wisdom and protection, policing the boundaries of what it meant to be a Black religious leader. To be a Black pastor did not include pastoring white people.

As long as African American pastors remained committed to multiracial churches, they risked being denied acceptance and legitimacy in the Black religious community.

Asian American Pastors

Much of what Asian American pastors learned about being a pastor is rooted in their Asian ethnic (Korean, Chinese, etc.) home churches, which are most often conducted in another language, uphold cultures and traditions from another country, serve a particular ethnic group, and are led by foreign-born pastors. There is no template for what it means to be an "Asian American" pastor, let alone an Asian American pastor of a multiracial church. This leaves Asian American pastors of multiracial churches with really only one viable path of leadership, and that is the one laid out by white Christian traditions. Pastor John Song's story illustrates this.

Pastor Song is a second-generation Korean American conservative Protestant pastor in his late forties who grew up in the Korean immigrant church. He served as an assistant pastor of both a Korean church and a predominantly white church before his present position. His church at the time of the interview was a multiracial, majority–Asian American congregation that he planted in a diverse suburb in California. Song is well known in both the Asian American and white evangelical communities as one of the few Asian American leaders who has (successfully) become embedded in predominantly white pastoral networks. He is thought to be someone who can uniquely speak about the Korean immigrant church, the Asian American Christian community, and the white American church experience.

Reflecting upon his childhood church experience, Pastor Song admits that he has come to view the leadership style he witnessed in his home church as undesirable. He says he does not affirm its Confucian-influenced "vertical" and "hierarchical" orientation, with its preoccupation with titles and status. Instead, he prefers the "American leadership style," which is more "egalitarian" and allows congregants to more freely associate with one another, including with pastors. Pastor Song describes this latter style, which he picked up while working in predominantly white churches, as "mature" and "spiritually healthy" relative to their Korean counterpart.

Like many of the other Asian American pastors in the RLDP, Pastor Song chose to disengage from his home church and adopt dominant white models of church leadership and organization. This choice, however willing, might be explained in part by differences in the expectations of first-generation and second-generation pastors. Pastor Song notes that second-generation Korean American pastors, like himself, are not really inheriting a "Korean" spirituality. He grew up in a large Korean immigrant church where the head pastor faithfully upheld Korean devotional practices. While the first-generation Korean pastors were expected to carry on these practices, the second-generation Korean American pastors were not. He explains:

> [A]ll of the Korean pastors were required to go to *sabekkido* [early-morning prayer] . . . one of those "Korean things" that require a lot of work . . . and *shimbang* [visit] everybody, showing up to everything. . . . But among the second-generation pastors, they didn't require [us] to do that.

Song adds that the Korean senior pastor at his home church was not only uninterested in mentoring him; the pastor also did not know how to mentor him. The senior pastor led his Korean immigrant church in the hierarchical Confucian Korean cultural ways and was therefore not capable of mentoring a young American pastor like Song who wanted to plant more egalitarian multiracial churches.

Song eventually decided to leave the Korean immigrant church and turned to a Swedish denomination for guidance and mentorship: "I said, 'I need more than this.' So I applied for the internship [at a Swedish denomination], and so that became sort of my journey into white evangelical culture." And it is in this "white evangelical culture" that he finally found mentors and "sound leadership" guidance that would help him to actualize his vision of planting multiracial churches. Now he is known as one of the most successful multiracial church planters, particularly among Asian Americans, and is respected by his peers both in and outside of his home church community.

Ambiguity and Success in the White Mainstream

Similar to Pastor Song, other Asian American pastors in our study do not have mentors from their ethnic home churches who could give them guidance on how to lead a multiracial church. Additionally, there isn't space for second-generation Asian Americans to be pastors in their ethnic home churches, largely because these spaces are organized around the needs and desires of the first generation. Thus, if they want to become head clergy of a multiracial church, they believe that they have to disengage from their ethnic home churches and turn to the established, predominantly white mainstream religious institutions for guidance.

When discussing what resources have been particularly influential in their role as pastors, the Asian American pastors in our study consistently point to those affiliated with predominantly white religious institutions. One pastor of a mainline church on the East Coast explains, "[M]ost of my intellect as well as my organizational leadership skills come from the white culture." Another notes that although he grew up in a Korean church in Korea, his theology and training have largely been in white institutions and that he enjoys reading "Tim Keller,"[44] along with "Luther and Calvin." And when these pastors are asked what pastors or preachers they admire or try to emulate, they invariably mention white pastors. One of these pastors shares, "If there is anybody I would want to emulate in my preaching stock, it would be somebody like Andy Stanley[45].... If you were to assess his preaching style, it probably is white middle-class."

By the time Pastor Song was interviewed, his interviewer had already heard several Asian American pastors share that they had adopted white Christian leadership styles. So the interviewer asked him what he thought might be distinctively "Korean" or "Asian" about his leadership or church. Pastor Song paused. He then said that he did not really know. With that, Song encouraged the interviewer to ask his associate pastor, a white man who has worked with him in the same church and denomination, what he thought was "Korean" or "Asian" about Pastor Song and the church. This pastor too had a difficult time answering this question. After giving it some thought, he shared that besides Song's "Asian work ethic," the many hours and late nights that he devotes to his job, he couldn't name anything particularly "Korean" or "Asian" about his leadership: "John has a very Asian work ethic. Do you know what I mean? He doesn't take a day off. At least not like I do." When asked about what might be "Asian American" about his multiracial but predominantly Asian American church, he paused again. He then surmised that while there are cultural differences in the homes of the Asian American congregants whom he often visits, such as in the way they decorate or the foods they prefer, the worship and organization of the church do not feel noticeably different from the white churches in the denomination that he grew up attending and serving.

It is noteworthy that Pastor Song either could not or would not explain how he, a Korean American who grew up in the Korean church culture, exhibited any signs of Korean or Asian culture within his multiracial church. It is also notable that Pastor Song directed the interviewer to a white colleague to identify how he or the church was "Korean" or "Asian" and that this white pastor drew upon characteristics associated with the "model minority" perception of Asian Americans. Pastor Song has an "Asian work ethic," but other than that, he affirms whiteness. As for the Asian American congregants, they leave their "Asianness" at home.

Hispanic American Pastors

Pastor Manuel Santiago is a forty-something first-generation pastor from Mexico. He is a brown-skinned, shorter man, perhaps 5'6", with thick black hair and a noticeable accent. He was raised in the mainline Protestant tradition that he is still a part of. As a young adult, after leaving a career in another field, he emigrated to the United States to work as a missionary alongside family members who were already in the country working as missionaries to migrants. Within a couple of years after arriving here, he decided to go to seminary. Upon getting his MDiv, he transitioned into pastoral ministry. One of his main assignments out of seminary was at a multiracial, multicultural church. It followed a multiservice model where each group had their own culturally specific worship service. Pastor Santiago was the associate pastor of the Hispanic service, which was conducted in Spanish.

At the time of our interview, Pastor Santiago had been at his current church for only a few months. He was still unpacking and organizing his office. His previous church was also racially and ethnically diverse, but that was not always the case. When he had arrived at this former church to be its senior pastor, he explained, "it was . . . ninety percent [white], and then a little bit of everything. . . . When I left, they were probably twenty percent to twenty-five percent nonwhite."

His success at diversifying his former church along with a significant decline in pastors within his denomination are what precipitated his move:

> When pastors retire . . . you have to move people around. So, in my case, I had been at that church for eight years. . . . I did not ask to move. I wanted to stay there. The pastor who was here also did not ask to move. She wanted to stay here. But with all those changes, you know, they began to make changes and move you. . . . Personally, I do think that there's also this process that is parallel to that in which the bishops and the district superintendents, who are the supervisors that we have, begin to look at the needs of the congregation and the gifts of the pastor and that's how they match you up. . . . [I]n my case, they saw this church as a good match for me . . . and I was a

good match for it because of my experience. Because this church also is in the process of wanting to become more reflective of the community.

Pastor Santiago believes he was pegged by his denomination as a diversity specialist. He had a good deal of success there, at least based on his and the denomination's key metrics of growth in attendance and reflecting the racial demographics of the neighborhood. The church increased in size during his eight-year tenure there, from 130 to 180 people.

Similarly, the community of his current church was rapidly changing, and his skills were needed there. In 2000, the community of his current church was 62% white. In 2019, four years after the interview, the proportion of white people was half that, 31%, and more than half of the community's residents were Black. The church at the time of the interview was about 70% white, and the second largest group in the church was Black, estimated to be about 10%. When Pastor Santiago was asked how he, a Hispanic, was a "good match" for this diverse church in a rapidly changing neighborhood, he chuckled a bit and responded, "I'm in the middle." He went on to explain what he meant by this:

> I hope that people see me as a pastor who happens to be Latino, not a Latino who is a pastor. . . . I also think that one of my gifts, I guess, is being able to connect with the community, regardless of racial boundaries. And so, thinking about what was happening here at this church, I think that this church is . . . a bigger congregation than where I was . . . but I think that in many ways, it's very similar to where I was when I started eight years ago at the other church. . . . And so . . . it was very clear that . . . God was sending me here.

He clarified what he has to offer this church: "I'm not white. I'm not Black. So maybe I can speak to both. And then, I'm also Latino, so I—I hope that I can bring a different perspective and experience to that."

Pastor Santiago's story is similar to that of Pastor Mills's in that he had proven experience heading racially and ethnically diverse congregations. His denomination recognized that and placed him accordingly. Unlike Pastor Mills, though, who longed for connection with Black pastors and Black church culture, Pastor Santiago did not express a need to be connected to other Hispanics. He saw himself as a person in the "middle," someone who could relate to a lot of people across racial lines.

ESTRANGED PIONEERS 59

Pastor Santiago also saw himself as someone who is in solidarity with people of color and as someone who is not white. This is clearer later in the interview when he talks about people not understanding the church's mission to be an inclusive congregation:

> I have a lot of people in the congregation who don't know what our values are. They don't know our mission statement. They don't know our vision. They don't know who we are. And yet, these people are the ones in charge of making decisions about how we're going to spend money, how we're going to spend our time, and how we're going to use the building. So, one thing that I'm—first I'm working with the staff.

The way Pastor Santiago talks about these congregants suggests that he does not feel very connected to them. The congregants who are in charge of making decisions in the church do not know the church's mission or vision. They do share the church's value of inclusivity, which is also his own value. Building inclusive congregations has been his pastoral focus. Pastor Santiago never says that these people in the congregation who don't know the church's values are white. The subtext, however, suggests as much, particularly when he says that all the staff he will have to work with to build a more inclusive congregation are white.

When we juxtapose these comments to how he talks about the way congregants of color interact with him, it becomes clearer how he sees himself and whom he feels more connected to. When asked how people of color in the congregation feel about him becoming the senior pastor, he responds, "They're very happy that I'm here. . . . It's like they feel like there's hope." Pastor Santiago had a bit of a hard time verbalizing what congregants of color think of him, because he largely gathered their thoughts about him from their body language and ways of interacting with him. "You can see it," he said. His congregants' body language, gestures, and facial expressions symbolically communicated to him that they are in solidarity with him. They are on the same side. When asked for more specific examples of this connection, Pastor Santiago explained:

> Well we—we—sometimes we make jokes about white people. You know, just little things, but I see it more in the way they look at me and the way they smile. You know what I mean? It's not just—they're very loving people. I mean . . . I think there's a connection that . . . people who are

not from the majority understand. You don't have to say a lot. It's just [there].

Joking is a tool people of color may use to defuse the tension that comes with managing themselves in white-controlled contexts, such as when white people do not seem interested in welcoming them.[46] It is a mechanism deployed to both resist suffering and strengthen bonds.[47] Taken together, the joking about white people shows a level of safety, comfort, and togetherness between Pastor Santiago and his congregants of color.

Managing Assimilation and Otherness

Pastor Santiago is a Hispanic man who "looks" Hispanic and has a noticeable accent. On the one hand, he wants to be seen primarily as a pastor who happens to be Hispanic, one who can traverse racial boundaries, as someone "in the middle" between Blacks and whites. Still, he experiences a sense of otherness and thus feels a stronger and more intimate connection with his congregants of color. This sense is both because of people's general value of inclusion and because of more personal experiences with whites in his congregation.

Wanting to be seen for their nonracialized identities, namely as a pastor or Christian, while also navigating how others see and interact with them is a common tension that Hispanic American pastors discussed. It is not that African American and Asian American pastors did not have similar desires to be seen for their achieved status by those they feel connected to. The difference lies in how they managed this. With Hispanic American pastors, there was a desire to both assert and not assert their Hispanicness. Where Asian American pastors were ambiguous about how to lead multiracial churches, Hispanic American pastors' ambiguity was more rooted in their racial identity.

Take Pastor Luis Montoya, a 1.5-generation Mexican American. He is fluent in Spanish and English and, like Pastor Santiago, started his ministry career as a missionary before planting a church and becoming a senior pastor. The conservative Protestant church in the predominantly and historically white denomination where he pastors is two-thirds Hispanic and almost a third Anglo, and the worship services are held in both English and Spanish. In the interview he said that he doesn't identify racially: "I'm a pilgrim. I don't. I don't because I'm nothing. . . . Literally nothing, racially."

It is interesting that while he is "nothing" racially, he sees himself as having a "sensitivity to" and a special "awareness" of race and "the conflicts that are involved" in regard to race. Specifically, he approaches "race and racial differences . . . lightheartedly." He is "more appreciative of the differences" and tries to "look for those aspects of race that correspond to beliefs and Jesus." He says that he does not struggle with discussions on race, unless he has "somebody who's really hell-bent on wanting to make race the great divide." When asked who is making "race the great divide," he answered:

> Well, mostly . . . Hispanic pastors who are primarily Spanish-speaking who make it a point to talk about the Anglo pastors in a negative light because they're Anglo. [Interviewer: What would they say about Anglo pastors in a negative light?] Uh, "They don't respect us. They don't appreciate us. They don't understand us. They don't like the way we do things. They don't treat us as equals."

He then notes, "[W]ithin that group of peers, I'm kind of an oddball."

Both Pastor Santiago and Pastor Montoya downplay their Hispanicness, not wanting to be seen as primarily Hispanic. What makes Pastor Montoya different from Pastor Santiago is that Pastor Santiago sees himself as being in solidarity with people of color. He isn't ignoring racial realities or power dynamics. Pastor Montoya, however, actively distances himself from racial categories and other Hispanic pastors. His rhetoric demonstrates a strong desire to eschew any connection with Hispanics. In his view, people of color—other Hispanic pastors, in his case—are causing division by naming their experiences with white people and the white-dominant power dynamics in the church.

Curiously, at the same time, Pastor Montoya wants to be seen as someone who understands race, indirectly drawing on his status as a racialized person to legitimize his capacity to talk about race. In fact, after the interview, the interviewer told him they were working with students on campus to deconstruct their feelings and thoughts about Ferguson. The interviewer wrote in their field notes:

> [Pastor Montoya] then shared that he would be happy to help in any way with having discussions/counsel on these issues . . . "because" he explained, "you can always fit another Mexican in. . . . [T]hat is a Mexican joke/common saying . . . that you can always fit another Mexican in the car. . . ."

[The interviewer] then said, "Wait, but you said you are not Mexican... you are just a pilgrim." Then he said something like "I still have the Mexican side or part in me."

Pastor Montoya did not fit in with Hispanic pastors. He was the self-proclaimed "oddball" in the group. Unlike Pastor Mills and other African American pastors of multiracial churches, he did not struggle with being excluded from Hispanic pastor circles. Rather, he seemed to look down on Hispanic pastors who are Spanish-speaking and culturally Hispanic and did not see their thoughts on experiences with Anglo pastors as legitimate. He was the more assimilated and evolved pastor. He was just a pilgrim, a Christian, that is, until it benefited him to not be—as a potential "Mexican race specialist." In this way, he may also be the "oddball" among the Anglo pastors in his denomination.

Exclusion from the White Hegemonic Structure

Despite differences in how African American, Asian American, and Hispanic American pastors experience alienation from their home religious communities, they all face exclusion from whites. This manifests in both subtle and outright racism, microaggressions, resistance to their authority, and institutional barriers to power and authority.

Pastor Mills felt he was able to move from being "in-between" whites and people of color to being "in-both." In his view, he gained sufficient understanding of white congregants' expectations to become "comfortable" heading a congregation with whites. Still, he found himself having to decipher what white congregants wanted, what they meant, and the extent to which they supported his leadership. In fact, he found himself questioning if his white congregants were acting out of racism or "just ignorance." He said, "It's one of those things that ... does get tiring. Sometimes you just think, 'Is this racist, or is this just ignorance? The person really doesn't mean anything by it?'" While Mills came to be more comfortable heading a congregation with a large proportion of whites, that he cannot distinguish between racism and ignorance among his white congregants belies his claim that he is "in" the community of white congregants. If he was "in," it stands to reason that he would know the difference.

Highlighting differences for Pastor Santiago also happened, but around his accent. He was the first person of color to head his congregation and had assumed the position just a few months prior to our interview. In his estimate, "there's some anxiety about those things, again." When asked if he could provide an example of how he experienced this, he responded, "Well, I mean, they will give you backhanded compliments. [Laughter]. On their line, on the way out [after the service]. You know, 'I'm glad I can understand everything you said. . . . I was afraid I wasn't going to be able to understand anything you said.'" When asked if white congregants literally said this to him or if it was something he surmised, Pastor Santiago clarified, "Literally!"

These pastors also had a sense of just not feeling like they belong, despite occupying the most senior pastoral position in the church. Pastor Mills's experience highlights that. So does Pastor Hong's, an Asian American pastor who planted a church: "There would be times when it would be a real struggle to feel like, 'Man, am I even in the right—I know I'm leading this, but I—I mean, I think I can do a much more effective job somewhere else, among people who are just, again, much more, at least, racially similar to me.'" Like other pastors of color, Pastor Hong's experience revealed the level of estrangement he felt in his role.

In other instances, the exclusion is very clear. Take, for example, the experience of an Asian American pastor on the West Coast. He shared what he faced on the first day on the job as the head clergy of a mainline church in what he described as a "very racist" town in California: "The first thing I saw . . . my first day in my office, there was a note that said . . . 'So and so left the church because they didn't want an [Asian] person.' That was my introduction." Not only did someone leave simply because of this pastor's race, but someone else in the church, who chose to remain anonymous, felt it necessary to let him know, suggesting that the racism went beyond a single individual.

While we cannot test this directly, our recruitment process of pastors of color that head multiracial congregations suggests that there are institutional barriers to heading multiracial churches, particularly for Hispanic Americans.[48] Starting out, there may be a shortage of certified seminary-degreed Hispanic pastors that denominations and religious organizations can hire to lead their congregations, multiracial or otherwise, given the Hispanic American community's mixed levels of assimilation into mainstream institutions. Moreover, the Hispanic pastors who are available, particularly those who speak Spanish, are often seen as specialists who can lead separate Spanish-speaking ministries and are chosen by their denominations and religious organizations to serve in those ethnic ministries over those who are English-speaking and multiracial.

Another barrier for Hispanic American pastors is the minimal or lack of institutionalized resources available to them for heading multiracial churches. Again, all pastors, regardless of their race, attest to this. White pastors in particular have access to resources through informal avenues, such as social ties to highly resourced benefactors and invitations to exclusive spaces, like organizational boards and meetings. In other words, they can draw on their whiteness and the privileges associated with it to find resources for themselves and their congregations. Pastors of color, with few exceptions, do not have these opportunities to leverage. But Hispanic American pastors consistently share an added institutional barrier: language. Some Asian American pastors in our study too have to navigate multiple languages in their congregations. Hispanics, however, are now the largest group of color in the United States. Not only that, but even though the group "Hispanic" encompasses many different ethnicities and cultures, they have a language in common: Spanish. This is not the case for Asian Americans, who are Koreans, Chinese, and Filipinos, among many others. These groups speak many different languages. It is for these reasons that the institutional language barrier in congregations stands out for Hispanics. They have one language in common, and they are the second largest racial group in the United States.

Father Rodriguez lays this out for us. In his many years of being a priest in the Catholic Church, he has come to believe the Church pays "lip service" to serving congregations with Hispanic Americans who are Spanish-speaking:

> The Catholic Church [in the United States] is primarily Hispanic today . . . due to immigration. . . . You hear . . . local bishops here, they'll even say . . . "Oh, we require Spanish of our seminarians and we really want to make sure that we support our Hispanic community," but . . . all the leadership is white. Even the one Spanish-speaking bishop is from Spain and, bless his heart, he is great. He is amazing. He is amazing but . . . but there's not the kind of . . . on that level there is not much leadership. The archbishop himself doesn't speak Spanish very well and appears not to care. . . . [I]f we're going to do it [effectively serve Spanish-speaking congregants] we should put resources into it. . . . There are Spanish training centers now, those are being developed, but with respect to clergy, it's not encouraged.

The Catholic Church at the local level, at least from Father Rodriguez's perspective, is not invested in providing the kinds of resources his congregation, as well as others that serve Hispanic congregations, need. This is ironic given that the growth of the Catholic Church in the United States is among the Hispanic population.[49]

The Emotional Burden of the Estranged Pioneer

Being estranged pioneers can come with the added emotional costs of low self-esteem or a sense of inferiority. This is particularly evident among some of the Asian American pastors in the study. Several express a constant, slow-burning concern that they are not accepted because of their ethnicity or race and that they are viewed as inferior to other leaders, particularly white leaders. This stems, in part, from their racialization as not only "second best" but also "less American" compared to whites, and perhaps even compared to African Americans.

One second-generation Chinese American pastor confessed that he feels like an "adopted family member" of his church. He wrestles with self-doubt and a sense of inferiority, which probably stems from his being "Asian." He goes on, "Even as a senior pastor, I'm going through this wrestle, I'm like having a hard time because . . . [e]ven though I am American . . . it's always hard when you feel like you're the minority . . . like you've been oppressed. . . . Is it my brokenness or reality?" He further confessed that sometimes he wishes he were white because that would make it easier for him to lead: "If I was just white, it would help." He qualifies all of this by saying, "Even though I am American."

Pastor Hong discussed at length how being Asian was associated for him with feelings of shame and inferiority. These feelings are not straightforward and are in fact a bit complex. Perhaps, he even speculated, they are what drove him to plant a multiracial church in the first place:

> I didn't realize how deep I had a sense that being Asian was an inferiority—like it was something I had to dig out from. And even . . . doing a diverse church. So, again, we're talking about the—the pros and the cons, but, I realized I like being part of a diverse church, because it makes me feel more significant. It makes me feel I'm doing something different, and I'm looking for all these ways to try to be special—trying to take away my

shame of what I feel is deficient in me and just having to come to grips with, "No. Those—those are not deficiencies. That's the way God made [me]." But deep in my psychosis [laughter] was this feeling of "Who I am is less."

Consistent with the messages other Asian American pastors communicated or received from their Asian ethnic home churches, Pastor Hong saw heading a diverse church as a step up; it made him feel "more significant." The context of the conversation suggests he felt more significant because he was doing something others were not doing, that is, other pastors who headed homogeneous churches. Diversity was a way for him to prove that he was not inferior, a way to undo the internalized shame he felt was associated with his Asianness. When we consider the broader messages about the value of whiteness and that he is a second-generation person, with all the pressures of assimilation that come with being an immigrant or child of immigrants, his feelings are not surprising. What is surprising is his willingness to be vulnerable and share those feelings.

Pastors of color of multiracial churches must negotiate a racialized social system that valorizes whiteness and devalues people of color. This is poignantly felt in their relationships with congregants or potential congregants. Their authority is questioned. There are also reports of flat-out rejection and racist microaggressions. White pastors experience challenges from their congregants as well, of course. Challenges from congregants are par for the course for any pastor navigating a religious social structure that is completely voluntary. In such a system, people will voice their opinions. Our findings suggest that, in addition to white pastors not having to endure experiences of racism or racial discrimination like pastors of color do, a key difference between white pastors and pastors of color is that while white pastors may be challenged, they are still accepted as legitimate authorities. And being accepted as a legitimate authority comes with significant social and material benefits.[50]

3
Managing the Challenges of Leading Multiracial Churches

Pastor Shin, a Korean American who planted a multiracial church in a southwestern city, told the interviewer, "I might leave ministry if I am done with this one. It's that much." As this statement suggests, starting a church is not easy, and starting a multiracial church is especially challenging.

Pastor Shin experienced many trials along his church-planting journey. For one, he was the only "Asian guy" in his religious network, so he had relatively limited support as a pastor. Also, his congregation was losing members fast, and he was encountering financial difficulty. After listing these and other challenges, Pastor Shin let out a long sigh. He confessed that he may leave ministry altogether if his church was to fold. And it seems it did. When we searched for his church online a few years after this interview, we could no longer find it. When we searched the pastor's name on the internet, we did find him serving in ministry elsewhere, but he was no longer pastoring a multiracial church. The stress of leading a multiracial church must have been too much.

As Pastor Shin's story suggests, leading multiracial churches is exhausting. It wears at a pastor's soul. This is the case for all pastors, regardless of their race, but pastors of color experience unique and added burdens leading multiracial congregations. This chapter addresses these distinct and additional challenges and examines how pastors of color try to manage them. We examine head clergy's responses to various questions of where and to whom they turn for support and how they manage the various expectations and challenges they face. We also examine their responses to our question about how they would advise other pastors who wish to lead multiracial congregations.

Pastors' responses to these questions reveal that they rely on three strategies to manage their additional challenges and compensate for the dearth of resources available to them in their positions. One strategy is to overachieve, or at least try to achieve more than their white counterparts. A second strategy is to hide or suppress their racial selves in their role as head clergy in an effort to minimize any negative effect that they perceive their racial minority status may have on their church. Although pastors of color can be quite critical of the religious structures and practices of their ethnoracial home churches—particularly in comparison to established white churches—many also find considerable and necessary social, psychological, and spiritual support from co-ethnic and co-racial ties, including those ties that come from their ethnic home church. This gives them the energy and courage to press on in their role as head clergy of multiracial congregations in what often feels like a wilderness experience. Thus, a third strategy is to get "recharged" by spending time with people, often other pastors, who share their ethnoracial identity. We then conclude with recommendations of what can be done to better manage the health and well-being of pastors of color in their role as head clergy of multiracial congregations.

The Racial Tax

Get More, Do More

In *Spirit Moves West: Korean Missionaries in America*, I (Kim) examined why and how a group of Korean missionaries evangelized white Americans in the latter part of the twentieth century.[1] I found that the Korean missionaries viewed white people as the most prized converts in their cross-racial evangelism and disciple-making efforts in the United States because, they reasoned, white people would make the most promising leaders in a society where white people are the most valued as Americans, Christians, and leaders, among other statuses. Recognizing the racial hierarchy they were working within, Korean missionaries' main strategy for evangelizing white people was to simply work harder than others. Summarizing her years of evangelizing white people, one Korean missionary said, "I just worked hard... *really* hard." In other words, she had to pay a racial tax as a Korean person evangelizing white people.

The burden to overachieve derives from a few sources, but it boils down to a simple reality: people of color are perceived as less desirable or less capable leaders compared to whites. Like the Korean missionaries in *Spirit Moves West*, pastors of color in our study are well aware of the racial landscape, that they are operating within a racial hierarchy that frames white leaders as normative, legitimate, and most desirable. This perception is among not only whites but people of color as well. To compensate for a subordinated racial status, pastors of color of multiracial churches pursue more credentials in the form of special training, greater experience, and more education. They strive to work harder than their white counterparts to prove to themselves and others that they can lead well. By working harder and being more competent and successful in their position than their white colleagues, pastors of color believe they can counteract the challenges they face in their job on account of their race. That is how they pay the racial tax.

Pastor Johns, an African American who heads a conservative Protestant church he planted in the Southwest, is one such example. He explains, "I just feel like across racial lines or denominational lines, education for an African American pastor [e.g., having a doctorate] is essential if he is to be embraced by others outside of the African American cultural context." In contrast, white pastors can become famous and "get into a lot of doors" without having many educational "credentials" at all. Pastor Johns made this point by giving examples of evangelical pastors like Mark Driscoll and Matt Chandler, who are widely recognized in the Christian community despite not having doctorate degrees. African American pastors, he reasons, would have to have "credentials galore" to gain the same amount of widespread recognition as these white pastors.

This is exactly what Father Angelo, a Filipino priest who has decades of experience working in a mainline Protestant denomination, believes pastors of color have to accomplish. Given the disadvantages that priests of color have, Father Angelo advises young priests of color to simply work harder, pursue higher credentials, and perform better than their white counterparts: "I was telling our fellows, if you are the same or equal in stature and ability and education like the white fox, you are not going to make it. You have got to go beyond. . . . If he [the white fox] is a star, you have to be a superstar." Whatever Father Angelo meant by calling a white person a "white fox," what is clear is that he believes one way pastors of color can deal with the racial prejudice and discrimination they encounter is outperforming their white counterparts in their denomination or tradition.

Sheep or Goat

While congregants of color prefer white pastors, it is white congregants, in particular, who have a difficult time following the lead of a pastor of color and "submitting" to their leadership. Many pastors of color believe this is because white (middle-class) people are simply not used to following anyone, especially someone who is not white. One second-generation Korean American pastor of a multiracial conservative Protestant church plant plainly stated, "White people just don't like to follow anyone, you know?" An African American pastor was more specific saying "Whites don't follow Blacks." Consequently, they work hard to demonstrate they are worthy of being followed, to please white people within their multiracial congregation and gain their approval.

Pastor Jackson, a conservative Protestant who planted his now medium-size multiracial church in the Southwest, shares how he experiences this dynamic. He too uses language like "try harder":

> I think it takes a little bit of an extraordinary person, somebody that is a little bit above the normal, to be able to pastor a multiethnic church if you are Black . . . because it took one to two years for people to trust me in this church. I had to earn that trust. . . . I had to build the trust and I think I would have to build that trust even if I weren't Black. I would have to build it, but being Black, I think I had to try a little harder.

While all pastors have to gain their congregants' trust, a Black pastor of a multiracial church has to try even harder. This is because they must counter a "negative stereotype of Black pastors" that paints Black people as less dependable, educated, or competent relative to white pastors. To do so, Pastor Jackson tries especially hard to "be excellent" in all he does. He makes sure he is "never late" to any meetings. He makes sure that he "effectively communicates verbally and in writing." Although he already has a Master of Divinity degree, he was pursuing even more credentials, taking online seminary classes, and was thinking of pursuing a doctorate. He spends twelve to fourteen hours on the Sunday sermon in order to make it "more than perfect." On top of all this, Pastor Jackson is bivocational. In addition to all the energy and time he puts into pastoring and ensuring he is sufficiently credentialed, he is holding down a full-time job because he does not get paid for heading his medium-size congregation. His church cannot handle the financial burden of paying him a salary. And not surprisingly, Pastor Jackson has never had a vacation from either of his two jobs.

Despite the extra work and sacrifices he made starting and heading his congregation, it took a long time for Pastor Jackson's congregants to trust him. Several white families would not give to the church even though they attended for over a year because they were not sure "if he was really real," or if he could be "trusted." Needless to say, Pastor Jackson is overworked. A major reason why is that he is a Black man heading a multiracial church with white people who are leery of trusting a Black leader.

Pastor Mills is another African American Protestant who heads a church of a few hundred congregants. And like many other pastors of color in our study, he is highly educated with multiple degrees. Pastor Mills confessed that he tries to do everything "with excellence," including having "excellent music" by "highly skilled musicians." While this seems to be working to attract Hispanic Americans and Asian Americans to his church, he has a hard time attracting white people because, in his view, they are simply unused to submitting to leaders in general, and especially leaders of color:

> I believe that it is difficult for white people to have Black leaders. I am as educated as any pastor that you would find.... We try to do everything with excellence here.... [We have] a trained opera singer who has a master's in church music.... This guy is highly skilled. Yet ... we find it difficult to attract and keep whites. We do not have that problem with Latinos. To a certain extent, we don't have that problem with Asians. What is my thesis for that? I think white people don't want to submit to leadership.

Pastor Mills tries his best to compensate for his race and does everything with "high excellence" in an effort to encourage white congregants to support his leadership. But even still, he has to accept that it may not be enough.

For women pastors of color, it is obvious that the leadership hierarchy is not only racialized but also gendered and patriarchal.[2] White men sit at the top of the clergy hierarchy. So congregants not only have a hard time accepting and following pastors of color; they have difficulty accepting and "submitting" to a woman as their head clergy. This puts an added strain on pastors of color who are women. They have to work even harder than their male pastors of color colleagues to be accepted and respected as head clergy.

This was evident to Pastor Taylor, who is one of the very few women in her mainline Protestant denomination to head a multiracial church. When asked about the challenges she has faced "as a Black woman priest," Pastor Taylor responded, "Well, first of all, it's to be seen as a priest. And I think that has a lot to do with being female." Just because she is a woman, some people won't acknowledge her as a priest. To address this misperception, she was advised by her supervisor to always come to work with a black clergy shirt and collar so as to look as priestly as possible.

> The first day I came to work I didn't have on a clergy shirt. . . . [My supervisor] said to me, "You are going to come to work in a clergy shirt and it is going to be black. Because you are going to have enough trouble with people recognizing you as a priest, so you are going to look as priestly as you can. Black. No pink, no blue . . . black shirts."

Still, despite dressing the part, Pastor Taylor receives little respect. People just do not see her as clergy. To illustrate her point, she recalls an interaction with a woman getting into an elevator: "I held the elevator [door] and the woman was like . . . 'Thank you, Sweetie.' I get 'sweetheart,' 'darling' . . . I mean . . . oh my gosh. I stopped getting upset about it because I would be upset all the time. I am saying to myself . . . 'Wait . . . I am in a suit. I have on my collar and I am Sweetie?'" Such language comes off as patronizing and particularly gendered.

Pastor Taylor has thus concluded that she simply has to work harder, not just more than white people but also more than men, to be accepted as a priest: "[M]en have advantages that we don't [have]. I think that we have to work harder. . . . In my faith, my experience tells me I have to work harder." In fact, her experience tells her there are congregants who will not accept a woman as their priest but would be willing to accept a man of color as their priest:

> As far as the parishioners are concerned who don't think that women should be priests, race does not matter. It is the fact that you are a woman. It is much easier to accept a Latino or an Asian male than it is to accept a woman even if [she shares] your ethnicity . . . whatever it is, because she is a woman. . . . For example, people asking about Hillary [Clinton, former U.S. presidential candidate]. . . . What is she going to do with her grandchildren? Really? What would [the women priests] look like at the altar when they are pregnant and they are kind of like that fat priest over there. . . ? It is okay if his gut

is over there, but if you are pregnant, that is not acceptable? Hello?! It looks the same.

Pastor Kay, another Black clergywoman who heads a mainline congregation, has the same struggle and burden. She shared the following when asked about the challenges of leading multiracial congregations:

> I think as a Black woman in charge of this place, I could never describe the nuance[d] challenge. . . . It's subtle, where one can feel that the old Black woman would rather have a white male pastor, a little bit more like Jesus or something. Where in our denomination . . . we still have a conscious clause that if you really don't want to hire . . . a woman, you don't have to. You can just say "The Bible says . . ."

These two Black clergywomen have to work overtime just to be "seen" and have any hope of being respected as head clergy. This is the case even in their liberal multiracial mainline Protestant churches. There seems to be no way around it.

When You Dis Yourself

In *The Souls of Black Folks*, W. E. B. Du Bois[3] reveals what it is to be both Black and American: "It is a peculiar sensation, this double-consciousness, this sense of always looking at one's self through the eyes of others, of measuring one's soul by the tape of a world that looks on in amused contempt and pity." It is seeing oneself and measuring one's self-worth against a "tape" fabricated by a white supremacist and paternalistic society. This soul-wrenching struggle relates to the social psychological concept of "internalized racism," when people of color come to accept and then "internalize" the dominant narratives of white superiority and their own racial group's inferiority.[4] Internalized racism carries emotional "psychic costs" people of color bear as the racist stereotypes, images, and ideologies propagated by a white supremacist society about their worth and ability impact their sense of self and self-worth. Living in a society where "white is right" and "white is best," "feelings of self-doubt," disrespect and even disgust for oneself and/or one's race emerges.[5]

This concept of internalized racism helps us understand a second way pastors of color deal with the unique and additional challenges these pastors experience heading multiracial churches: they try to distance themselves from the negative frames assigned by the white supremacist superstructure to their race by dissin' themselves and at times their ethnoracial group as well. Pastors of color, particularly those who planted their own churches, report hiding or suppressing their racial identity in an effort to disassociate it from their congregation. They believe their racial minority status might diminish the success of their churches. Many also dis their ethnoracial home churches and, in the process, reveal a rather strong partiality for white religious culture and structure.

One of the pastors who took this approach is Pastor Park, a second-generation Korean American pastor who planted a multiracial church on the West Coast. He grew up in predominantly white neighborhoods in the Midwest, "always had only white friends," and attended private prep schools. His Korean immigrant parents discouraged him from learning Korean to ensure his success and assimilation into mainstream society. He became a Christian during his college years, almost by chance, through an evangelical Korean campus ministry. He left a secular career to serve as the assistant pastor of a predominantly Asian American young adult ministry housed in a larger, aging white conservative Protestant church that was headed by a white pastor. With this white pastor's guidance, Pastor Park eventually branched out to plant a church several miles away.

One of the main strategies he employed when planting his church was to minimize his racial and ethnic identities. Pastor Park intentionally omitted any photos of himself on the church advertisements so as not to signal to people that the pastor of this new church in the community was Asian. He reasoned that if he included a picture of his face in church advertisements, people would quickly pin the church as an "Asian" church and lose all interest. To make this point, he shared how another Korean American pastor who wanted to start a multiracial church in the neighborhood swiftly failed because he put a picture of his entire Korean family in the church advertisement. The church was then pegged as an "Asian church" and never made it off the ground. Pastor Park made it clear he was not omitting his face because he was ashamed of who he is. Instead, he was simply accepting a reality that non-Asians, mostly white people, who predominate in the neighborhood would have trouble picturing themselves in a church led by an Asian person: "I mean, with the exception of Francis Chan [a well-known pastor who is Chinese American]... who do you have that is an Asian pastor over a non-Asian Church? I mean I can't name anybody." He assumes others would also have trouble imagining themselves in a church headed by an Asian pastor, even if he is an attractive and likable person, born and raised in the United States.

Pastor Park's conservative Protestant church had grown considerably since it was planted, becoming one of the larger churches in the community. Even after such growth, he remained cautious: "I [still] don't want to put my face on [anything]." Even today, the face of his "right-hand man," who is white, is more prominently displayed on the staff pages on the church website than his own face. He seems to reason, that having a white person's face, or no face at all, is better than having his Asian face associated with his church.

Like Pastor Park, Pastor Jackson planted his church out of a predominantly white religious network. He too omitted any photos of himself on church materials. The church, he says, has "been very intentional to keep my face off of anything, because there is a stigma that comes along with an African American." The stigma associated with his Blackness could negatively impact his church. Fewer people would come to his church if it was obvious that the church was headed by a Black person. Pastor Jackson was so committed to this belief that it was not until the lay leaders affirmed him, expressing to him that they were not ashamed but proud of him, that he relented and agreed to have his face on church materials. He recounts:

> This year is the first public advertising that we have done with my face on it. So we have kept my face off of everything until this year, where, you know, our leadership team says, "Why are we doing this? You know you are who you are. We are not ashamed. We are proud of you. So, we don't have no problem."

Even with this assurance from his leadership team, Pastor Jackson is still reluctant to make it evident that the audio sermons available to the public online are by him, a Black man. He is intentional about disassociating his Blackness from his sermons because he wants people to be drawn to his sermons and consider visiting his church based on the "word," the quality and content of the sermons, rather than the color of the person who is delivering the sermons. Like Pastor Park, Pastor Jackson emphasizes that he is not hiding his race because he is personally ashamed. Rather, it is simply a practical strategy to draw people to his church, which is located in a "white neighborhood" that is not comfortable with having even "a marginal percentage of Black people." He explains, "I said, 'Look guys, are we considering the community that we are in, the neighborhood that we are in?' Because if people see a Black face in a white neighborhood . . .'" Pastor Jackson is so certain of the negative impact his race would have on the church he has even concealed from visitors his role as head pastor:

> I would be out in the lobby and I would meet them and everything. And they would say, "Well, who is the pastor?" And I would say, "You know, I don't know." I would say, "He is in there somewhere." And then I would get up, and then they would be like, "You are the pastor."

He does this so that people would stay and attend his church service for "the Word of God" and not for who is delivering the word. "So just to get their minds and their eyes and their hearts away from who that guy is . . . Does it really, really matter as long as you are hearing the Word of God in a way that you can understand and that you can apply it to your everyday life?" He continues to suppress and disassociate himself because, like Pastor Park, he believes "it works." Perhaps there is some truth to his view. Unlike many other African American pastors who have tried to plant a church in the neighborhood and failed, his church plant is still standing.

Dissin' Your Background

Almost all the pastors of color in our study dissed their ethnic home church, describing it as lacking in one way or another when compared to the mainstream or white-majority church, which was perceived as better and ideal, friendly and egalitarian, collaborative and team-oriented. Asian American, Hispanic American, and African American pastors viewed the leadership, teaching, preaching, and general culture of their ethnic home church as wanting when compared to that of white-dominated Christian religion.

Pastors of color described the leadership they found in their ethnic home churches as subpar compared to that of mainstream majority-white congregations. Many were not particularly fond of the hierarchical leadership structure of their ethnic home churches, often framing it as authoritarian and dictatorial. One African American pastor describing the leadership in the churches he grew up in asserted that "The pastor is Jesus" and the church was run "with an iron hand." He much preferred the leadership approach he learned while in a predominantly white seminary because, in his view, it favored shared governance and collaboration.

Korean American pastors, in particular, described the Korean church, whether in the United States or in South Korea, as lacking when compared to predominantly white Christian communities. The leadership structure, preaching style, and organizational culture of the church were of concern.[6] Pastor Park, for example, was quite familiar with what he described as the "passionate Korean preaching style," which he became acquainted with during his college years in a Korean campus ministry. He admits his preaching may even be a bit "Korean" because he preaches more passionately than most other pastors he knows in his denomination. When asked later about his preaching style and role models, however, Pastor Park quickly named a white pastor. He also specified that the preaching style he follows is most like a "white middle-class" style:

> I probably emulate or want to emulate, my preaching style, more off of somebody like an Andy Stanley [a well-known pastor who is white].... If there is anybody I would want to emulate in my preaching stock, it would be somebody like him.... Then, if you were to assess his preaching style, it probably is white middle-class.

The same goes for how Pastor Park views his leadership style. Korean pastors, he says, lead Korean churches in a hierarchical authoritarian fashion, as if they were Moses standing on the top of the mountain, the dominant and indisputable head of the flock. That, however, is not his leadership style:

> In the Korean American culture... you had to have what we call "the aura" in order to make it as a... "Korean" American pastor. And the aura was that they were unapproachable, they were prophetic, and that they were dominant.... I am just not that person. I am "just an extroverted, funny, inappropriate, we are just going to hang out and be friends" [type of a person].... Even with my staff right now... I don't come to the staff and say, "This is where we are going." I don't. I sit down with everybody and I go, "Where do we perceive that God is leading us in the new year?" This is my leadership style.... For the most part, I lead by consensus.

Rather than leading his followers like an almighty prophet with an iron hand, which he believes is common for other Korean pastors, Pastor Park treats his staff and congregants like his friends. They lead together, which in his mind is the more commonly white "American" versus "Korean" way of leading a church.

Interestingly, Pastor Park names the white pastor who helped launch his church as an important role model. The church ministry that he led prior to planting his multiracial church was predominantly Asian American. He had plenty of Asian people that he could have recruited to help launch his church plant. Instead, the small group of people that helped start his church were white. Pastor Park's "right-hand man" is also white. This was a deliberate choice. He explains that "the beauty of a church plant is that you get to establish your culture and identity." As the head church planter, he gets to dictate the culture of his multiracial church plant. And the culture that he has chosen for his church is admittedly "white middle class": "Even though our church is multiethnic, we are probably monocultural [white middle class]."

Pastor Park's church is multiracial and located in a city that is racially very diverse, with the most sizable population being Hispanics, followed by Asians, and non-Hispanic whites. He is very familiar with the "Korean" style of preaching and leading and the Korean immigrant church culture. He even became a Christian through a Korean Christian fellowship. Yet, from the way he preaches and the way he leads to the songs his church sings, the unstated culture of his church is white.

Pastor Jackson would also say that the multiracial church he planted has more of a white middle-class culture. He explicitly states that his church follows a "white" preaching, teaching, and leadership style rather than an African American or Black church style. His rationale for this is simple and practical: that is the only way that a church plant can hope to survive in a predominantly white city in the Southwest, even if that city is in the most racially diverse county in the state.

Pastor Jackson "grew up in some Black churches," so he "know[s] the Black church scene." He is also an "ex-military guy" and had the opportunity to travel the world and be exposed to different people and cultures. Along the way, he "visited all kinds of churches, Japanese, Korean." Despite his familiarity with the "Black church scene" as well as a variety of cultures of people who are not white, Pastor Jackson does not preach like African American pastors. He says, "I don't preach like my ethnicity. Right. So African American pastors have a reputation of preaching very warm, powerful, charismatic, culturally directive sermons. I don't." Instead, he chooses to preach in a way that would be more amenable to white people, a capacity he developed having been trained in historically and predominantly white seminaries and embedded in an equally white denomination and religious network. Pastor Jackson even advises other Black pastors who have struggled to start a multiracial church to not preach "Black" and instead preach in a way that will suit the white people in the community.

> They expressed their struggles. They said, "Man, it's hard. We can't. We don't have the money. We can't get people to come to the church." . . . And one of the things that I shared with them very gently is, "Guys, you can't bring your traditional Black Pentecostal service into a white conservative community and think you are going to thrive. . . . You think you are going to be the T.D. Jakes [a well-known pastor who is Black] of [this city], it is not happening." It is not impossible, but it is really hard. So the church should look like the community.

Like him, the Black pastors he is advising are choosing to plant churches in white conservative communities. He encourages these pastors to let go of their own culture with the express intention of attracting conservative white people. Indeed, the city that Pastor Jackson is working in is predominantly white. But the broader county is very racially diverse and international. Additionally, there are several racially diverse cities and towns nearby. Thus, Black pastors hoping to plant multiracial churches in the community don't have to cater to just white people in order to grow. Pastor Jackson, however, advises them to do so anyway, suggesting he places a greater value on attracting white people to his church than people of color.

Like many conservative Protestant pastors who lead multiracial congregations, Pastor Jackson tried to stay out of politics. Yet this position mostly only served the interests and predilections of white congregants. Around the time of the interviews, the murder of Michael Brown in Ferguson, Missouri, had occurred and Black Lives Matter protests were taking place there as well as other places in the country. Yet Pastor Jackson did not talk about Ferguson, Black Lives Matter, or, as he put it, "African American issues" with his church. He also does not celebrate or mention Black History Month. And even though the second largest group in his congregation after whites were Hispanics, he does not take a stand on undocumented immigration. Instead he preaches that while people ought to help those in need, this does not make it okay to "break laws." Thus, he indirectly opposes undocumented immigration, a position that most likely suits the politics of his conservative white congregants.

The same goes for church music. For what he calls "lobby music on Sunday morning," his church plays music in the background as people enter the church for worship services. They intentionally "mix up the music" at this time. "They have on a Black song, one white song, one Black song, one white song, one Latino song, one Black." But when it comes to the actual worship service, the music and singing are "white." The worship leader is biracial (Black/Asian American), and the church's "worship is actually white, because [the worship leader] doesn't know any Black music . . . he is more of a Hillsong [type of worship music commonly associated with white contemporary Christian worship] guy."

Like Pastor Park, who eschewed the leadership approach of his Korean counterparts who head Korean immigrant churches, Pastor Jackson does not want to lead like his Black counterparts who head Black churches, people he disparages as irrefutable leaders of the church, who act as a "talking head" of the church with an attitude like "I am the only guy here. And I am the pastor here . . . and if you don't hear me, you ain't going to hear nobody else, and I run this place!" Instead, Pastor Jackson too chooses a collaborative leadership style, wanting others to join him. He prefers to lead with a team, one that includes people engaging in a variety of different teaching, leadership, and preaching styles. Thus, his assistant pastor, who also preaches, is white. Describing his preaching staff, he says, "They don't look like me, and I don't want them to look like me. . . . I don't want them to preach like me, I don't want them to be anything close to who I am." Although Pastor Jackson is Black and is familiar with the Black church tradition, he does not preach, worship, or lead like a Black pastor. Instead, in his attempt to be open to a broad audience in his multiracial church, he ends up preaching, worshiping, and leading in a way that would be most amenable to white people. In this, he suggests appealing to whites is paramount.

Pastor Song, a 1.5-generation Korean American, shares the perspective of Pastor Park and Pastor Jackson. Before becoming a head pastor of a multiracial church, he worked in Korean as well as predominantly white conservative Protestant churches. For part of his career, he was an assistant pastor in one of the largest Korean churches on the West Coast. Yet Pastor Song received "zero mentorship" from the Korean head pastor. This was attributed, in part, to the church's leadership structure. The head pastor's leadership style was heavily influenced by Confucian culture and was quite hierarchical. The status of the head clergy was not to be challenged. The head pastor of the Korean immigrant church would also be ill-equipped to mentor a person who wanted to head a church other than one that aimed to serve Korean immigrants.

In contrast, a well-known white pastor in his denomination whom he names as his primary mentor was "a very strong leader," yet humble and approachable. Even though this white pastor is a "world-renowned" speaker and leader, he had an accessible "horizontal" leadership style. He worked with his staff as a team. Pastor Song notes that this kind of egalitarian leadership style fostered trust among the staff and congregants and generated a healthy spiritual climate for the church: "I had the privilege of working under him and with him ... an amazing man. I learned a lot ... in terms of what we call truth, grace, trust. Their big thing was trust. If you have trust, then we can work together." This white pastor taught him how to be a strong leader, one who cultivates a team approach and builds trust among his staff and the congregation. It was this white pastor, not the Korean pastors he served under in the Korean church, that provided needed guidance on leading a multiracial church movement.

Pastor Song claimed that Korean churches have an unhealthy culture, epitomized by the prevalence of "parking lot politics." This occurs when congregants who do not feel they can express their concerns during formal gatherings air their grievances afterward, in the parking lot. White churches, on the other hand, have white pastors who are more likely to have egalitarian relations and communication with their staff and congregants, according to Pastor Song. The perception is that white churches don't have the same level of "parking lot politics" as Korean churches because people can share what they want with leaders during meetings, and even express critical comments. That means "once the meeting was done, it was done," as Pastor Song put it. In white churches, there was no need for a post-meeting in the parking lot. To him, this promoted more positive "relational dynamics" and was an indicator of a church being more "spiritually healthy" than the Korean churches he encountered.

Pastor Song was not alone in his less than positive view of his home church. Some Hispanic American pastors dissed their home church communities, preferring the cultures of white churches. Pastor Luis Montoya is one of these pastors. He is a bilingual 1.5-generation Mexican American who was hired by a historically and predominantly white conservative Protestant denomination to lead a small multiracial church. When Pastor Montoya was asked why some Hispanics would come to his church rather than a Spanish-speaking Mexican American church, he described the shortcomings of the "ethnic church" as a remnant of the old country and a hard immigrant life. In his view, an upwardly mobile Hispanic American would be eager to leave behind the ethnic church and choose to be a part of the broader mainstream church once they had success in the new country:

> If you have had any kind of upward mobility in your life because you are a small business owner . . . now [you have] a house on the other side of the tracks, or you have gone off to college, and you have your degree and you are living on the other side of the tracks, you did all of that to leave the neighborhood, including the ethnic church.

Successful Hispanic Americans who have assimilated and been educated in mainstream institutions don't want to go back to where they came from. They won't go to Spanish-speaking immigrant churches that are typically underresourced and have "immigration issues." Instead, they want to go to the predominantly white churches in the mainstream, which is a measure of success. They will go to a church like his that is connected to a mainstream denomination, "where they get the kind of teaching, camaraderie, kind of networking, the kind of connections for themselves and for their kids" that they want as upwardly mobile Hispanics.

Other pastors of color also saw their ethnic home churches as generally deficient when compared to white-majority churches. The ethnic home church was described as lacking theological rigor and soundness. Its services and worship style were characterized as emotional and unsophisticated. Pastor Charles, for instance, a young African American pastor who planted a multiracial church in the Midwest, makes this point when explaining why he left the Black church:

> I had left the Black church in part due to the lack of theology or depth of theology in some, but not all, of the worship music in the African American church. You could take an artist like Hezekiah Walker who writes very repetitive kinds of songs, over and over. He repeats the same phrase over and over again. It just lacks depth. . . . [T]he song is more self-centered rather than outward vertical centered . . . like "God, get me through this" versus "How can we build in songs that teach about the character and nature of God?"

If Pastor Charles wants to sing songs that have more theological "depth," at least as he understands depth, he will have to go elsewhere.

Pastor Charles also does not like the preaching style associated with Black pastors of Black churches. He does not like to "whoop" or think he ought to take "three hours" to preach a sermon. He also does not like to wear a suit on Sunday. He dresses more casually and takes only about an hour to deliver his sermons. Although Pastor Charles is not explicit about the source of the style that he likes to follow in lieu of the Black church style, the preaching and presentation style that he describes following on Sunday at his multiracial church would align most closely with what one would find in the white conservative churches.

Although pastors of color who planted churches say they don't receive much support from any churches, white or otherwise, they especially note that their ethnic home churches provide little or no resources compared to the broader white churches. Pastor Johns, another conservative Protestant pastor who planted a multiracial church, points to the lack of help from the Black church community. In his view, the Black church is generally not trusting of potential rising leaders because there is but one king and one pastor within any single Black church. Other leaders may challenge the pastor's reign. A rising star, perhaps an assistant pastor, may challenge the head pastor's leadership or, worse, take some of their congregants to start another church. Thus, instead of supporting one another, Black church leaders fight with one another for Black congregants' respect and loyalty. Pastor Johns shared the following when asked whether or not he received support from Black churches to plant his church:

> That don't exist. . . . African American pastors typically do not help African American planters. That is specifically things that I know. . . . Because ultimately the Black pastor does not want to disciple and prepare the guy to plant the church, because if you leave me, then you are taking some of my people with you possibly, so the African American church, or lead pastor primarily, has been really neurotic about, first of all, who he actually has standing in his pulpit to preach to his people. Then, when you staff, let's say a young adult pastor and after a couple of years, I will either fire you because I can't trust you any longer because you may try and start your own church. So it is this whole crab in the bucket mentality. . . . As soon as . . . a crab tries to crawl out of the bucket . . . what will happen? Before he gets out of the bucket, another crab will pull him back down.

This explains why he hasn't received "a dime" from his family members, all of whom are leaders in the Black church. When asked if he found resources or support from the white church, Pastor Johns was also disappointed that he has not received much from them either. What little support he did receive, however, what Pastor Johns refers to as "small resources," like education and training on church planting, came from white religious organizations and networks. When asked how the "white church" has supported his church-planting endeavors, he replies, "Small resources, but nothing major. Training, you know, invited to a conference, have my plane ticket, hotel . . . those types of things paid for. All to educate me, but not to support me. Do you get what I am saying?" While Pastor Johns adds that these resources are small and merely educational, what assistance he did receive came from the white church, which he did not grow up attending or have any familial connections with.

Thus, on the whole, one of the ways multiracial church pastors of color cope with the estrangement they experience from their ethnic home church is to criticize them in favor of white churches, which, from their perspective, provide better models and guidance for their multiracial churches.

Recharging from Home

Curiously, although they criticize their ethnoracial home churches, some pastors of color, specifically African American pastors, manage the stresses of being the pioneers of multiracial congregations by reconnecting with their ethnoracial home church. While they find the Black church wanting in various respects, African American pastors are able to recharge through the familiar and close-knit social ties, the homophily that they can enjoy in their home churches. The Black church community is where they can be in the majority, the norm, and be among that which is familiar and find some respite from the white-dominant world where they work and often live.

Asian American and Hispanic American pastors did not turn to their ethnic home churches to recharge like the African American pastors did. This may be because these are
communities largely geared toward serving an immigrant ethnic population. A co-ethnic, primarily non-English-speaking immigrant congregation may not be a space where assimilated Asian American and Hispanic

American pastors of multiracial, English-speaking congregations feel they can rest and recharge. These immigrant congregations, which are largely the product of the post-1965 immigration wave, also lack the history and years in U.S. society to have developed an established culture and identity like the Black church. That said, all pastors of color found some semblance of comfort through co-ethnic social ties, whether in or outside of their ethnic home churches.

Take Pastor Mills, an African American pastor of a mainline church who, as we noted, tries to do "everything with excellence." He heads a 175-person multiracial congregation where the two largest groups are whites and Asian Americans. Although Pastor Mills grew up in a predominantly Black community and attended a Black church for most of his life, he has pastored only predominantly white or diverse churches. As such, he misses the Black church. It is in the Black church where he can get fed, where he can get rejuvenated and recharged:

> There's something about the Black tradition—the singing, the Spirit, the movement—and I miss that. Every other year, I go to a convocation of pastors of Black churches. I'm not in a Black church, but I go. . . . My soul is set on fire and I get fed. And I come back and I'm ready to go. I'm just rejuvenated.

Pastor Mills is not alone in finding respite through the Black church. Pastor Johnson, who is in his sixties, grew up in the Black Baptist church and is ordained as a Baptist minister but currently heads a historically white but currently diverse mainline Protestant church in the South. He is a classically trained musician and has received several ministry related degrees, all from historically white Presbyterian seminaries, and years of experience in ministry. Before he preaches on Sunday mornings at his church, he commonly visits a Black Baptist church nearby. He does this to get "fed" and "inspired" before he preaches at his own church.

> Normally every Sunday morning I go to a Baptist Church that is a mile from our building and I just simply sit in the pew and get fed and inspired at that very traditional African American Baptist church. . . . I go there at seven-thirty a.m. and then we get out about nine and I go over to [my church] in time for our Sunday school. . . . Why? I just think it is very important, healthy for you to get outside your own place. . . . [I] wanted to hear

preaching other than my own.... I wanted to go and sit somewhere and just simply be ministered to before I went someplace else and ministered.

Ironically, Pastor Johnson is one of the African American pastors who found the Black church leadership style wanting in various respects. Yet in order to be "ministered to" before he has to minister to people in his multiracial church he goes to the "very traditional African American Baptist church." This reveals the complex relationship Black pastors of multiracial churches can have with traditional African American congregations.

The Black church is often described as being more hospitable, providing more community, and being a place where African Americans can "exhale" after days of going to school and working in a society that is predominantly white. In describing the critical role the Black church plays for African Americans, one African American pastor says, "That is one place you go to, when you know you are going to be in the majority, that I can kind of let my hair down." The Black church is a place where African Americans can take a break from living and working in white spaces.

Another African American pastor who heads a large multiracial church explains the downside of not being able to just relax and be Black. He says Black pastors in his position are always educating and explaining "racial issues" as the head of a multiracial church. Black Lives Matter was already underway and there were heightened tensions revolving around the shootings and deaths of unarmed Black men during the time of our interview. But his church wasn't a place where he could simply exhale and get support. Instead, he had to educate, tread potentially dangerous waters lightly, and explain "racial issues" to his diverse congregation. He could not take anything for granted, including that everyone would agree that "Black lives matter." If he was in a Black church, however, he could expect people to be on the same page on this matter. He would not have to explain himself or the issue at hand. He could simply exhale and find support and lament. He explains:

> When it comes to racial issues like Trayvon Martin or Michael Brown, I feel like those conversations are harder. They are more challenging, difficult, because you just have diversity built into your congregation. So it is harder to just vent and to have that cultural exhale and say, "Man, I am just frustrated with being a Black man," because you have got people that you have got to understand and that don't understand that. You have got to educate them. So you are always educating. You are always having a conversation.

> You are always trying to explain. You don't get the chance just to exhale, at least in your church context.

This pastor continues to be committed to leading his multiracial church and having the hard conversations about race, because that is where he says the "greater Kingdom fruit comes from." To manage the stress that comes from having to have these difficult conversations, however, he takes time out to "exhale" and get together with other African Americans who share his experiences and perspectives.

> You have very long, great, challenging conversations, and you say that the greater Kingdom fruit comes from this route. So we want to go after the greater Kingdom route. . . . And you get together with those that live like you and vote like you, and then you exhale. You just don't do that on Sunday morning.

If they cannot go to the Black church on a Sunday to "exhale" after a long week of being Black in America, they can at least get together with other Blacks who "live like" them. Taking time out with colleagues who "get them" and share their racialized lived experiences can help relieve some of the stresses of being the lonely pioneers of multiracial congregations, doing the hard work of bearing "Kingdom fruit."

As discussed in previous chapters, the Hispanic American pastors in our study are relatively more assimilated than those in the Hispanic immigrant church community. All of the Hispanic American pastors in our study are immigrants or the children of immigrants who come from majority-Hispanic neighborhoods and Spanish-speaking ethnic home churches. Despite this, all of them were assimilated enough to be hired or appointed to head primarily English-speaking congregations in historically and predominantly white mainstream Christian organizations. For these more assimilated pastors who have entered mainstream associations in their profession, going back to independent Spanish-speaking and primarily immigrant Hispanic congregations was not appealing. The immigrant congregations they left behind serve as a place of comfort and shelter for immigrants seeking to worship in their own language and culture and to find support for their lives in a new land. But it may not be a place of refuge for bilingual or English-speaking Hispanic American pastors who have married Anglo women and found leadership positions in mainstream associations and institutions.

These immigrant congregations also lack institutional power, history, and resources compared to the white mainstream congregations and even compared to the Black church, which has a longer institutional history and presence in the American religious landscape.

Similarly, the immigrant church dynamics as well as the much shorter history of Asian immigrant churches compared to both white churches and Black churches in U.S. society may help explain why Asian American pastors did not turn to their home churches to recharge. The literature on Asian American congregations, particularly Korean American, which predominates studies of Asian American congregations, reveals intergenerational strife between the first and second generations.[7] The immigrant Korean church is in many ways viewed as a church for the first, not the second, generation. The services are held in Korean; the congregations support Korean culture and traditions, however reimagined; and they are led by first-generation Korean Americans. Thus it may not be viewed as a "home" church in the same way that the Black church may be for African American pastors.

One Asian American pastor in our study, however, Pastor Hurh, had a uniquely positive relationship with his home church, an independent second-generation Korean church. This church was born out of a Korean immigrant church as an "English ministry" for the children of immigrants. In time, it became a separate independent church that attracts later-generation young Asian American adults who want a "church of their own." His home church actually supported his church-planting efforts financially and spiritually, which is unusual.

As we mentioned, support for church plants, if there is any, tends to come from white religious networks and denominations. Similar to other Asian American pastors in our study, Pastor Hurh does not find comfort in an Asian ethnic immigrant church. However, like African American pastors, he does find comfort and community, a place where he can "exhale," in religious contexts where he can be among other second-generation, bicultural Korean Americans. Thus, with time and greater intergenerational diversity, we can expect there will be more Asian American congregations that can serve as sites of refuge for a broader group of Asian Americans, including those who head multiracial churches.

The church, however, is not the only place where people can be among their own people. Beyond the ethnic home church, Asian American pastors, similar to African American pastors in our study, found familiar connections and comfort with fellow co-ethnics elsewhere. Although they did not find their ethnic home churches to be appealing places to rest and recharge, being with other Asian Americans, whether as friends, colleagues, or congregants, was valuable. In these contexts, they don't have to think or be concerned about their "race"; they can let their "race" down, so to speak, in ethnically or racially homogeneous settings.

For example, Pastor Hong is a second-generation Korean American who grew up in an immigrant Korean church, although he lived in "mostly all-white neighborhoods." He now heads a multiracial church in a predominantly white area on the East Coast. Pastor Hong says that as an Asian American pastor, he feels he has "more to prove," that he has to work harder to show that he can lead his multiracial church:

> You feel a sense to have to prove yourself, even to your own church, because in your mind, you are thinking... Well, there is always tension and conflicts in church. But in your mind, it comes back to, "Well, it is because I am Asian." So you almost feel like you have to work harder to try to prove that wrong.

Thus, he has additional stress in leading his church because he is Asian American. However, after more Asian Americans joined his congregation, he found himself becoming more comfortable and feeling like he does not have to work so hard to prove himself: "There has been a sense at our church, especially with a lot of the Asian influx, I have been feeling much more comfortable in our church." With more Asian Americans in the congregation, he has not been as stressed about leading.

In addition, Pastor Hong notes that he does not have any "real friends" he can "just hang out with." Nevertheless, he says that the few pastors that he has "more of a friendship" with are "Korean guys."

> In terms of real friends, I mean... I don't think I have had that since I was younger.... Other, you know, and those are other pastors as well.... [I]t became more of a friendship level, and those are Korean guys as well. So that is one thing I realized. There is a sense of friendship and closeness that, it doesn't feel as much work just to be with people who, again, share certain cultural similarities or affinities.

While he does not have many friends, those he has found kinship with are other second-generation "Korean guys" who pastor congregations. They have more in common; there is "a sense of friendship and closeness," a "taken-for-grantedness" that allows him to be more relaxed. He does not have to work so hard to connect with them.

On the whole, Asian American pastors do not find their ethnic home churches to be places where they can "exhale" and recharge. Their ethnic home churches are immigrant churches, which are "home" primarily for their immigrant parents, not themselves. While lacking social support from these home churches, they confess being with fellow Asian Americans, particularly those who are also bicultural, is comforting. They can "vent," relax, and take more for granted with fellow Asian Americans who are also Christians and share their liminal experiences as 1.5- or second-generation Asian Americans. As more Asian American churches grow and mature over time, we can expect that there will be more ethnic home churches that can serve as places of rest for a broader demographic of Asian Americans, including Asian American pastors seeking places to recharge as they pioneer multiracial congregations.

Finding Their Own Tribe

Pastors of color do not have the same amount of support as white pastors to help them manage the stresses of their job, either from their home churches or from their broader mainstream religious networks. They are more "alone" than their white pastor peers in their role as head clergy of multiracial congregations. Nevertheless, pastors of color are not without help. They too have peers they can turn to. One of the ways pastors of color can counteract the unique and additional challenges they encounter in their position as head clergy is to find and build a community, a support system of their own—their own tribe of estranged pioneers of multiracial congregations.

When pastors of color are asked about the people who provide them support, they most commonly mention their partners, husbands, or wives or other close family members. They also list their friends, pastor colleagues, and mentors. What all of these different supportive people have in common is that they are also committed to multiracial churches. They are co-pioneers on the journey to lead and grow multiracial congregations.

A Chinese American pastor in the Southwest who planted a multiracial church coming out of a Chinese immigrant church named three people as his greatest source of support: his wife (also Chinese), a white American scholar and mentor who has helped start a multiracial church movement, and an African American pastor who leads a multiracial church in his denomination. What all of these people have in common is their passion for the multiracial church movement. In one way or another, they are all fellow pioneers of multiracial churches.

Father Angelo is the priest who advises other Filipino priests in his mainline Protestant denomination to work harder than white pastors in order to succeed. He was able to come as far as he has as one of the few "stars" in his denomination, not simply by hard work and doing more than his white colleagues. He has also had the support of other pastors of color. When asked who he relies on for support, Father Angelo quickly named three people of color, one African American, one Hispanic American, and one Native American, who are part of "the diversity team in the national office" of his denomination. These people of color, including himself, are committed to diversity and to expanding multiracial congregations within their denomination.

> We have [these] four, I call it the four aces of [our denomination] that are really engaged in diversity, [in] not just training but [also] working together. We have a conference for young adults of color that we sponsor every year. We have developed a new community . . . for all races coming together . . . peer support for the multicultural kind of training.

This group comes together regularly to plan conferences and foster conversations about diversity and support different races "coming together" in his historically and predominantly white mainline denomination. There are only four of them, including himself, representing each of the largest communities of color in his denomination (Hispanic American, Native American, African American, Asian American). Nevertheless, they exist. They are helping to make the denomination more diverse, multiracial, and egalitarian. Even though he is the only Asian representative and leader in this denominational network, he has fellow pioneers working in different parts of the community toward the same goal of achieving diversity and inclusion in their denomination.

We see this with Pastor Hurh as well. Although his home church consisted primarily of second-generation Korean Americans, the church's leadership was very sympathetic and practically supportive of Pastor Hurh's efforts to plant a multiracial church. They too shared the dream of having more racially inclusive churches in the United States, particularly those started by Korean Americans. Thus, their ultimate source of connection and support stemmed from the shared desire and goal for multiracial congregations. Additionally, Pastor Hurh named African American as well as white pastors who support him. These pastors are on the same journey leading and growing multiracial congregations in his religious network. There are only a few of them, scattered near and far. Pastor Hurh counted only five people, including himself, who are devoted to multiracial churches within his Protestant church-planting network. And, as far as he is aware, he is also the only Asian in this network. Nevertheless, he knows he is not entirely alone in the struggle, which provides him comfort and reassurance as he presses on in his efforts to pioneer a multiracial church.

African American pastors too named fellow tribe members, whatever their racial makeup, as sources of support. What all these supporters had in common was their devotion to the struggle of leading and growing multiracial congregations.

Recall Pastor Charles, who found the Black church's support lacking and who was critical of the Black church's leadership style. When asked where he found support, pastoral guidance, or advice, he quickly noted a "consortium of multiethnic church pastors" within his historically and predominantly white denomination, which actually consists of only a few people he can count on one hand. They are not nearby, so he cannot meet with them regularly. Nevertheless, they are there, and he can reach out and speak with them on the phone or the internet about "issues of multiethnicity." He explains:

> My denomination has a Department of Church Growth and Evangelicalism and within that a consortium of multiethnic church pastors. So, many of the church plants coming into the [denomination], particularly in the last five years, if they are multiethnic, I know who they are, and so we have a monthly phone conversation to talk about issues of multiethnicity. One is a Caucasian pastor in [a midwestern city], another Puerto Rican pastor in [an eastern city]. . . . We talk regularly about what is happening in our churches, how we are addressing these issues, what do we dream about, for our future.

Pastor Charles mentioned two other African American pastors who have successfully planted multiethnic congregations and whom he calls upon for support. Again, these pastors are not nearby, and there are only two of them. But they provide invaluable support for him. He says, "They understand my pain, that lamenting, we don't wish things to be like this [so difficult] forever, the fact that the strategy that we were each taught to plant a multiethnic church [within the historically white denomination] doesn't necessarily apply in our multiethnic demographic." With these fellow African American pioneers of multiethnic churches, he says he can lament, connect, and air the frustration over having to lead multiracial churches without sufficient models and guidance from his denomination.

Looking Ahead

The three main ways pastors of color of multiracial congregations manage the stresses of their job are working harder than their white counterparts, dissing themselves and/or their ethnoracial community, and recharging in safe spaces with people who share their ethnoracial experiences. These are the strategies they find available to them to pursue the work of heading racially and ethnically diverse churches. None is ideal.

Working harder means they must use greater stores of resources, in time as well as energy—physically, emotionally, and spiritually—to head their congregations. What a burden this is! The energy they could be using to take care of themselves and their loved ones or growing their church in the ways they value is being used just to stay in the game. This is largely because they are not given the same benefit of the doubt their white colleagues enjoy.

It is also quite normative for racially subordinated people to reinforce the white supremacist structure by internalizing the dominant narrative which valorizes whiteness and views their own racial group, on the whole, as less capable, desirable, and worthy than the dominant group. Being estranged from the home church and being marginalized as "less than" white leaders in the broader multiracial church world can understandably lead them to feel they have to suppress their racial selves and make attempts to disassociate from the ethnoracial religious communities they left. It may in fact be protective for them, at least in the short run, to diss their own ethnoracial selves and community and align with the white power structure. In the long run, however, doing so only reinforces the white supremacist system and invalidates the very religious communities that people of color hail from and call home, places many actually return to for safety when they need replenishing. It may even be damaging to their own sense of self and worth. Furthermore, it counters pastors of colors' ultimate pursuit of a more inclusive and egalitarian, if not just, multiracial Christian landscape. Finally, dissing and distancing themselves from their ethnoracial home church community diminishes their ability to function as people who can bridge the segregated church communities in the broader society.

Pastors of color of multiracial churches are in a unique position. They have the capacity to nurture connections to their ethnoracial home churches while also sustaining a connection to the broader mainstream white church through their position as heads of multiracial congregations. However, since the racialized religious system, as it exists, does not facilitate or support pastors of color of multiracial churches coming together, they have to make a special effort to support themselves and start their own group. They cannot navigate the structure well on their own. They need allies. They need help. We therefore encourage pastors of color to first and foremost choose to validate themselves as well as their ethnoracial home communities racially and ethnically. We encourage them to maintain and foster the social ties they have with their ethnoracial home communities, while also finding and building support with their own tribe of multiracial church pioneers.

4
Advantages to Leading as Pastors of Color

"Why Would Anyone Want to Do This?"

In June 2019, the Religious Leadership and Diversity Project (RLDP) conference was held. Religious practitioners and interested laypersons from across the United States and even a contingent from Australia were in attendance. The RLDP team presented several key findings from the study, much of which we are discussing in this book. A main takeaway from one of the first presentations was that pastoring is hard. Pastoring a multiracial church is very hard. And if you are a pastor of color of a multiracial church, buckle your seatbelt because you are in for a real struggle! Perhaps not surprisingly, someone in the audience exclaimed afterward, "Why would anyone want to do this?!" Good question!

Compared to homogeneous congregations, Emerson and Smith[1] speculated, "the cost of producing meaning, belonging, and security in internally diverse congregations is usually much greater—because of the increased complexity of demands, needs, and backgrounds, the increased effort necessary to create social solidarity and group identity, and the greater potential for internal conflict." Subsequent research, including our own, repeatedly bears this out. Multiracial congregations are costlier to pursue and less durable and stable than more racially homogeneous congregations.[2] People of color endure most of the costs of participating in multiracial congregations,[3] and pastors of color who head these organizations face additional challenges because of their race.[4] Given the tremendous pull of homophily and the reality of racial segregation in the American religious landscape, it is altogether reasonable to ask why anyone, particularly a person of color, would want to pay the significant costs of leading multiracial congregations.

In an effort to address this important question, this chapter explores the advantages that pastors of color have as leaders in multiracial spaces. We analyze what the African American, Asian American, and Hispanic American pastors shared in our interviews when we asked them the following questions: "Do you think your race affects how you lead your congregation? Why? How? Or Why not? Does your race help you in any way as a multiracial church pastor? Does it limit you?" We also analyze how pastors responded to questions on how their congregants' expectations of them varied by race, if at all, as well as questions on what they thought of contemporary U.S. race relations.

We find that pastors of color tend to have three main advantages. One is that they are multicultural. By this, we do not mean their heritage is multicultural; rather, they are experienced in traversing more than one culture. They are most likely familiar with, for instance, the behavioral norms, values, ideologies, theologies, ways of speech, language, and style as well as material culture, like music, food, clothing, art, and technology, of their own ethnoracial culture and the dominant white culture. Another advantage is that they are better able than white pastors to see and comprehend the racialized social system as a result of their experiences as racialized minorities. A third advantage is that they have the potential to act as bridges between their ethnoracial religious community and their current religious network.

In every case in this study, the current religious network of pastors of color is almost all white as they are all affiliated with predominantly white denominations or religious associations, something common for pastors of multiracial churches. With the exception of two African American pastors who grew up in fairly mixed churches and neighborhoods, the rest of the African American pastors in our study grew up in churches and neighborhoods that were predominantly or entirely Black. Excluding a biracial Asian American pastor, all of the Asian American pastors in the RLDP are either immigrants or the children of immigrants who come from an ethnic Asian home church (e.g., a Korean church) in the United States or abroad. All of the Hispanic American pastors, including the two biracial white/Hispanic American pastors, are bilingual in Spanish and English and grew up in and/or have worked in Spanish-speaking congregations, whether in the United States or abroad. Thus, all of the pastors of color in the RLDP are familiar with at least one other ethnoracial culture besides the majority white culture.

We hope that exploring the advantages of leading as pastors of color will help address the broader question of why anyone, particularly people of color, would want to head multiracial congregations.

Being Multicultural: A Valued Credential

As noted, all of the pastors of color in the RLDP had some level of multicultural competency, a credential most white pastors in the study lacked. Minimally, this meant pastors of color were sufficiently fluent in and had the ability to engage in the ethnoracial culture they were raised in as well as the white majority culture within the same space. By the time they were in ministry, having multicultural competency had simply become a part of their lives—a byproduct of living as racial and cultural minorities who often traversed white-dominated spaces. While there are differences in how they understand their ethnoracial background and how that background helps them navigate their world, pastors of color share the common experience of traversing multiple cultures.

African American Pastors

Whether they call it code-switching, color-switching, or simply being able to understand and inhabit multiple cultures, multicultural competency is part of African American pastors' biography. It is who they are. African American pastors have the ability to navigate different cultures, which they picked up by simply being racial minorities in a white-normative dominant culture. They received their multicultural competency training involuntarily through the "school of life." While the training may not have been pleasant at times, it equipped them to take on the many challenges that often beset them as leaders of multiracial and multicultural communities.

Pastor Hart, one of the few African American conservative Protestant pastors who planted a large multiracial church on the West Coast, was clear about his multicultural competency (in interviews, the term that was commonly used was "cultural competency") and where he got it. When asked if he received "any kind of cultural competency training" to plant his multiracial church, Pastor Hart responded, "Yeah. Yeah. Yeah." When asked where he received such training, he quickly said that such a question is really for white pastors who have not had to navigate a culture other than their own majority culture. Pastors of color, however, cannot go through any part of their life without having to navigate white culture in addition to their own ethnoracial culture. Pastor Hart explains:

> Most minority pastors have to learn cultural competencies through on-the-job training because . . . as a Black man, I have always had to learn what it is to navigate a majority cultural world. As a majority culture person, they would never need to know how to navigate my world. . . . [T]hey can go their whole life and never need to know how to navigate my culture or my world. I cannot go five minutes without having to know how to navigate theirs. So cultural competency—I have been learning that ever since I went to school, as a child.

White people can move through life without having to be familiar with navigating a culture other than their own. Pastors of color, however, "can't go five minutes" without having to navigate the white majority culture.

Another African American conservative Protestant pastor shares the same story. He explains what it is like being Black in America:

> In our world, at least in America, Blacks are having to be in situations where they are the minority, and so having to integrate and assimilate into environments that are not predominantly Black are things that we can't avoid. . . . [Y]ou can't live in America and at some point not do that . . . whether in your job, where you live. You are going to have to be okay with being a minority at some point.

This pastor continues by noting how, from his perspective, the situation is different for white people:

> Where for many whites . . . [in] many contexts in our nation, you can live a life without ever having to consistently be part of a community where you are the minority. You can go have a career and a job where you don't have to be a minority. You can go to school where you don't have to be the minority. You can go to a neighborhood where you don't have to be a minority.

In short, many Blacks have to be "okay" with being a minority and assimilating into a culture other than their own. It is simply a fact of life in America. Many whites, in contrast, do not have to do the same.

Having to learn how to navigate other cultures, especially without any choice in the matter, is certainly not easy. Such efforts, however, are not in vain. All of the African American pastors, in one way or another identified themselves as being culturally competent and unequivocally agreed that being so advantaged them in myriad ways in their role as head clergy of diverse congregations.

When asked if the cultural competency training he received in the "school of life" by simply being a Black man in America has helped him in any way as a leader, Pastor Hart had no doubts: "Of course! God . . . You know, you grew up having to navigate. Yeah. It is much bigger than you, and you have got to know that in order to get any type of degree that is worth its salt or any type of job outside of your community. You have got to know . . . how to navigate other cultures."

We had no shortage of African American pastors who agreed with Pastor Hart. One of the two Black women pastors in our study was Pastor Taylor. Like all other women head clergy in this study, she heads a multiracial church in a predominantly white mainline Protestant denomination. She explains how her diverse background helps her lead her multiracial church: "[It] has helped me lead a multiethnic church because I can translate across cultures. I can do that. If I meet with something that I don't understand, I am pretty good at figuring it out, like observing and going, 'Okay, causality.' This always brings this response." Pastor Taylor's lifelong experience interacting with multiple cultures as a child and a woman of color gives her the tools to "translate across cultures" and know how she should proceed in diverse situations.

Father James also has multicultural competency. Seeing the white dominant culture for what it is and being self-reflective about his own biculturality, Father James is able to steer his largely Hispanic and Anglo congregation through difficult times. One of the ongoing challenges he has as head clergy is building a more inclusive community in a church where the older Anglos who think they "own" the church are prejudiced against the newer, Spanish speaking Hispanic members, many of whom are immigrants. Being able to see and understand the U.S. racial structure and having the capacity to traverse different cultures, Father James first approaches the problem by understanding the broader cultural historical context. He understands that the Anglos' prejudice against the Hispanic members is part of a broader sociohistorical pattern of immigrants being viewed as inferior and being excluded from the majority community. He explains why the Anglos clash with the Spanish speakers:

> Because [in] our history as a country . . . immigrants are always known to be dirty, lazy, they steal. . . . That is what they said about the Italians and the Irish and the Polish and the Hungarians. And that is what they said about

Blacks and now they are saying that about the Hispanics. . . . For example, Anglos say, "Oh, they don't give anything to the church, and they are so dirty. Whenever they come, there is always Cheerios [on the floor that their children dropped]." It is the same thing.

Seeing the broader context, Father James takes extra steps to include the Spanish speakers in his congregation. When the Anglos complained that the Hispanics were not doing their part and not participating in church activities, Father James asked the Anglos, "Did you ask them in Spanish? Did you send out the invitation in Spanish?" They had not. Once the Anglos asked in Spanish, however, Father James said, "Boom," the Hispanics participated. It was the same when the Anglos complained that the Hispanics and especially their "rowdy children" were wearing the church property down and not helping with the upkeep of the congregation. In response, Father James asked for volunteers, including the Spanish speakers, to spruce up the building, and the Hispanics came out in droves to help. "For example, when we painted the building over there . . . we asked for volunteers, and the Spanish community came out with their paints and brushes . . . and then people said, 'Wow.' We took pictures and publicized that. 'Oh, now, they are helping.' Well, they were never invited." As a multiculturally competent leader, Father James understood that Hispanics were not being included within his historically white English-speaking church, that they were "never invited" to be a part of the church. He therefore took active steps to include them, and his efforts have eased tensions and benefited everyone in the church.

Pastor Kay, another Black clergywoman in a mainline denomination, also has multicultural competency and is clear about the importance of having it to lead multiracial congregations. As head clergy of a diverse multiracial church, she says she has to be what she calls "multivocal" and to develop "borderness." In other words, she needs to be conversant with multiple worldviews and cultures and have that be reflected in everything that she does. She explains:

Because my congregation is multiracial and multicultural, I am responsible to be culturally competent. In my work, I talk about being multilingual or multivocal. How do we develop our borderness. . . ? What do I read? What do I listen to in terms of music? What are the commentaries that inform my writing? What novels inform my imagination? What movies. . . ? We need to be conversant with more modalities, more cultural markers, more so you can make illustrations that make sense when you are preaching. So when you are counseling somebody, you have a sense of where they live and breathe, because you are walking around a bit in their world.

Pastor Kay's multicultural competency is therefore reflected in everything from her preaching to her counseling. It is also evident in her ability to easily "color-switch" and connect with a variety of people, whether at staff meetings, board meetings, or at the pulpit: "I switch colors often. I am fluent in white-male-speak, academy-speak, Black-woman-playful-speak . . . pound-cake-and-champagne-speak. I studied Spanish [and] German. . . . My best gift is to be fully me so you can be fully you." Pastor Kay not only speaks multiple languages; she is also multivocal and versed in multiple cultures and communities. Her "color-switching" is simply part of who she is. Moreover, by being her full "color-switching" Black woman self, she believes she helps others be fully who they are as well.

Pastor Jackson, an African American pastor in his early fifties who planted a nondenominational conservative Protestant church, can also "color-switch." When asked how he fosters diversity in his thoroughly multiracial church of whites, Blacks, Hispanics, and a few Asians, Pastor Jackson pointed to his biography. He grew up in the "Black church" and lived in the "middle of the cornfield" where Black people were "lynched." He also spent years living in Japan and South Korea and "traveling all over," "visiting all kinds of churches" as an "ex-military guy." As a result, he has become multicultural, and this helps him foster diversity and lead his church.

Pastor Jackson goes on to say he is "culturally versatile and can adapt to various settings depending on the audience." To illustrate his point he says:

> It is the manner in which I speak. . . . I am from Brooklyn, New York. So I can go, "Yo, man. What's up? Hey. Let's get this thing going. Let's get down with it." Or I can say, "Hey. Good morning, everybody. Glad that you are here. . . ." There is a difference. It is a different flow based on where I am at . . . the audience I am dealing with.

Pastor Charles, another African American Protestant pastor who planted a multiracial church, is younger than Pastor Jackson and not as well traveled. Yet he too says one of his assets as a multiracial church pastor is his capacity to "code-switch." He learned to do so growing up as one of the few African Americans in diverse but predominantly white settings:

> The strength of growing up as the only African American in white groups? I think number one is the codes. You know . . . code-switching . . . an ability to understand—not fully, but to a degree—to understand my white friends and then be able to explain my white friends to my African American friends.

In short, Pastor Charles has what all of the African American pastors of color in our study have in one form or another: multicultural competency. They are sufficiently familiar with more than one culture and are multivocal. They have the potential to speak and connect with multiple cultures and peoples in a variety of different contexts, which is no doubt an advantage in leading diverse congregations.

Asian American Pastors

Like the African American pastors in our study, having multicultural competency is simply a part of who Asian American pastors are living in the United States. Their level of multicultural competency may certainly vary, and the ethnoracial culture(s) that they are familiar with may differ. Nevertheless, all of the Asian American pastors are multicultural at some level and have the capacity to serve in multiple cultural contexts, which can be an asset as head clergy of multiracial congregations.

Pastor Song, the 1.5-generation Korean American pastor who is viewed as a "star" in his circles for coming out of the Korean immigrant church to plant a large multiracial church, is sure of his multicultural competency. He says that 1.5- and second-generation Korean Americans who grew up in the Korean American community while also being versed in the dominant white culture have a "bicultural edge" in leading multiracial congregations. Because they were "forced to be culturally agile" in various situations with different people, they have an edge when it comes to leading in diverse contexts:

> Korean Americans have a certain kind of an inherent advantage because they are bicultural. . . . They have a bicultural edge, because they were forced to be culturally agile at school and at home, at church, at different places. They learned to be flexible depending on the context and the culture. . . .

> We are multifaceted. We don't treat our parents the same way we treat our friends.... The way we act is slightly different, especially if they speak a different language, [in a] different cultural context, we adjust to them.

Multicultural Asian Americans like himself can be culturally flexible. They are multifaceted and are able to adjust to interact with different people in varying contexts.

Being multicultural is also part of who Father Angelo is, particularly as someone who grew up in the Philippines. Father Angelo explains that Filipino culture is itself a pliant culture, an amalgamation of Western and Eastern cultures. Thus, he is culturally agile and familiar with living and leading in a mix of cultures:

> I grew up in a more flexible Filipino culture. They say that Filipinos are pliant like the bamboo. They bend a lot.... So I think I have that kind of thing. I really bend a lot in many cases and try to understand others. So I would say that my cultural background, at the basic core, seems to dictate how I approach ministry.

Father Angelo's pliant cultural background, in addition to his years of experience ministering in several countries, including the United States, makes him culturally agile. This is no doubt an advantage for him as a leader of multiracial, multicultural communities.

Not all Asian American pastors were as explicit as Pastor Song or Father Angelo about their multicultural competency. Still, in one way or another, all of the Asian American pastors communicated that they have it. This is the case for Pastor Lee, a Korean American conservative Protestant pastor who planted a multiracial church. When asked if his race affects his leadership, Pastor Lee shared that "being Asian" might be an advantage because he can naturally and easily "cross cultural boundaries." He says, "[It is] just who I am . . . where I can kind of cross cultural boundaries pretty easily and naturally." Because he is culturally fluid, he has the capacity to understand the varying expectations that the different groups in his congregation have of him. For example, he understands that white congregants want to treat him "like a friend," while his Asian American and African American congregants want to treat him with more deference as "the pastor." White congregants want to call him by his first name, Kevin; his Asian American and African

American congregants want to refer to him as "Pastor Lee." Understanding both sides and, moreover, why there is a difference, he tells his congregants to call him "Kevin," "Pastor Kevin," or whatever else works for them.

Hispanic American Pastors

Unlike other pastors of color, none of the Hispanic American pastors in our study willingly planted a multiracial church. Whether they were born in Mexico, Colombia, Chile, or the Bronx, they were all assigned to a church or asked to plant one, most likely because they were seen by their denomination or religious network as Hispanic diversity specialists who spoke Spanish. Whether or not they liked being pegged as diversity experts or felt suited for the position, all of the Hispanic American pastors had some form of multicultural competency.

Pastor Luis Montoya explains how he came to lead his small, predominantly Hispanic multiracial congregation within his nearly all-white conservative Protestant denomination: "They didn't look at my credentials. They didn't ask me any questions. They just said, 'You are Hispanic, you are bilingual, we can use you.'" Pastor Montoya has two seminary degrees and years of experience in ministry. What made him most suited to lead his multiracial congregation, however, was his bilingual, bicultural background—the fact that he is culturally competent in the Mexican American culture that he grew up in as well as the broader white majority culture that he knows so well.

Pastor Garcia also works in a conservative Protestant denomination. He too was appointed to his small, predominantly white and Hispanic multiracial congregation because, as he explained, he is bicultural, bilingual, and presumed to have multicultural competency. His denomination was correct in making this assumption. When asked if his congregants' expectations of him as head clergy vary by their race and ethnicity, Pastor Garcia replied that he is well aware of varying cultural expectations because he comes from "a different culture"—a culture different from the white majority culture. He was born in Chile, raised in Mexico, and trained to be clergy in a predominantly white Protestant denomination in the United States. He explains how his diverse cultural standpoint helps him to better understand the different cultures in his congregation:

> I am aware of expectations, cultural expectations because I come from a different culture.... There are warm cultures, for example in Latin America and some countries in Asia.... People are more important than time, planning, and schedules in that context. It is much more expected that the pastor visits you if you are sick.... He is the one that has to be there ... a little bit more relationally present. And then there is the cold culture.... If the Caucasian family is sick, they don't want me to visit them at home.

He says that people from Latin American cultures are more flexible with time and schedules than those who are from cold cultures, like the "Caucasians" or whites. People from warm cultures are "okay" with his showing up at their home at any time. For the whites from "cold cultures," however, he must schedule the visit ahead of time.

> If I send my text saying, "It's okay to show up?" "Yeah sure anytime you want." It is because [in] ... warm climate cultures, time is very flexible. They tend to arrive later.... But people who are from cold climate cultures, they tend to be more punctual. And you schedule much more.... So if I want to meet somebody from this context, I know that I need ... at least two weeks in advance [notice].

Being aware of these cultural differences as someone who comes "from a different culture," Pastor Garcia describes his multicultural, multiracial church as an amalgam of warm and cold cultures. His church is "highly relational," like the warm cultures, but "not to the extreme." He recognizes that "schedules have to be done in advance" to accommodate the cold-culture people. Balancing these two cultures, he encourages his congregants to be flexible with themselves and with one another and embrace their differences. Pastor Garcia provides an example of how he creates an "atmosphere" in the church to make this possible, "an atmosphere [where] people feel much more freedom, relaxed to recognize the differences and talk about them":

> For example, "I am a cold-culture person here on this team so, you know, we have five minutes left, I need to go in five minutes." Or asking a warm-culture person, "What time do you want me to start or arrive?" ... This is kind of like how marriage is like.... You embrace the differences; you learn to take them for what they are.

Pastor Garcia recognizes that accommodating cultural differences isn't easy, and he certainly doesn't always get it right, but it is an important part of being in a diverse congregation.

Like the African American pastors, one of the Hispanic pastors pointed out that people of color are already used to being bicultural and inclusive because they are familiar with not only their own ethnoracial culture but also the broader white-majority culture. Unlike most white people who can largely go about their lives without having to be familiar with a culture other than their own, most people of color have to be culturally competent in the "white culture" in addition to their own ethnoracial culture. This pastor explains, "Black culture and Hispanic cultures live in a white culture already. So . . . we are already inclusive. You know what I am saying? Because Blacks and Hispanics live in a world that is white, they are already inclusive." People of color are already culturally inclusive by necessity; they are familiar with navigating more than one culture.

Pastors of Color as Potential Bridges

When asked how they manage their role as head clergy of a multiracial congregation, white pastors often talk about relying on "bridge people," who are invariably people of color, to help them understand the different cultures and connect with the ethnoracial group(s) in their congregation. In contrast to white pastors who seek out these "bridge people" for guidance, pastors of color talk about themselves as serving in this role. In their own way, many of the pastors of color in our study described themselves as "bridges" that can potentially connect and broker disparate communities within their congregation.

African American Pastors

Pastor Jones heads a small multiracial mainline Protestant church. His voice, he says, is not the "main voice" in either of the two primary communities that he is part of—his Black home church and his predominantly white religious network. Despite this, he has a unique and "versatile voice" which helps him to connect these two separate communities. This is his advantage as a pastor of color who heads a multiracial church. He is the pastor called on by the African American pastors of Black churches in his religious network when they need intel on how to deal with white people and how white people think about a particular situation, such as the Ferguson uprising following the fatal shooting of Michael Brown by a white police officer. He is also the pastor called on by white people to provide the same intel on Black people. Pastor Jones is explicit about being "the bridge" between these isolated networks: "I am familiar with 'white and Black.' I am familiar with what white and Black [people] are thinking about... not just what Black people are thinking about. The bridge, for lack of a better word."

Many other African American pastors likened themselves to a "bridge." Pastor Charles, who grew up in predominantly white spaces, refers to himself as a "spokesperson" who decodes Blacks to whites and vice versa, which he says makes him a "bridge builder." This is how he responded to our question about how his race helps him to lead a multiracial church:

> I was the only African American in my AP Chemistry class in high school. So I was comfortable being "the representative" of the entire Black race, if you will. And that is a responsibility that I accept fully.... And I don't consider myself a spokesperson for African American males, but I am a representative of that group.... It makes me a bridge builder ... [which is] the greatest strength for pastoring this multiethnic church.

Pastor Charles does not consider himself to be a spokesperson for African Americans; he is clear about that. Just by being an African American pastor of a multiracial church working in a predominantly white church network, however, he is thought of as the de facto "representative of the entire Black race." However unfair and overwhelming that may be, Pastor Charles accepts his role as a spokesperson—to serve as a bridge for segregated communities that do not know each other well.

Pastor Gates, a pastor of a small, predominantly Black and white mainline Protestant denomination, is also a bridge. When asked what his congregants expect of him as head clergy, he says that one of their expectations is that he will "create a partnership" and function as a bridge between the Blacks and whites in his community. He is expected to help the two largest racial groups in his congregation and neighborhood to connect and better understand each other. Pastor Gates explains his efforts to fulfill this expectation by helping the white people who run some of the social service programs in his community better understand the Black people who make up the majority of the people who utilize these services and vice versa:

> If you are white and you are trying to reach out, you had better know who your customers are.... One of the first things [the white people] did when we first had all of the children out here... "Well, where is the Black parent? What is that parent going to say to me?" And then I let them know, "It's okay." And then I also talk to my Black parents. "If you send your child here, that child is going to be chastised or corrected by a white individual, so get used to it or don't come." I am not afraid to say that is a risk.... I have set the stage for both Blacks and whites.... That is a risk, but it is a risk that, if you are pastor, if you serve the community, you must take. If you don't take it, you won't get anything done.

Pastor Gates thus functions as a bridge between two segregated communities to provide pertinent information and counsel that help the two communities work together. He emphasizes that setting "the stage for both Blacks and whites" to cooperate with one another is a "risk." He says that he may get attacked from both sides, that the two sides can "blow up" on him at any moment. Being a bridge is not easy. One can be walked all over by multiple groups. However, someone *has to* take that risk in order to serve a diverse but divided multiracial community. Without someone like him filling the holes in the structural network, "you won't get anything done."

Asian American Pastors

When asked about his primary responsibilities as head of his predominantly Asian American and white multiracial congregation, Pastor Song talked about what other pastors in his predominantly white network talked about. He talked about vision casting, leadership development, and pastoral care, but he also talked about the senior pastor serving as a "bridge" and connecting the various cultures in his church. For example, he intentionally pulls examples from Asian American culture as well as the local white American culture to make the sermons resonate with his congregants. As a pastor who is familiar with the Korean immigrant as well as the Asian American experience in addition to the broader white American experience in the majority culture, he is able to serve as a bridge that gets to inform how a multiracial church that is predominantly Asian American and Caucasian is done.

Pastor Hong also serves as a bridge in his multiracial conservative Protestant church that he planted in a city on the East Coast, which is also predominantly Asian American and white. He sees himself serving as a bridge because he recognizes that he has to go out of his way to make those who are not in the majority culture feel cared for and welcomed in the church. Recognizing the shortage of Asian Americans in leadership, he personally encouraged several Asian Americans to take the initiative and assume leadership positions in the church, a large majority of which were held by white people. While encouraging his Asian American congregants to be more active in the congregation, he also makes sure that his white congregants do not feel neglected. When he hired several Asian American staff members, he made sure to hire a new white staff member as well. In this way, Pastor Hong sees himself as a key broker, a bridge that encourages two otherwise distant communities to be more connected and "get along" in a multiracial context.

When asked how race affects his leadership, Pastor Lee, a 1.5-generation Korean American pastor of a mainline Protestant congregation with whites, Asian Americans, and Blacks, also talked about being a bridge. Pastor Lee said that being an Asian who is Korean and leading a church like his is, "at first," a challenge because people doubt that he can lead since he is "not white." As a leader, he starts out with a deficit because of his race. He adds, however, that once they get to know him, his congregants come to realize that it is a "plus" that he, an Asian person, is their leader. This is because he serves as a bridge for the two largest groups in his congregation, Blacks and whites. Although he is not central to or the most knowledgeable about either of these two communities, he is sufficiently familiar with both and can therefore serve as a bridge. He explains that although he is not Black, he is familiar with being a racial minority. Although he is also not white, he is familiar with having some privileges as the so-called model minority. Thus, while he is not a key player in either of the two communities, he is sufficiently familiar with and connected to both that he can serve as a bridge between the two groups:

> It helps [being Korean]. Because I am not white and because I am not Black. . . . At first, it is a challenge . . . people looking down at you and kind of thinking, "Can you really lead this group? Really?" And then they get to know me and they are like, "Wow, this is a plus." You know . . . when you get into the inner dynamics of who you are, this is a plus. You are that bridge.

Pastor Lee is not a central player in his home Korean church or in his predominantly white church network. He is also not recognized as a major figure in the Black community. Yet he knows enough about these communities and is sufficiently connected to them to function as a bridge for his white, Asian, and Black congregation.

Hispanic American Pastors

Unlike the African American and Asian American pastors, none of the Hispanic American pastors used the term "bridge" to describe themselves. Nevertheless, all of the Hispanic American pastors in fact served as a bridge between at least two segregated communities, namely the Spanish-speaking Hispanic community and the English-speaking Anglo community.

Pastor Martin, who identifies as "half-Latino" but self-describes as looking "all white," talks about serving as a bridge between the Spanish speakers and the English speakers in his multilingual, multicultural, multiracial conservative Protestant congregation. He says that although he looks like a white person and can "do white," he can also "go into Latino mode at any point." Because he is bilingual and bicultural, he says that he "communicates like a Latino" and moves his hands a lot when he preaches. When it is time to pray, he easily flows back and forth between English and Spanish. "When we get up to pray, I pray in Spanish for a minute and then I will finish the prayer in English." This is natural for him because, he explains, "I am bilingual, that is the way I grew up." And he prays in both Spanish and English intentionally because it "gives some people a reminder that, 'Okay, it is not just a white person up on stage.'" Being bilingual and coming from a "diverse heritage," he is able to connect with his multilingual congregation filled with whites, Hispanics, Blacks, and Asians. Moreover, he is asserting his identity as someone who owns his "Hispanicness" despite how he may be perceived based on how he looks.

Serving as one of the few bilingual bicultural Hispanic American head clergy of a multiracial congregation is not easy. Various Hispanic American pastors talked about being alienated, "neither here nor there." They shared that they are not fully comfortable or able to "be themselves" in either the Spanish-speaking Hispanic or the English-speaking predominantly Anglo communities. Pastor Montoya, one of the few bilingual Hispanic American pastors in his predominantly white conservative Protestant denomination, explains: "The Hispanic pastors, they have their group and everything is in Spanish. But I don't really feel comfortable with that. . . . [A]nd then Anglo pastors, they welcomed me and we had good relationships, but there isn't a sense of great camaraderie."

Pastor Morales, a Colombian American pastor of a largely Hispanic and white mainline Protestant congregation in the Southwest, laments the "special expectations," the extra burden that is placed on bilingual Hispanic pastors like himself in his predominantly white denomination. In addition to serving his large bilingual congregation, Pastor Morales is called upon by the denomination to translate materials or offer his opinion on all matters related to Hispanics. Although he serves as a key informant for his denomination, he describes himself as the "lonely only" within his predominantly white religious network. He is also no longer a key player in the predominantly Spanish-speaking religious network that he left to serve in his mainline Protestant denomination.

Unlike the African American and Asian American pastors who were more accepting of the often challenging role of acting as a bridge between multiple ethnoracial communities, Hispanic American pastors in the study did not always appreciate this role. It was thrust upon them by their predominantly white religious denomination. It left some feeling further alienated. Yet, despite the estrangement and alienation they encounter, Hispanic American pastors still function as bridges that can unite racially diverse but divided communities.

The Potential: Keys to the Imagined Multiracial Future

In her groundbreaking work on the sociological significance of Black feminist thought, Patricia Hill Collins[5] argues that "black female intellectuals" have a distinctive standpoint as "outsiders within." In the world of academia, a culturally and numerically white-dominant space, Black women occupy a marginalized social location or standpoint that gives them a special insight and perspective on the social world, one their white and male counterparts do not have access to by virtue of their racial- and sex-dominant social location. As a marginalized population, it also means Black female intellectuals are often otherized and excluded from the power structures of the ivory tower.

Collins's[6] concept of the "outsider within," however, does not apply just to Black female intellectuals. Ultimately, anyone who is marginalized within society has a special insight and perspective on the social world as a result of their standpoint and personal and cultural biographies. We therefore propose that pastors of color are uniquely positioned to lead multiracial congregations. More specifically, we contend that the standpoint and personal and cultural biographies of leaders of color mean they have access to certain distinctive qualities and capacities that make them particularly suited to head multiracial communities.

What distinctive qualities or capacities do they possess? One quality they have is what we call *racialized multicultural competency,* meaning fluency in more than one culture, minimally one's own ethnoracial culture and that of the dominant white society, as well as a capacity to see, understand, and navigate the white supremacist social system, not only intellectually but emotionally. This fluency and capacity are a direct result of their distinctive standpoint as a racial and cultural "other" within a white-dominated social world where personal experiences with racism are all too common. Racialized multicultural competency is available to anyone who meets these criteria. This form of cultural competency is multicultural because it denotes a capacity to navigate multiple cultures within a single context, that is, a multicultural space. Moreover, it is a racialized competency because it is specifically rooted in one's standpoint as a member of a marginalized racial group and informed by a seeing and understanding of the white supremacist system. Racialized multicultural competency is a particular advantage that pastors of color can have in leading multiracial communities.

Our term "racialized multicultural competency" is extending the work of Kathleen Garces-Foley and Russell Jeung,[7] who proposed the concept of "racialized multiculturalism" in their article on the unique contributions Asian American evangelical leaders can make to multiracial church ministry. They argue that Asian American evangelical leaders who grew up in bicultural backgrounds have a "racialized multiculturalism," "a combination of sensitivity to racialization and appreciation of diversity."[8] Garces-Foley and Jeung suggest that Asian American evangelical leaders' "racialized multiculturalism" is distinct from the color-blind approach commonly associated with most white churches. It is also different from the social and political activism practiced by many Black churches which often emphasizes issues related to race.[9]

We build on Garces-Foley and Jeung[10] in several ways. Racialized multiculturalism is a viewpoint specific to Asian American evangelicals and it is particular to their position as a racialized group lodged between the Black and white U.S. racial divide. However, all leaders of color, not just Asian Americans, have access to racialized multicultural competency by virtue of their standpoint as members of a marginalized racial group in a white supremacist society. More than a viewpoint, racialized multicultural competency is a capacity to navigate at least two ethnoracial cultures: one's own and the dominant white culture. This competency stems from the experiences, however diverse or nuanced, that all people of color share by being the racial and cultural "other" in the white-normative and white-dominant racialized system. We further argue that racialized multicultural competency is more than a viewpoint or approach to diversity. It is the ability, the potential to see and understand the racialized social system and be sufficiently familiar with and, by extension, interact with more than one ethnoracial group.

In essence, racialized multicultural competency is a form of specialized cultural capital—an accumulation of knowledge, behaviors, and skills that people of color can uniquely tap into in their position as leaders of multiracial communities. Whereas cultural capital[11] is typically used by sociologists to describe the set of cultural assets (knowledge, skills, tastes, and ways of behaving commonly obtained through one's upbringing) that contributes to one's educational and subsequent economic mobility, racialized multicultural competency is a set of cultural assets uniquely advantageous for individuals leading and navigating in multiracial contexts. While the contours and levels of their proficiency will no doubt vary, our findings reveal that leaders of color, regardless of ethnoracial and Christian background, have a form of racialized multicultural competency that makes them most suited to lead in multiracial spaces.

As already discussed, pastors of color who lead multiracial congregations are estranged from their ethnoracial religious home community as well as their predominantly white religious network, and thus are not key players in either of these groups. They have a shortage of what sociologists refer to as "bonding capital"—the strong social ties that exist among homogeneous groups of people.[12] These pastors of color, however, have another valuable and unique form of capital, what sociologists refer to as "bridging capital," a type of social capital that can connect people who are otherwise divided and isolated from one another.[13] Multiracial church pastors of color thus have the opportunity to act as brokers.

People generally build relationships and communities within particular social worlds. These social worlds have their own norms, values, and structures that organize how people interact and who they interact with, as well as who gets access to resources embedded in that social network. This often includes important information and knowledge, favors, and introductions to others. Brokers are situated between two distinct and segregated social networks. This is why brokers are so valuable. Pastors of color of multiracial churches, in particular, are valuable as brokers who—due to their unique structural location as people connected to a group of color as well as to white people in a society that is highly racialized and segregated—have an opportunity, the potential, to bridge otherwise isolated and segregated ethnoracial religious groups.

Stovel and Shaw[14] explain that "the crucial characteristics of brokers are that (a) they bridge a gap in social structure and (b) they help goods, information, opportunities, or knowledge flow across that gap." There are additional factors that impact how resources flow through brokers from one social world to the next. A broker might be more embedded in one social world than the other. There may be higher expectations for conformity in one social world compared to the other. Still, without brokers to bridge gaps that exist between distinct social networks, resources like these would remain restricted to particular social worlds. Moreover, as a result of their exposure to separate, distinct social worlds, brokers also have a culturally diverse portfolio.[15] In the case of the pastors in our study, they have racialized multicultural competency.

Multiracial church pastors of color can act as brokers because of their capacity to fill a gap in a social network between the predominantly white religious community they are embedded in and their ethnoracial religious home community. Because these two religious communities, on the whole, do not interact with one another, pastors of color of multiracial churches have knowledge and resources that neither of these segregated communities is privy to. This not only gives them the power to serve as brokers; it also enables them to decide when and how the brokering will occur. However, their capacity to leverage the power that comes with being a broker, that is, to control and manage the transfer of resources, including, among other valuable social goods, knowledge and introductions, depends upon the extent to which they can foster authentic relationships based on trust and mutuality with both their ethnoracial religious home community and their predominantly white religious community. The greater the authenticity, trust, and mutuality, the greater their power to bridge the gap between these segregated and distinct religious communities.

Recognizing their strategic value and position, we recommend that pastors of color embrace who and where they are within the social matrix. We encourage them to be comfortable being an "estranged pioneer" and be "okay" with the tensions they are feeling in their position. Social identity is group based and reinforced by cultural markers that define who is "in" and "out." What has happened to pastors of color by leading multiracial congregations, without their even knowing it, is that they have relinquished one of those cultural markers. Pastors of color have lost some bonding capital with their ethnoracial home communities by leading multiracial congregations. However, they have bridging capital, important and unique assets that suit them as leaders of multiracial spaces.

With this in mind, we also recommend that pastors of color reinforce their identity and embed themselves in social communities that affirm who they are. We encourage them to find and connect with their own tribe of bridge makers. They should not look for their identity to be met, confirmed, or reinforced in both of the communities they broker. The essence of who they are will not be in either. Instead, it will be with other estranged pioneers. That is their tribe—the tribe that holds the keys to a multiracial future.

5
White Pastor Privilege

Jay-Z has a song called "99 Problems" in which he lists the travails of being a Black man in America. Among all of his problems, "girl problems" wasn't one of them. In a different way, it is the same for white pastors. White pastors may have their own "99 problems" as heads of multiracial congregations. But pastoring while white is not one of them.

In this chapter we examine the experiences of white pastors who head multiracial congregations. For sure, heading a multiracial congregation is challenging for them. No matter who you are, creating a racially and ethnically diverse religious community in a society that is as highly racialized and segregated as the United States is challenging. There is an emotional toll associated with trying to bring people together from different racial and ethnic backgrounds into a single community regardless of whether that person is a white pastor or a pastor of color. However, the difference between white pastors and pastors of color is white pastors do not experience any problems or disadvantages specifically associated with being white.

We might suspect that white pastors would experience some disadvantages associated with their race. It is reasonable to think, for example, that lacking racialized multicultural competency would be a detriment for white pastors when heading a multiracial church. Our data, however, show that this may not be the case. Lacking racialized multicultural competency is not problematic for white pastors in their leadership, nor is it a barrier to gaining or maintaining their position as a pastor of a multiracial church. It is also noteworthy that having a version of racialized multicultural competency for people who occupy a dominant standpoint is not something white pastors spoke about needing to have to navigate their role. To put it another way, a white pastor could be fluent in only one culture (their own) and have no awareness of the historical and sociological implications of systemic racism and white supremacy and still be a pastor of a multiracial church.

Still, there are white pastors who recognize a deficit in their racial and cultural understanding. To compensate for this, some intentionally pursued relationships with peers who are people of color, sought mentors who are people of color, or took courses to increase their fluency in a culture other than their own. A few chose to educate themselves on systemic racism by reading books or taking classes on the subject. This is in fact noteworthy because there are no real negative consequences for them, like being viewed as inferior or disrespected as a leader, for not doing so. These white pastors chose to go the extra mile when they did not have to.

Nevertheless, this is not the norm. More important, it reinforces the point rather than undermines it. White pastors have white privilege—the various unearned assets that go along with being white in a white-normative and white-dominant society. This privilege affords them greater freedom to choose how they will lead. They may choose to pursue ways of gaining multicultural competency, but they don't have to. They may choose to learn how racism and the racialized social system matter for them and their congregants, but they don't have to. It is up to them. It's their choice. Thus, while white pastors have universal challenges that beset all pastors that head multiracial congregations, they do not have unique problems leading a congregation on account of their race.

Neither being racially and culturally competent nor having an understanding of how the white supremacist system impacts their life and the lives of their congregants emerges as an important qualification for white head clergy of multiracial churches. Their denominations or religious associations do not indicate these are critical for them. Their congregants, both white and those of color, do not either. It simply is not a part of *their* job description. This is in contrast to pastors of color, who do need to possess racialized multicultural competency to access and navigate the role of multiracial church pastor.

In short, white pastors have *white pastor privilege* even as leaders of multiracial congregations. We unravel the basic components of this privilege and how it advantages white pastors in their role as head clergy of multiracial congregations. We then discuss what white pastors are doing or not with this privilege and why.

White Privilege: Checking the Power Box

When asked how being white affects him in everyday life, Pastor Roberts responded quickly, "I get the benefit of the doubt all the time." He then described an antiracism training that he did at his Ivy League seminary to try to understand the "position of the oppressed." In this training, he took a twenty-question test on power positions. Pastor Roberts said that he "checked the power box on all twenty categories" and that he got "the benefit of the doubt at every turn." To explain what he means, he continued: "Why did I get to become the priest of this place after being a priest for two years in a system that doesn't allow the assistant priest to become the priest?" The reason? Being white had a lot to do with it. He concludes, "That is my experience in life. Anywhere, as long as I walk in like I belong, everybody just assumes, like, 'Who is that guy?' 'I don't know, but he looks like he belongs.' I can go farther than others." Pastor Robert heads a midsize mainline Protestant congregation in an affluent midwestern suburb. He is describing having "white privilege."

White privilege is a concept that largely gained momentum in the public sphere with Peggy McIntosh's[1] "White Privilege: Unpacking the Invisible Knapsack," an essay on the unacknowledged benefits that white people have in the United States. In this and related works, "white privilege" is defined as an unearned systemic advantage, entitlement, power, and conferred dominance associated with being racialized as white.[2] White privilege is the product of being in a social system that is entirely set up to work for white people.[3] Keeping in mind that race intersects with various other identities and positions, such as class, gender, sex, and sexuality, it remains true that being white comes with multiple unearned advantages. There is conferred authority, dominance, legitimacy, power, and the privilege of being the norm and being considered the standard for what is acceptable, conventional, and legitimate in society. Having white privilege means one can be treated as an individual and not have to "represent one's race." It also means that an individual can be unaware without fault about their race privilege as well as the experiences of those who lack such privilege. Being oblivious to other cultures besides their own is generally not a problem.

These advantages are all reflected in what we call "white pastor privilege" among white pastors who head multiracial congregations. Drawing on the concept of white privilege, white pastor privilege encompasses unearned advantages enjoyed by white pastors that are associated with being white in a society that is structured by white supremacy. These include legitimation of their authority, the normativity and affirmation of their ethnoreligious culture, and easier access to financial, social, and cultural resources.

Unraveling White Pastor Privilege

While only the pastors of color identified what we call "racialized multicultural competency" as an important quality for leading in multiracial spaces, all pastors, regardless of race, sex, or denomination, acknowledged white pastor privilege. Whether Black, white, Hispanic, or Asian, all pastors, in one way or another, spoke of the unearned assets that come with being white leaders of multiracial congregations. Compared to all pastors of color, white pastors are the most preferred by congregants. They have the most agency and freedom to just "be themselves" in their role as head clergy. Moreover, leading in multiracial spaces gives white leaders another advantage: a more enhanced racial identity. By leading multiracial congregations, they become socially vaccinated against the one conceivable drawback to being white in a multiracial society—being considered a racist, an oppressor, or someone ignorant of other cultures—and any guilt that may be associated with benefiting from whiteness. Thus, along with other privileges they enjoy, white leaders of multiracial churches can often gain a more positive self-perception as good, nonracist white people.

We examine white pastor privilege by analyzing pastors' responses to questions on how their race affects their leadership, how it advantages and disadvantages them in their role as head clergy, and how race affects them in everyday life. We also consider pastors' responses to how, if at all, they talk about race and racism in their multiracial congregation.

Most Preferred Leader

When asked how being white affects his role as head clergy of a multiracial megachurch in the Southwest, Pastor Jones thought for a while and then said that it certainly did not limit him in any way and that being white was wholly advantageous. He shared as a matter of fact, "I could not have become the pastor of this church had I not been a white guy." He added that although his church was located in a diverse area, his church was "not in a place of calling an African American senior pastor." Whatever Pastor Jones, a man from the Deep South, meant by this, one thing is certain: being "a white guy" helped him to get the job to head this megachurch. In fact, he did not even apply for the job. The church search committee scouted him from across the country and pleaded with him over several months to come out for an interview.

Being a white guy was also an asset for Pastor Roberts. As previously stated, he became the head priest of his mainline Protestant church after serving for only two years as an assistant priest "in a system that doesn't allow the assistant priest to become the priest." Defying the system and becoming head priest so quickly was possible because he is white. Pastor Roberts shared that when the previous head pastor retired, the church had an "open search." However, they really had only one candidate in the running: him. The experiences of white pastors like Pastor Jones and Pastor Roberts communicate that a "white guy" is the preferred leader for the position of head clergy.

Pastors of color are clearly aware that white pastors are the preferred head pastors. Father James, whom you already met, is an African American Catholic priest in his sixties who, like Pastor Jones, grew up in the Deep South. He talked about the preference he saw white priests experience within his organization. Even in his large multilingual, multicultural, multiracial parish in the Midwest, all congregants, regardless of race, preferred white priests:

> You would have the older whites asking, "Why did we get the Black priest?" Like if the patient comes in and says, "Why did I get the Black doctor?" . . . But then some of the Blacks were saying, "Why did we get the Black priest?" in a negative way . . . because they have always had white priests. Negative, like "What did we do to get a Black priest?"

The bottom line is white priests are preferred over priests of color. Getting a Black priest instead of a white priest is perceived as a punishment by congregants, including Black congregants.

Father Angelo shares how churches in his mainline Protestant dioceses on the East Coast accept priests of color only when the churches are struggling, backed into a corner, and cannot afford to pay a full-time wage for a white priest. If they have abundant resources and funds, however, "they would accept the white guys." "White guys" are favored as head clergy no matter the racial makeup, denomination, or size of the congregation. Congregations will take priests of color only out of desperation because white priests, it is inferred, wouldn't take such a position or perhaps the congregation wouldn't feel it was appropriate to offer white priests such a lowly position. Either way, priests of color are perceived as less valuable than white priests.

Women pastors who served as head clergy in the more liberal mainline Protestant denominations were also clear about the preference for "white guys." As we noted in the previous chapter, Pastor Kay, even as she heads her large multiracial church as the first Black woman in her position, has the nagging feeling that her congregants, including other Black women, would prefer to have a white man as their head pastor. The preference for white men is pervasive.

Most Normative Leader

One of the basic features of white privilege is that one can be viewed and treated as the norm, that is, the model for what is acceptable and good in various aspects of American life.[4] This is certainly evident in the church. White pastors and their leadership style were viewed as normative and the standard for all head clergy. From how a pastor should look to how they should preach and how they lead, white pastors were the unstated model for what is good and acceptable. This was especially apparent from the perspective of pastors of color.

Here, it is important to draw upon the perspective of those who are not understood to be "normative leaders" to understand what is normative. They are the ones who would be most aware of multiple leadership styles as well as the positive and negative feedback one would experience when enacting or embodying one style rather than another. In many ways, this further affirms what we discussed in Chapter 3. The ways in which pastors of color compensate for the dearth of resources available to them is by knowing and aiming to emulate what they have come to learn is acceptable and normative leadership for multiracial church pastors.

Physical appearance is one way a leader aims to be normal. Pastor Johnson, the conservative Protestant African American who recently planted a multiracial church, struggled with how he should "look" as a pastor of his new church plant. Growing up in the Black church from a long line of Black pastors, Pastor Johnson is more than familiar with how a Black pastor should look: In the "African American church, you better come to church in a suit, man. You can't 'get in the pulpit' without a suit and a tie." Although he knows that "a suit and tie" is the standard for a pastor in many Black churches, particularly those he comes from, he eventually chose to dress more casually for his multiracial church plant. He says, "I don't wear shirts and ties on Sundays. I wear jeans and a shirt." This more casual style is not simply a personal fashion choice eschewing the conservative conventions of the Black church. He wanted to dress more like the typical pastor who heads a multiracial church. Pastor Johnson explains that in order to pastor a diverse Protestant church, a pastor has to dress a particular way: "If you want to be diverse ... you got to dress a certain type of way. You have got to have ripped jeans and kind of the ultimate kind of picture of the hip multiethnic pastor." And the pastors who embody the "ultimate kind of picture" of a cool multiracial church pastor are white pastors in jeans, preferably a little ripped.

Besides physical appearance, the normative leadership style is perceived as relational and egalitarian. This became apparent as African American as well as Asian American pastors in the study discussed how they tried to alter their leadership style to distance themselves from the more hierarchical dictatorial style that they saw growing up in the Black or Asian ethnic church and tried to follow what they perceived as a more modern, desirable, and egalitarian, team-based leadership style, which they associated with white pastors and white churches. What is critical here is that the normative leadership style is understood to be how white leaders lead. This was particularly evident among African American pastors like Pastor Perry.

Pastor Perry's heritage is Caribbean, though he identifies as simply African American, having grown up in a predominantly Black inner city on the East Coast. He says he went to schools that were "ninety-nine-point-ninety-nine percent African American" and went to a Black church, which his mother forced him to attend. Once he was old enough to decide for himself, he stopped going to church until a few white Christian mentors helped him to "meet Jesus" and become a real Christian. These white mentors from an affluent, predominantly white multiracial church showed up to his basketball games "when no one else did," invested their time and money in him, and showed him that "another world" was possible—that boundaries can be crossed. These mentors also eventually helped him to get several degrees in conservative Protestant seminaries and be the pastor that he is today.

With this background, Pastor Perry explains the differences in leadership style between the Black and white church. He shares first about the leadership style found in the Black church:

> You don't see a lot of leadership books for African American churches because there is one style of leadership, one methodology: "Do what the pastor says." That is the type of leadership that I am accustomed [to] from

the Black church. Whatever the pastor said is what was done. One African American pastor put it this way: "My job is to lead and feed," and he would point at the congregation, "Your job is to follow and swallow."

In contrast to this top-down "follow and swallow" leadership style which Pastor Perry associates with the Black church, he explains that the leadership style he learned from his white pastor mentor had far more "checks and balances" and was more of a team effort. It is this latter style, which Pastor Perry associates with the white church, that he follows as he leads his midsize conservative Protestant church in a major city on the East Coast:

> I want people to buy in, which means I have to spend a lot of time just making sure where I want them to go, convince them to go, which means that I have to make sure that where we are going is the right direction for everyone involved. I have to be less selfish. There are so many checks and balances. . . . [A white pastor mentor] impacted my leadership style more so than anybody else. . . . He has had a bigger impact on my ministry than anybody else.

Pastor Perry confesses that his natural inclination is to lead "like an African American male" who sees "the world through the lens of an African American male." He notes that the team-based style, with "many checks and balances," which he picked up from his white mentors, is the leadership style that he struggles to adopt. He pursues this model knowing that "white people have a difficult time submitting to Black leaders" like himself.

Pastor Johnson serves as head clergy of a liberal Protestant congregation in the South. Like Pastor Perry, he adopted white models of leadership. Pastor Johnson notes that he grew up in a church that was run like a "dictatorship" where "the pastor is Jesus." But by going to his predominantly white seminary he learned to pursue an alternative model of leadership, where the pastor "is not Jesus" and where leadership is shared within the church body. He explains:

> I had to learn it [to share, not be Jesus], because my upbringing was a dictatorship. My pastor led with an iron hand. He had a pretty strong hand. And nothing got done unless the pastor was part of it or in it or approved it or something. . . . So I did have to learn that, because . . . the model that I am now working [with] was not the model that I grew up under.

Asian American pastors made similar adjustments to follow the more normative white American leadership style as head clergy of their multiracial church. Korean American pastors in particular often described their immigrant ethnic church as hierarchical and dictatorial, where the pastor single-handedly ran the church. In contrast, they want to run their multiracial congregations using the more egalitarian democratic style of leadership, which they say they picked up by attending white churches, working with white mentors, and attending predominantly white seminaries.

Pastor John Song is a 1.5-generation Korean American conservative Protestant pastor who grew up in the immigrant Korean church and has experience serving in the Korean church as well as a predominantly white church in the same denomination. He has worked with both Korean pastors and white pastors and has decided to pursue the leadership style of white pastors to lead his predominantly Asian American multiracial church. He eschews the "vertical . . . very hierarchical" leadership style that he associates with the Korean church and is pursuing the "very horizontal" leadership style that he learned from his white pastor mentor. The latter is understood to be the better, more suitable leadership style.

Pastors of color who head multiracial conservative Protestant congregations idealize and normalize white leadership styles in how they dress, which is more casual, and in how they relate to their congregants, which is more informal compared to the churches in which they grew up. Although the Black, Hispanic, or Asian conservative Protestant churches they grew up in conferred significant respect to their clergy and referred to them using formal titles like "Pastor," "Reverend," and "Doctor," as pastors of color of multiracial churches they opt to follow the more informal custom common among white churches and refer to themselves simply by their first name. Thus, Pastor Daniel Lopez might be referred to as "Reverend Lopez" in his Mexican church, but he is simply "Dan" or maybe "Pastor Dan" in his multiracial church.

Another characteristic of pastoral leadership style is preaching style. The normative preaching style is associated with that of white pastors. African American pastors were clear about the "Black pastor" style of preaching as well as the more "white" mainstream style of preaching. And they often aimed to emulate the latter style in their own multiracial congregations. Pastor Johnson says he "grew up with a Black American pastor who did the celebration and the whooping." As an African American pastor who heads his multiracial church plant in the Southwest, however, he preaches "more like Andy

Stanley, Steve Furtick, and Craig Groeschel." These are white male pastors. Pastor Johnson adds that he gave up "hollering, whooping . . . walking the pews" like the Black preachers he grew up watching "a long time ago."

Pastor Perry says the same: "My pastors would squall and holler. It is called 'whooping' in an African American preaching style, just 'aaah.' You won't hear that here," in his multiracial church. Similarly while both Pastor Perry and Pastor Johnson grew up in the Black church like all of the other African American pastors in our study, where you "better bring a lunch" because the services last a while, they both, like other African American pastors who head multiracial congregations, try not to preach for more than an hour. Preaching for a shorter period of time, while not explicitly stated, is a standard associated with white pastors and their congregations.

African American pastors were certainly not alone in following white pastors' preaching style. A conservative Protestant Korean American pastor who was born and raised in the Midwest but became "saved" through a Korean American church and has experience working in Korean immigrant churches, explains the preaching styles he believes are available for him to follow as a head pastor of a large multiracial congregation: "Either I am going to be a straight talker like Mark Driscoll or try to be intellectually engaging like Tim Keller or try to be just witty and funny like Matt Chandler." These are all popular preachers in his conservative Protestant religious association who are white. Although he says that he preaches like the "passionate" Korean pastors he grew up hearing, he identifies his preaching style as most closely resembling Matt Chandler's style.

In these ways, whether white pastors recognize it or not, they have the privilege of looking like the normative pastor. They have the privilege of having their leadership and preaching style considered to be the standard for all pastors, including pastors of color who head multiracial congregations.

Most Respected Leader

White pastors are more likely than pastors of color to come from church communities where the position of pastor does not command as much respect and authority as it does in church communities of color. Despite this, another unearned asset that comes with leading as a white person is they are most respected and bestowed the greatest authority among all pastors leading in multiracial spaces. White pastors do not report experiencing challenges to their authority, as do pastors of color in multiracial congregations. For sure, congregants express disagreement or discontent with them or their decisions. But this is not the same as not seeing them as legitimate authorities. On the whole, white pastors experience a respect surplus, while pastors of color experience a respect deficit in their role as head clergy of multiracial congregations.

This respect surplus is extended to white pastors no matter their sex. White pastors recognized that they get the most respect and have the most weight and authority as leaders because they are white. A white mainline pastor shares:

> There are advantages to being a white male. . . . As a minister you walk in the room, there is going to be a general sense of your authority. . . . Nobody is going to be wondering where you are from or if you have a record, those kinds of things just aren't going to come up in people's minds like they do if you walk in as a Black male.

White pastors are respected. They are presumed to be qualified and competent. They start out with a "general sense of authority" and legitimacy as leaders by virtue of being white, which is something that their counterparts who are people of color do not have. Another white mainline pastor explains how this advantage also exists among clergywomen. She observes that her African American women colleagues are not given the same level of respect and authority that she enjoys as a white pastor:

> I have too many African American friends who are clergywomen, and . . . even though they are very strong women, they just don't have the opportunities that I have because they are African American women. . . . And so they are way down the run. . . . Unfortunately, all the different cultures are going to listen to me before they listen to Mary, who is African, or before they listen to my friend at [a nearby church in the denomination] who is African American.

What white pastors have to say, regardless of gender, carries more weight. It has more value.

Another white Protestant pastor explains that an important component of white privilege is that white leaders have the power to be heard. What they lay down on the table matters:

I think the blessing that comes with the privilege, with white privilege, is that you have the power to lay down.... If a white person lays down their life, that is acknowledged by everybody in the circle as valuable, then obviously you are putting something on the table. And if you are obviously putting something on the table, I am almost obligated to do something to put something on the table. And once there is something on the table, there is an opening.

A white woman mainline pastor shares a similar observation serving in an interfaith council and local government:

I am part of a system . . . where I am given power and majority-group status. There is a lot that is going to be easier for me, but also in terms of [city] power dynamics my being white was also a factor in the interfaith council.... Whenever I brought up a concern, . . . [questioning or doubting the] gravitas to the perspective that I brought was just not existent.

Thus, one of the "blessings" of white privilege is that you can create an opening and enact change because what you say carries more weight. White leaders have the "gravitas" that commands respect and demands a response.

The value of having a caring and responsive pastor is also weighed differently based on race. A caring and responsive white pastor who reaches out to congregants, especially to congregants of color, is more admired and highly regarded than a pastor of color who does the same. A caring and responsive white leader is more valuable than a caring and responsive leader of color. Being welcomed, accepted, and wanted by a white pastor is most desirable. A white pastor of a conservative Protestant multiracial congregation explains what an African American congregant shared with him on this point:

People expect me to love them, listen to them, and they expect me to be the person who takes the lead in helping other people understand them.... An African American has said to me, "Pastor, I don't think you have any idea how much impact it has on them for you, as the senior pastor of the church, a white man, to be looking them in the eye with a smile on your face and saying, 'I would like to invite you to our church.'" For a pastor to want them, not just accept them, because there is a big difference.

A warm and caring pastor is valued, as he tells it, by his African American congregants. Perhaps, given that this pastor is a man, what is especially valued is a warm and caring white male pastor. An African American, Pastor Johns, who heads a multiracial conservative Protestant church, adds that even Black people will follow a white leader over a Black leader. Even if Black people may have more in common with other Black people and better connect with a Black leader than a white leader, they will still follow a white leader over a Black leader in a multiracial context. Pastor Johns explains:

> We go into a room full of white guys, ten Black guys in there, those ten Black guys will have more in common with me [a Black man], that will connect with me, faster than they will connect with you [a white man]. Now, when it comes to following, they will follow you before they follow me.

When asked why this may be the case, Pastor Johns replies:

> It is easier for Black people to follow a white guy than it is for white guys to follow a Black guy. It's just easier. It may be due to four hundred years' worth of slavery, oppression, just the mentality, that African Americans have. . . . Growing up as an African American primarily . . . heard, "White is right." If I say, "Jesus has a beginning," and a white guy says, "Jesus has a beginning," the Black person will more likely receive it coming from the white guy than they would coming from the Black guy, even though they feel like Jesus doesn't have a beginning, they'll just believe theologically what the white guy says before they will what the Black guy has to say about it.

From Pastor Johns's perspective, not only are white people more likely to trust the leadership of white pastors over Black pastors, but so are Black people. Black people perceive "white as right." This is in line with what white pastors know about themselves. They receive greater respect, authority, and legitimacy as leaders of all communities, including communities of color, in multiracial settings. This is no doubt a very valuable privilege and advantage white pastors have over pastors of color. This is why there is a respect differential: white pastors experience a respect surplus; pastors of color experience a respect deficit.

Father Russo is a white senior priest of a large multiracial, multilingual, and multicultural Catholic parish on the East Coast. He says he is uncomfortable with the tremendous amount of respect and authority he receives from his congregants, particularly from his congregants of color. Such a high level of respect is not what he is used to growing up in a predominantly white Catholic parish, but it is something that he has come to accept and even enjoy in his congregation, which has significant numbers of Hispanic and Asian congregants.

When Father Russo was asked about the advantages of leading a multiracial congregation, he first discussed the cultural diversity that he enjoys, like attending the different cultural festivities that his congregants put on annually. One aspect of this cultural diversity, which made him uncomfortable at first, is his congregants' "tremendous reverence" for him. He describes how the cultural festivities for the New Year put on by his Chinese congregants could not start until he, the senior priest, showed up. He then describes how the congregants made him sit in a special chair, almost like a throne, and honored him:

> I was late [to the celebration] because I forgot, but they could not start anything until I was there because I was the elder. And I had to sit in a very special chair and nothing began until I sat on this chair. And I had to do a special ceremony over the dragon. They do the dragon dance and all that stuff, but as the elder, my presence was . . . nothing could begin until I was seated there. And the tremendous reverence, it made me, like, really uncomfortable. . . . Every kid came up to me [and] wished me "Happy New Year". . . . The same thing with the Hispanics. . . . It is a different way of approaching the church and a different way of seeing the pastor.

The Chinese and Hispanics who predominate in his congregation are used to giving their senior priest tremendous respect and honor. This is not what Father Russo is used to. But it is a "different way" of approaching the church and seeing the pastor, which he has come to appreciate and identify as an advantage of leading a diverse congregation. White clergy like Father Russo get more respect and honor than they expect from their congregation in their role as pastors, thus experiencing a respect surplus. When we compare how he is treated by his parishioners to how the parishioners of color in particular treat Father James (an African American Catholic priest) and Father Angelo (an Asian mainline Protestant priest), the respect differential between white pastors and pastors of color becomes very clear.

Similar to Father James and Father Angelo, Pastor Charles, the thirty-something African American who heads a small multiracial conservative

Protestant congregation in the Midwest, encounters a respect deficit as a Black pastor, especially from some of his white congregants. Pastor Charles notes that various types of people in his multiracial church plant "give him suggestions" on how to improve the church. An older Black woman as well as a middle-aged Asian American woman regularly give him "suggestions." Perhaps this has something to do with expectations of authority within communities of color. As a young person, regardless of his role as pastor, he should respect those who are older than he. Further, these women may expect that, as a person of color, he understands these informal norms guiding relationships, something they may not expect of white people. However, these women are not the only people in the congregation who regularly give him "suggestions." He must also navigate those of a white male congregant who has a habit of making far more suggestions than they do. Pastor Charles has chosen to address the barrage of thoughts and suggestions of the white male congregant by simply ignoring them: "There is a Caucasian male in the church, anything he shares with me, I have the hardest time even hearing. I get at least five emails from him a week. I see his name, I delete the email. I don't even open the email. . . . [He is not] respecting of my authority as pastor." Of course, all pastors, even white male pastors, hear from church members. But the extensive amount of input, correction, and feedback Black pastors get stands out relative to what white pastors receive.

Pastor Charles's status is subtly challenged in how he is referred to as well, at least given his cultural background. Like nearly all the African American pastors in the study, he comes from a Black church tradition where the clergy position is highly regarded and where congregants address their leaders by formal titles. However, unlike other Black pastors in the study, who have accepted being called by their first name, Pastor Charles maintains the perspective that the pastor should be respected and be more formally addressed as the head pastor, referred to as "Pastor Charles" (calling them pastor using their last name) or "Pastor Joseph" (calling them pastor using their first name). Although the African American and Asian American congregants refer to Pastor Charles as "Pastor Joe," the majority of his white congregants just call him "Joe."

> African Americans call me "Pastor Joe." The majority of Caucasians just call me "Joe." There is no "pastor" title or anything in front of that. Not all of them, but the majority of them. So there is that sort of difference. And so

this particular gentleman [who is white] brings something to me, it's "Joe."
It is kind of condescending.

White congregants, like the white man who regularly likes to volunteer "suggestions," casually refer to him by his first name and disregard him in his role as head clergy. Pastor Charles finds this insulting. Needless to say, being shown "tremendous reverence" by his congregants is not one of the advantages that he experiences as a pastor of color of a multiracial congregation.

Most Resourced Leader

Having access to resources, like financial and social capital, is no doubt important for leaders of any organization. We find that white pastors in the RLDP are embedded in networks with greater access to these critical resources. This can make all the difference in sustaining a congregation in a country like America, where religious participation is completely voluntary. As one white mainline Protestant clergywoman said, "I wouldn't have the privilege that I have. I wouldn't be able. I wouldn't have gotten in the doors that I got into if I was Black, if I was Asian."

Compared to multiracial or nonwhite networks, white networks, whether they are religious or secular, contain the most financial, social, and other forms of capital that are valuable for leading and navigating organizations, including a multiracial congregation.[5] In the multiracial church world, white people—including white women—have nearly exclusive access to these robust white networks. This is one of the major findings in Christopher Munn's[6] work on race and access to social capital based on RLDP data. Munn finds that white people "intra-racially hoard" material and social resources within their homogeneous networks, which house the most resources. White people naturally form mentorship groups, peer networks, and religious committees and informally exchange resources among themselves. This then limits access to these resources to white people. Moreover, Munn finds that white people further exclude people of color from accessing these resources by devaluing their contributions to these networks. They are not perceived as valued, equal, contributing members to the networks, despite their fluency in what we call racialized multicultural competency. When they are given occasional access, it is as a "diversity representative." While they may be connected to these networks, they are still otherized and excluded from accessing the robust social and financial capital embedded in these networks. Thus, in the end, what we have is white clergy having access to the most resources among all clergy of multiracial churches, which is yet another unearned asset enjoyed with white pastor privilege.

In discussing how race affects how they lead or any advantages they experience leading their multiracial congregation as a white person, white pastors commonly confess they have access to social networks that house the most resources. They also note that they have exclusive or primary access to these resources because they are white. White mainline Protestant pastors were especially forthcoming about this advantage.

Take Pastor Michaels, a young white pastor who planted a small mainline Protestant congregation in a midwestern city. He is a bit unusual because he was one of the few white pastors who planted a church instead of being hired or recruited to head a church in his denomination. Even more unusual, Pastor Michaels planted a church thanks to the support of a pastor of color. Not only did he benefit from his connections with a pastor of color, he also benefited from his access to other networks which provided him the kind of support essential for building his small church plant in an underresourced neighborhood. Pastor Michaels had to turn what was once an "old dilapidated building" into a space where people can comfortably gather to worship. In getting the funds to make this renovation possible, being white and having access to white people with resources helped. He explains:

> Being white is a privilege in certain ways here, like being able to network with people that have money to build a church out of this old dilapidated building and have a lot of connections to be able to say, "Hey, because I am a white pastor and you are a white church or youth group or college group, you feel more comfortable probably connecting with me." And if I convince you that my family lives here and that we have been here for [so many] years and we are safe and we have learned a lot, you are probably more likely to come here. So I get this privilege of having a network and being able to connect with people who have resources that can make donations.

Being white, he can connect with white people in white churches, youth groups, or college groups that will feel comfortable giving him money. Being white, he can convince white families who tend to have more resources than families of color in the city to come to his primarily Black and white church and make financial contributions. Being able to access these resource-rich white networks enabled him to renovate his church and keep its doors open.

Pastor Michaels says he is fully aware that he has an advantage in accessing resources because he is white and that people of color would not be able to obtain similar kinds of resources. Moreover, the resources a person of color may be able to access, for example through nonwhite networks, would not be valued. He shares the experience of one of his Black staff members to communicate this point: "I have a Black brother who is interning with us. . . . One of the big challenges [of having Black people on staff] is, like, their network isn't going to be usually as robust."

Pastor Williams is another mainline protestant Pastor who heads a small, primarily Black and white congregation in a diverse city in the Midwest. Unlike Pastor Michaels, Pastor Williams did not plant his church. Like Pastor Michaels, however, Pastor Williams finds that being white helps him connect with white people with money, which helps him to obtain resources for his church and the programs that it funds. When asked how being white affects how he leads his congregation, Pastor Williams said that simply putting his clergy collar on as a white man and attending galas with the "movers and shakers" in the city opens doors to tremendous resources:

> It is amazing, because [the collar] cuts instantly, just eliminates all the small talk. "Where do you pastor?" "Well, let me tell ya." . . . And so it is a way to get that out there, so I think my whiteness, if you will, and my affluence, and being in those circles, opens a lot of doors . . . yeah! . . . I can see potential funding coming through the networks for the church.

Although he pastors a small church in a struggling transitional neighborhood, Pastor Williams gets invited to a lot of special events funded by private businesses and wealthy white people in the city thanks to the connections that his wife, who is also white, has in the community. Once he is at these gatherings, he is able to easily make connections with people who can be beneficial for his church. Thanks to these networks, Pastor Williams says that he has a "stack of business cards" that he can use to "send out letters and get donations" for his church.

Besides financial resources, white leaders have access to more power, that is, to political capital. This is because white voices matter the most. They carry the most weight in any kind of space. If a white leader speaks up on behalf of their church or their cause, others listen. A white Catholic priest who heads a primarily Hispanic yet multiracial parish explains how he, as an Anglo male, is able to access local and state government leaders and be heard and "do more" on behalf of his congregation. This is what he shared when asked how his race affects how he leads his congregation:

> Politically, an Anglo is able to do more.... Their voice is heard a little louder when we go to talk to senators or, um . . . you know, there is political clout. A white male in the United States, unfortunately . . . has more clout than most others. [Interviewer: So you are saying that politically, it is fortunate to be an Anglo?] Yes, absolutely.

Being white is an advantage because white people have the most political power. Among all voices, their voices matter the most and are most likely to be heard by everyone, including people in positions of power. This can prove beneficial not only for the white pastors but for the congregations and programs that they head.

In addition to having the most financial and political capital in the broader community, white pastors have greater access to social resources within their religious organizations, including, for example, mentorship, training, and peer networks. A primary reason for this is homogeneity. Most of these networks, which house valuable social support and information, are exclusively or primarily white. All of the pastors in our study, regardless of race, sex, or nationality, were trained in historically and predominantly white seminaries and organizations. The denominations, religious networks, and religious orders they are part of are equally white. These structures house formal and informal networks that most readily and easily accommodate white people. A racialized history and present means that resources are not only housed within segregated white networks but are generally reserved for white people.

Perhaps the only resource that white leaders may lack compared to pastors of color is multicultural capital—the knowhow to work with and within ethnic, cultural, and racial groups other than their own. Having access to exclusively white networks does not help them gain cultural insight on leading a racially and ethnically diverse group of people. Still, because they can easily access people of color to serve as multicultural liaisons on their behalf, white pastors are able to do rather well as leaders of multiracial churches.

It is important to point out that white pastors did not identify their general lack of multicultural competency or unfamiliarity with diversity as a weakness or a disadvantage associated with white people, including white leaders like themselves. Part of having white privilege means that you can be unaware of other cultures and the experiences of other racial groups without consequence. It also means that you can quite easily outsource the diversity work to others, namely to people of color. When asked who supports them in their job heading a multiracial congregation, white pastors commonly mentioned "bridge" people who were invariably people of color. These people helped them manage the diversity in their congregation. Although some pastors of color mentioned that they too had "bridge" people, as discussed in Chapter 4, they themselves, more often than not, served as "bridges" for the church.

The extent to which white pastors relied on people of color to serve as bridges or liaisons to help manage the diversity within their congregations was overwhelming. The most common strategy monolingual white clergy used to address the challenge of leading a multilingual congregation is to hire a bilingual pastor of color. No matter the denomination or religious organization, the most common solution to managing a diverse multilingual congregation is hiring a pastor of color who speaks the language of the non-English-speaking population in the church, whether it be Spanish, Mandarin, Tagalog, Vietnamese, or Somali.

Take Pastor Jacobs, who heads a small Protestant congregation in the Midwest with a sizable number of Spanish speakers. To accommodate both his English- and Spanish-speaking congregants, he holds separate services. Since he can speak only English, he has two Hispanic, Spanish-speaking pastors on staff who serve as translators. He explicitly notes that they serve as bridges for him: "They are both bilingual. I am the only one that is not bilingual. So I have—in order to deal with this diversity that is on the table—bilingual people around me all the time that will help me bridge into that." Pastor Jacobs deals with his congregation's diversity through bilingual people of color. He confesses that if he "got off the high horse" and learned Spanish, attendance at his congregation would "blow up" because he could more directly connect with his Spanish-speaking congregants. He chose instead to rely on his two Hispanic American assistant pastors to serve as bridges between himself and his Spanish-speaking congregants.

Notably, several white Catholic priests in our study who have Spanish-speaking congregants report learning Spanish, even if not becoming fluent, to better minister to their Hispanic parishioners. However, it is still common for them to rely on people of color who are not on staff as "confidants" or cultural liaisons to help connect with their Hispanic congregants. For example, a white Catholic priest shares that in addition to bilingual priests, he "utilizes" his bilingual congregants in his predominantly Hispanic multiracial parish as important "translators." They help him to understand and connect with his congregants: "Sometimes, when I really am in a situation where someone really needs to tell me pastoral things, I will often grab Sister Maria or another person I trust and say, 'Help me understand what this person is trying to tell me.'" Even if he cannot directly connect with his Spanish-speaking congregants, he has co-ethnic co-lingual congregants who can help bridge the divide.

Besides functioning as translators and "cultural bridges," people of color are also used to help white pastors understand "race issues" and function as "race bridges" between themselves and communities of color. This is the case of Pastor Daniels, a white conservative Protestant pastor who heads a primarily African American and Hispanic American multiracial congregation on the East Coast. Pastor Daniels, like many other white pastors, has a lot of support to do his job. He does not feel lonely in his position:

> I have got really a good group of just pastor friends. . . . My wife is ordained. We have four churches [nearby], good friends with every one of the pastors, had dinner with them, we know their kids. Really good friends. I have got pastor friends around the city . . . from the Mayor's Interfaith Council . . . got Pentecostal friends who are Black, friends who are Latino . . . pick a color, denomination. . . . There are about eight of them [in my inner circle], one is a senior vice president of the largest Christian radio station in the country. . . . He is a dear friend of mine. He and I get together at least once a month for breakfast.

With so much support, Pastor Daniels has pastors of color in his city whom he can easily turn to for help to understand "race issues," like the Ferguson protests, which were going on during the time of our interviews:

> I will go to these guys and say, "I don't get this . . . this whole Ferguson thing that is going on." I said . . . "Help me here! I got a lot of pissed-off Black people at my church." And I am not . . . I am siding with the White cop, and I feel bad about that. Help me understand.

Pastor Daniels does not understand what is going on with the Ferguson protests. He does not know why he has so many angry Black people in his congregation. His natural inclination is to side with the white police officer who shot Michael Brown. And he feels bad about that, so he needs his Black pastor friends to help him understand and better connect with what his predominantly Black and Brown congregation might be thinking, what they are going through.

Thus, in the end, the one resource that may not be provided to white leaders by being connected to resource-rich white homogeneous networks can easily be compensated and filled by people of color who can readily function as bridges and cultural resources for white pastors. Moreover, white pastors tend not to consider their lack of racial and cultural competence as a problem in the first place. Therefore, white leaders' resource surplus remains strong.

Free to Be

"Be your true self." "Don't apologize for who you are." "Do you!" These are popular self-help assertions in contemporary American society. They suggest that you should be free to be who you are. You should not hide aspects of yourself from others. Such advice may seem a bit farcical for sociologists like Erving Goffman[7] who view human beings as actors who are constantly putting on multiple "faces" and performances in everyday life in an effort to be seen favorably by others. Goffman argues we are all putting on a show, revealing only certain aspects of ourselves. We change how we present ourselves to others depending on the context. Pastors are no exception.

Although all pastors aim to present themselves so as to be embraced and accepted by their congregants, peers, and denominational or other religious leaders, white pastors have the greatest freedom and flexibility to "be themselves" in their presentations. Whereas pastors of color find themselves feeling a need to apologize for their racialized selves, white pastors of multiracial congregations never express feeling such a need. They do not discuss having to suppress or hide aspects of their whiteness. This is yet another form of white leader privilege: they have the greatest freedom to just "be" who they are.

When pastors of color were asked how their race affects how they lead, some talked about censoring or concealing aspects of who they are in order to lead. White pastors, in contrast, did not apologize for their race or try to conceal aspects of who they are. Most white pastors understood that being white affected how they led. They did not mention, however, the need to alter, suppress, or hide their race in their position as leaders of a multiracial church. This was clear for various white pastors, like Pastor Burke.

Pastor Burke heads a small conservative Protestant congregation in a diverse city in the Midwest and identifies himself as a "white Irish guy." When asked if his race affects how he leads his multiracial, multinational congregation of white, African American, Asian American, and Hispanic American congregants, Pastor Burke immediately responded, "It totally does." He added, "The stories I tell, they are white-guy stories." He also said that being a white guy means that he doesn't have to apologize for being who he is:

> I, you don't have to apologize for being who you are. You just have to love people for who they are and not make who you are, like, an essential thing for people to have a relationship with you. . . . I hope the Black guy in the church . . . I hope he feels like he can be a Black man in our church just as much as I feel like I can be a white man, and I hope we can figure out how to do it together. But, yeah, I can't undo my whiteness.

Pastor Burke does not have to apologize for who he is. He realizes that as a white man he tells "white-guy stories." Moreover, he hopes that the Black men in his congregation feel empowered to be themselves just as he does. It wasn't until the interviewer asked a follow-up question about whether he thinks that the Black men in his church are actually free to be "a Black man" as he is free to be "a white man" that Pastor Burke confessed that he had not thought about how being oneself may work differently for a Black guy. He then guessed that it would be harder: "If I was a Black guy trying to do the same thing, it might be harder. Yeah. It probably definitely would be harder. I hadn't really thought of it that way."

On its face, Pastor Burke's decision to just be himself and love people sounds right. But on closer analysis, he reveals in this brief quote both the benefits and challenges that come with whiteness. On the one hand, Pastor Burke's perspective is limited by his own admission, coming from that of a "white guy." At the same time he asserts that one should not have to make who one is "an essential thing." The benefit here is he can be himself without consequence. The challenge is his perspective is limited and he doesn't see this as problematic for a pastor of a multiracial church. His limited perspective becomes clearer when he compares his options to that of a Black man in his congregation. He hopes that a Black man could just be himself, as he is just himself in his congregation. He was able to maintain this perspective until he was asked to make sense of it. This means that he has held this view for a very long time. Prior to the interview, and perhaps even after it, he easily decontextualized racial identity from the racialized social system, allowing him to minimize both the advantages associated with his race and the disadvantages associated with being Black. In other words, he sees race not as systemic but personal. He can enjoy the advantages of his whiteness, which flow from a white supremacist system in which he is embedded, and be blind to how that system advantages him while simultaneously disadvantaging people of color.

When another white pastor of a small church was asked how being white affects his daily life, he answered that it makes life generally easier: "I think it is really, really easy to go through your life, you know, especially as a male, a white male, as a majority person, majority among majorities. It is just really easy to go through your life and make assumptions about the way life should work because it does for you." This perspective extended to his congregation. This pastor was also clear that race affects how he leads:

> I think, from a majority standpoint, you know, for better or for worse . . . I think I have just like a level of confidence. I am not concerned really that people are judging me. They very well might be. I am not saying they are not. But, it just doesn't . . . "What are they thinking of me? Are they? Are they looking at me that way because I am male? Are they looking at me that way because I am white?" Again, they may be, but it is just not in me to worry about that. . . . So there is just a level of easiness.

Being a white male no doubt affects how he leads. It makes him a more confident leader—one who does not worry so much about what others may be thinking of him or his performance as a leader. He can be free to be who he is as a leader without being concerned about his race negatively affecting how he plays the role of head clergy.

Pastor Feltner is another white male who heads a small mainline Protestant congregation. Pastor Feltner served in only "all-white" congregations as an associate or assistant pastor before he was appointed as a senior pastor of his current congregation with Asians, Africans, and Hispanics, most of whom are immigrants. Given that he had no prior experience leading a diverse community, he was asked how he met the various needs and expectations of his congregation. He responded that he had no problems. His church members got along well:

> The church does a great job. . . . It's a blessing to be in ministry here because of how they get along and work together and all of that. They really even had . . . one solid vision before I got here. Uhm . . . some of my ways of communicating . . . some of my sermon illustrations and stories . . . I don't always feel like they connect, and my wife says sometimes she is the only one laughing . . . and that has certainly been true. . . . But I have also found I need to be myself. I need to be true to myself . . . and they are accepting of that.

Pastor Feltner did not have any problems managing the various expectations of his multiracial, multilingual, multinational congregation because he says the congregants already had the vision for diversity and got along. His sermon illustrations and jokes do not connect generally with his diverse, predominantly immigrant congregation. But he is not worried about that. He is not suppressing his white male stories or illustrations. He needs to be true to himself. And thankfully, from his perspective, his congregants have accepted who he is, a white guy, and how as a white man he leads the church.

Being free to be white and having congregants accept them for being white, just who they are, was a common thread in the interviews with white pastors. When asked how they identify themselves racially, white pastors easily identified themselves as white, and many were proud to be white. White is who they are. They will not pretend to be anything else. They felt free to be white and "act white." A white male conservative Protestant pastor of a multiracial congregation says of his racial identity:

> [I am a] white male. I grew up out in a little town . . . with no diversity at all. I don't try to be anything other than white because that is what I am. People don't expect me to be like them. They just expect me to love them and listen to them. There is something fake about trying to be like them.

This white male pastor does not put up a front. He just tries to be himself, a white male. As far as he can tell, other people also expect him to be who he is. His congregants expect him to be himself and just love them and listen to them. Trying to be anyone other than a white man would be a lie.

This assuredness in who they are didn't exist just for men. White women pastors similarly embraced who they are. One shared that she was upfront with her diverse mainline congregation from the beginning of her appointment that she is white and that they better accept that about her: "I have told this church since I got here, 'If I don't fit what your expectations are, then tell me to go somewhere else, because this is who I am and I can't be something else. I am expecting to grow and change, but I am not going to pretend like I am something else.'"

Being confident and true to one's racial self means that white pastors do not apologize for having their own racialized perspectives. For example, some of the white clergy sided with law enforcement and the white police officers during the various Ferguson protests over the shooting of yet another Black man. As community leaders, a few of these white pastors even spoke up publicly on behalf of law enforcement and admitted that they had their own racial perspective. They did not, however, feel guilty or shy about their position. They were not troubled by the fact that they did not understand or share the perspective of most of their Black and Brown congregants. White clergy accepted they had a different perspective on the matter as a white person. They had no qualms about it.

Take Father Carry, a Catholic priest in his seventies who headed a small and financially struggling, predominantly Black and Hispanic parish. He had been called upon by local news to discuss his perspective on the Black Lives Matter protests and police brutality against unarmed Black men. With close friends in local law enforcement who are white, he sides with the police officers:

> I am white and a lot of [the congregants] are Black, and I don't know. Especially, most recently, with all of this Black/white stuff and the cops being killed. I don't know. It's very hard for me to know. I can guess. But I can be wrong too. I think [my Black congregants] want leadership, want me to be on their side.... But they don't know that ... in addition to being the pastor of this parish, I am also the clergy liaison to the local precinct.... The police asked me to take that on, and I am also chaplain to the local fire department. And the people know I am close to both of them.

Father Carry then adds that he is not sure how his Black congregants felt about his press response to the Black Lives Matter protests, in which he sided with law enforcement. His Black congregants may even think that he is a racist; he isn't sure. But if they were to think that he is a racist or accuse him of being racist, he says that they better recognize that having him as a clergy of an underresourced predominantly Black parish in the city is a privilege. He made the hard choice to be in that parish. No one else would want to serve such a parish, particularly someone who is white. Thus, in the end, Father Carry does not lose sleep over what his congregants may think of him. He can be his true racial self and hold his own racial perspectives.

There are several points to take away from this. Father Carry's position at the local precinct may be a conflict of interest. Can he effectively empathize with and care for the Black congregants of his parish? It seems he can't. He suspects they may perceive him as racist, suggesting he knows they may not trust him. Moreover, he doesn't really value his congregants. His perspective is that they should be grateful he even took on this assignment.

It is important to highlight here that Father Carry does not represent all Catholic priests in our study. Most other white Catholic priests in the RLDP held more progressive views on white police officers shooting unarmed Black men and the various movements that erupted as a result. In fact, several of the white Catholic priests as well as some mainline pastors in our study were actively engaged in progressive politics in regard to Black Lives Matter. Indeed, among the white pastors, Catholic priests were on average the most progressive. Conservative Protestant pastors were, well, conservative. The point here is the racial perspectives of white leaders do indeed vary and are no doubt heterogeneous. What remains consistent, however, is that white clergy have the most freedom to have and hold their own racial perspectives, whatever they may be. Their congregants willingly give them this freedom. One of the white Catholic priests who is actively engaged in progressive local politics shared that his congregation told him, "Listen, all that we have had here is white pastors. We know how to deal with you, don't worry about it.... Yeah, we know about this, so just be yourself and you will be alright." He is given the freedom to be himself in his role as a white head clergy by his Black and Brown congregants. This is explicit.

Thus, white clergy can be themselves in their role as head clergy of multiracial congregations. They can even be confident in and embrace their whiteness. They can think and lead like a white person, and their congregants, their primary audience, give them license to do so. There is no racial self-hatred, self-dissing, self-censoring, or self-veiling. This racial self-acceptance and affirmation is good for white pastors' personal well-being.

Self-Enhanced Racial Identity: Good White People

Several years ago at a conference, I (Kim) asked Peggy McIntosh, an anti-racism activist and author of the popular essay "White Privilege: Unpacking the Invisible Knapsack," a question: Why would white people like her want to fight racism and inequality and potentially sabotage the privileges that they enjoy in society as white people? Her response confirmed the resilience of white privilege. She explained that white privilege is like "a never-ending fountain." White people don't have to worry about losing their privilege by fighting racism. The beauty of white privilege, as long as it doesn't do any real damage to the white supremacist superstructure, is that it does not run out, no matter how often you use it or for what purpose you use it, including using it to fight racism and intolerance. In fact, McIntosh suggested that using white privilege to be more racially and culturally inclusive can give white people even more benefits. People of color won't fear them; they will trust them. White people actually end up diversifying and expanding their networks. As she put it, "Now Black people will be your friends." By gaining the trust and approval of people of color, white people eliminate one conceivable wrinkle in being white in a multiracial world: being accused of being racist by people of color. By pointing to their trusted connections with people of color, they can deflect criticism directed at them for being a racist. They also gain an even more positive racial identity as good, nonracist white people and, in a way, "save themselves" from the weight of being implicated in racial oppression.

We find this holds true for white pastors of multiracial congregations as well. By leading in multiracial spaces and being seen as pursuing ethnic and racial inclusivity, however willing or successful they may be, white pastors can, in essence, be somewhat shielded from being accused of being culturally intolerant and racist by people of color. Leading a multiracial, multicultural community can give them a more positive self-identity as they can think of themselves as relatively good and inclusive nonracist white people.

Multiculturally Connected and "Woke"

When asked about the advantages of leading a multiracial congregation, white pastors commonly discussed how they are personally enriched because they get to learn about different cultures and worldviews by virtue of leading a diverse congregation. For example, a white Catholic priest of a large multilingual, multicultural, multiracial parish on the East Coast talked about being blessed to learn about the different cultures among the various ethnic and racial groups in his church: "I am the most blessed priest in the world. I am never bored. I never know what is going to happen next." A white pastor of a Protestant church similarly shares:

> Advantages. . . ? I am a suburban Anglo boy, a baby boomer. It just opens up a world that is unknown, it is just a broadening experience to be working in a multiracial community. . . . Coming here, knowing the language, being able to get into that world just opens up a whole other culture, another whole way of looking at God, and spirituality. . . . It is just broadening and that is the great gift.

Another white Protestant pastor notes the same benefit. Although he grew up "very Caucasian, very Midwest," and "ignorant of different cultures," leading a multiracial congregation opened up a "whole new world": "Richness, different cultures have different views of life and there really is a beauty in there. It is a profound beauty. . . . I didn't know much about different cultures, the way they see it, different dresses, way of expressing themselves, way of praying spiritually, singing, all beautiful stuff." Being exposed to a diverse group of congregants, white pastors of multiracial congregations get to see a "whole new world" of diversity and can come to identify themselves as good, multiculturally "conscious" white people.

By leading in multiracial spaces and trying to foster a multiracial community, regardless of how egalitarian and inclusive they actually are, white leaders can get a "pass" on being a racist and can avoid the guilt or discomfort that may be associated with it. This was the case for Father Carry. He shared that he grew up in "a very racist family" and that the community that his current parish is located in is known as a place with "a lot of racist white people." When the interviewer asked him if he has been lumped in with the white people in the community and accused of being racist, Father Carry responded angrily:

Oh, nobody would ever dare say anything in front of me. It is just not allowed. I don't allow it. . . . To that point, people are dishonest with me. I don't know how they feel. I don't care how they feel. Fuck them. I don't care. You know, but they are wrong.

Father Carry does not let people of color accuse him of being racist. Thus, some people may not be honest with him about what they really think of him, including thinking that he is racist. Still, he doesn't care, because he says they are wrong, that he is not racist. And he shuts down any possible claim made by Black and Brown congregants that he is racist, and he uses the fact that he heads a multiracial, predominantly Black and Brown parish as his defense. According to him, he could easily be at another parish that is more financially well off and white. But he "chose" to stay and head this poor, predominantly Black and Brown parish. Thus, people of color, especially those in his congregation, cannot accuse him of being a racist:

Early on in my tenure, I made it very clear that I would not let race be a trump card in any conversation. Never accuse me of racism. I mean I choose to be here with you. I am old enough and smart enough to be at a nice cushy parish someplace. I don't have to be here. I choose to be here.

White pastors like Father Carry who don't "have to" lead a multiracial community have white pastor privilege. White pastors have options; they can be elsewhere. Therefore, they can deflect accusations of being racist. They can assume an identity as a good white leader who does not deserve to be called a racist.

What to Do with White Pastor Privilege?

White pastors have white privilege. That is clear. What matters, therefore, is what they do with that privilege. We find that white mainline Protestant pastors, particularly women, are the most likely to actually use their white privilege to become more culturally competent, confront issues of racism, and fight against systemic racism.

Pastor Dillon, for example, is honest about her white privilege and aware of the reality of systemic racism in U.S. society. She also actively tries to do something about it. When asked if she talks about race at her small Black, white, and Hispanic church on the West Coast, she laughed out loud. Of course she does. Pursuing "racial justice" is one of the core values of her congregation. She self-identifies as an "antiracist activist."

Pastor Dillon knows that she has white privilege. She has had advantages and access to resources that people of color have not had because she is white. She admits that she was able to get accepted into various leadership positions in her local community and the school board because she is a white woman who can easily connect with other white people in power in the city. She therefore uses her white privilege and access to power to help others who lack such access. She started the Committee for Racial Justice after a local school district tried to cover up a racist incident at one of their schools. She opened up the investigation and held the predominantly white-led school district accountable. Pastor Dillon also invites local politicians to come to her church to discuss racial injustice and racial profiling. She mobilizes and organizes rallies for Black Lives Matter. She is part of the NAACP, Justice Not Jails, and various other local and national programs that aim to reduce racial inequality. Pastor Dillon is also a member of an antiracist alliance of white people.

Pastor Dillon keeps doing this work even though she gets reprimanded by her supervisors in the denomination for being too activist and neglecting traditional pastoral care and preaching. Indeed, her Sunday services are more like a community organizing rally than a worship service. Nevertheless, she presses on. This is who she is as a clergywoman—a white woman who understands her white privilege and is actively engaged in antiracism and racial justice.

There are also white male pastors who see their white privilege as well as structural racism and who actively try to combat racism in and outside of their church. Take Pastor Roberts, the Ivy League–educated pastor who, as he put it, "checked the power box on all twenty categories." When asked if he talks about race with his primarily white and African American upper-class congregation in the Midwest, he says, "I preached on it many times." He has talked about "structural inequality and race," Trayvon Martin, Black Lives Matter, racial profiling, and the mass incarceration of Black men and has read Michelle Alexander's *The New Jim Crow*. After the Ferguson uprising, he shared before his sermon, "I stand in solidarity with the Black Lives Matter movement," to which his liberal mainline Protestant congregation, who he says usually "don't applaud at anything," erupted in applause. Pastor Roberts even wrote his application essay for his current position as head clergy by quoting from the book *The Elusive Dream: The Power of Race in Interracial Churches* by Korie Little Edwards.

Thus, Pastor Roberts is a white pastor who understands his white privilege, sees structural racism, and tries to do something about it. When asked if he gets any pushback for talking about racism, he said he isn't sure. Most congregants have been receptive. He then guessed that congregants who are not on board with confronting racism and embracing antiracist activism "will leave," because "there is no doubt" where his church stands on the matter.

These two pastors, however, are the exception. The majority of the white pastors in our study, particularly those who are from conservative Protestant denominations and associations, are not using their white privilege to actively promote cultural inclusivity, pursue social justice, or fight racism. This, however, is not simply a product of white conservative Protestant pastors' personal shortcomings. This may have as much to do with the broader social structural conditions that they are working in—the culture and structure of their religious denomination and association.

Among white evangelicals, there is a "witch hunt" of sorts for "liberal" evangelicals who pursue racial social justice. In fact, during the time of our study one of the white conservative Protestant pastors who wanted to be more engaged in racial justice and the Black Lives Matter movement feared being put on a "blacklist" in his conservative religious association for being a liberal who preaches a socialist "social gospel" in lieu of "the Gospel." Following the Ferguson uprising, white evangelical elites like Pastor John MacArthur of Grace Community Church created a list of "legitimate" conservative evangelicals, which chastised and excluded evangelicals who call out systemic racism and pursue racial justice. The latter type of evangelicals were branded as social gospel fanatics and lost their credentials as "legitimate" Christians.[8]

The cultural climate of the religious organizations that many conservative Protestant pastors operate in is not conducive to talking about racism or combating systemic racial inequality. In fact, it is anything but. On the whole, conservative Protestant institutions are not particularly supportive of racial social justice. Any talk of racism or antiracism may brand pastors who do speak up as Marxist "critical race theory" heretics.

For many mainline denominations, talking about social justice, including racial social justice, is part of their culture, mission, and identity. The motto of the United Methodist denomination, for example, is "Open Hearts, Open

Minds, and Open Doors." One of their core identities is pursuing "social justice." Being inclusive of people of color is part of their congregational identity and culture, which makes it easier for white United Methodist clergy to choose to be more multicultural, talk about racism, and participate in social justice.

There were also several Catholic priests who were proactive about fighting racism and being culturally inclusive. This too, we suspect, is related to a different organizational climate for Catholic priests compared to conservative Protestant pastors. "Catholic," by definition, means encompassing inclusiveness and diversity. The Catholic Church is a global church. The Catholic churches in the United States, for example, have multiple ethnoculturally informed masses held in various languages, often by priests from around the world. Moreover, liberation theology, which advocates social justice for the oppressed, is part of the Catholic canon.

Many mainline pastors and Catholic priests have more protection in their job as head clergy than conservative Protestant pastors. Their religious organizations are episcopal polities. It is the bishops, superintendents, or directors over their parishes, regions, or orders who have authority over their pastoral assignments. Many mainline clergy and all Catholic priests are appointed by their religious organizations to serve as head clergy. In contrast, most conservative Protestant pastors head churches that have a congregational polity. They have either started their own congregations or have been hired by their churches. This makes them far more vulnerable to the whims and passions of their congregants. People can vote with their feet and leave the church, which can leave the pastors jobless, or the congregation can literally fire them! Catholic clergy as well as many mainline Protestant clergy who serve in episcopal polities therefore have greater freedom to be more activist and racial-justice-oriented because they have more job security and protection compared to conservative Protestant pastors.

We have seen that white leaders are the most preferred, normative, respected, and resourced leaders among all leaders. They have the most agency and freedom to "be themselves" in their positions as pastors. White leaders simply have more options, including the choice to use their white privilege to fight intolerance and racism—or not. Those who lead voluntary multiracial spaces can also enjoy an enhanced self-identity as good and tolerant nonracist white people.

While this is true, white leaders who choose to combat white supremacy head-on bear costs, and these costs vary according to the type of organization they are navigating. Given the nature of their organizational culture and structure, white conservative Protestant pastors face more risks and will have to pay more costs than mainline or Catholic clergy for choosing to battle white supremacy. The freedom to use white privilege for racial justice and inclusivity thus varies depending on the cultural and structural context of the white pastors' position.

This suggests that the solution to moving toward a more racially equitable and just religious landscape lies in changing religious structures. It is not simply about changing "hearts and minds." For white pastors to have more freedom to use their white pastor privilege to be inclusive and fight against racism and for racial justice, there needs to be institutional change in the culture and structure of their religious denominations and organizations. It is not enough for white pastors to personally see injustice and want to use their privilege for good. They need to be in institutional spaces where these views and actions are embraced and supported as well.

Conclusion

Estranged Pioneers

In this book, we have looked at pastors of multiracial churches with a focus on pastors of color to examine what it means to lead in racially diverse spaces. What are their experiences heading racially diverse churches? What are their challenges and successes? How did they come to head racially diverse religious spaces in an institution that is still overwhelmingly racially segregated?

Heading a multiracial church is not for the faint of heart. Any person, regardless of race, gender, or religious affiliation, who is aiming to do this kind of work in a society that in many respects works against racial diversity, justice, and equity faces an uphill battle. Pastors of multiracial churches are essentially on their own. They do not get additional help or support for this kind of work, even though it is something that is praised and framed as laudable by those in and outside of their religious circles and denomination.

To understand their experiences leading multiracial churches, we began by looking at pastors' biographies to see what events or experiences are common across their lives to understand how they came to head racially diverse churches. We highlighted three common patterns, or what we refer to as "dots." These are common events or experiences we see across pastors' lives.

One common dot is that the vast majority of pastors of multiracial churches across race—if they were raised in Christianity—grew up in churches made up of people who share their ethnoracial identity. For instance, African Americans grew up in African American churches; Asian Americans grew up in Asian ethnic congregations, usually immigrant centered; Hispanic Americans grew up in Hispanic congregations, in the United States or elsewhere; and whites grew up in white congregations. Despite this, a large majority of the pastors of color in our study were raised in religious traditions that were a part of white Western-controlled denominations or religious associations. This is by necessity for Hispanic and Asian Americans.

There is no "Hispanic church" or "Asian church" as there is a Black church in the United States. Still, several Black pastors and their families came from Black churches embedded in white Western Christendom as well.

A second common dot along their journeys is going to college, seminary, or divinity school. This event is particularly consequential for pastors of color. It is when they commonly and for the first time experience sustained interaction in a Christian space that is largely white and controlled and infused with the ideologies, theologies, and religious culture of white Western Christianity. This places them at greater risk of leaving their ethnoracial religious home communities.

A third common dot is the polity of the pastor's denomination or religious affiliation. The polity determines where a person will pastor. There is no substantive difference in the ways in which pastors who are a part of denominations or religious affiliations with episcopal polities talk about how they came to head their congregations. They are simply assigned. There is, however, a difference across race among pastors who are associated with denominations or religious affiliations with congregational polities. These are conservative Protestant or evangelical pastors, all of whom are men. White evangelical head pastors were by and large hired by their congregations. Very few had planted their churches, and those who did not do so with the explicit aim of starting a multiracial church. Conversely, 85% of the Black and Asian American conservative Protestant pastors in the RLDP planted churches with the explicit intent of starting multiracial churches.

We also paid attention to how pastors experience being head clergy of multiracial churches. Regardless of religious affiliation, pastors of multiracial churches are pioneers. They are going against the odds, doing something that few of their peers are doing. This work is in many respects easier for white pastors of multiracial churches because they are leading in racially diverse religious spaces that are embedded in a larger white Christian universe. They can maintain connections to the Christian community with which they are already comfortable and familiar and maintain a religious identity that affirms who they are. Pastors of color of multiracial churches do not have such a luxury. They are not just pioneers; they are what we call "estranged pioneers." When they head multiracial churches, they are leaving their ethnoracial home communities pretty much altogether. What's more, their endeavors are not valued or celebrated as something that will potentially benefit the communities they come from. Their ethnoracial identity and connection to their ethnoracial religious community is destabilized in the process. They experience alienation. They are also othered by and perceived as inferior to their white peers within the new communities that they lead.

It should therefore come as no surprise that the pastors of color carry a heavy load as they aim to build a racially diverse religious community. They rely on three strategies, which are not always the healthiest for themselves or the community they lead, to manage the load. First, they overachieve, or at least try to achieve more than their white counterparts to manage the challenges of leading as a pastor of color. They feel that they need to pay a "racial tax" and work harder than their white counterparts in their role as head clergy. Second, they reject, minimize, or hide their racial identity, particularly in their roles as head clergy, often because they see embodying and embracing their ethnoracial identity and culture as a threat to the stability of their racially diverse churches. A third strategy, which is the healthiest option of the three, is to reconnect with people, often other pastors, who share their ethnoracial identity. This helps them to refuel and provides temporary moments of belonging.

Although pastors of color suffer varying levels of alienation from their ethnoracial home churches, are othered as racial inferiors, and carry a heavy load in this work, they are advantaged as leaders in multiracial spaces in distinct ways. They are multicultural, able to move in and out of more than one ethnocultural community. Their standpoints as racialized minorities in a white supremacist world provide them a lens through which they are better able than white pastors to see and comprehend the racialized social system. These advantages together, we suggest, give pastors of color of multiracial churches what we call "racialized multicultural competency." Moreover, pastors of color of multiracial churches have the potential to act as brokers, uniquely situated between two separate social networks, to manage and negotiate the sharing of resources. In their case, it would be their ethnoracial religious community and the larger white Christian circles in which they are currently embedded. Enacting this role greatly depends upon their ability to foster authentic relationships based on trust and mutuality with both their ethnoracial religious home community and their predominantly white religious community.

In Chapter 5, we turned our attention to the white pastors in the study. They have what we call "white pastor privilege." That is, they have a set of unearned advantages enjoyed by white pastors that are associated with being white in a society that is structured by white supremacy. This manifests in various ways, but most notably in how their authority is legitimated. White pastors are often preferred by both white congregants and congregants of color. Their leadership style is viewed as normative and the standard for all head clergy. White pastors do not report resistance to their authority, as do pastors of color. Finally, white pastors have greater access to resources. This is, in large part, an artifact of white pastors of multiracial churches still being embedded in religious networks and religious associations or denominations that are largely white and rooted in white Western Christendom.

Religious Racial Diversity and Whiteness

This study demonstrates that multiracial churches are a product of white Western Christianity.[1] I (Little Edwards) intimated this in other work where I argued that multiracial churches work to the extent that white congregants are comfortable.[2] Whiteness is normalized in these spaces as well, even in spaces where people of color are the numerical majority and the head pastor is a person of color. These churches work in this way because they are governed by white hegemony. Similar to the pastors in this study, the congregants of color participate in the reproduction of a space where whiteness is valorized and the beliefs, values, culture, and preferences of people of color are made secondary. To put it another way, their sense of belonging is less important than making sure white people feel they belong. Ultimately, racially diverse religious spaces might look inclusive and equitable, but they quite often do not foster authentic, equitable, and just religious communities.[3]

Omi and Winant[4] argue that in the U.S. context, people are regularly participating in racial projects as a way to reproduce and establish what race is and what the categories of race mean. Racial projects, they say, are "simultaneously an interpretation, representation, or explanation of racial identities and meanings, and an effort to organize and distribute resources (economic, political, cultural) along particular racial lines."[5] In multiracial religious spaces, congregants, including congregants of color, can perceive pastors of color as inferior to whites; pastors of color minimize their racial selves, also treating themselves as inferior to whites; and decisions are made to minimize or eliminate the religious culture valued by people of color to make sure the church is racially diverse. All of these are ways that both pastors and congregants, those who are white and those who are people of color, reproduce a racial hierarchy that places whites at the top and people of color below.

Then we have to take a broader view of multiracial churches and consider where they are situated. Multiracial churches are not just about maintaining diversity at the expense of the souls of people of color. They are also about ensuring white people are sufficiently comfortable so they won't leave and the church can stay racially diverse. Looking at the experiences of the 121 multiracial church pastors in the RLDP, we can see more clearly how multiracial churches are products of white Western Christendom. Multiracial churches and the people who lead them are almost exclusively embedded in white Christian religious communities or organizations. One pastor of color in the RLDP started a multiracial church out of a religious space of color, a Korean church. This was a rarity indeed. Still, this pastor's church is embedded in white evangelical circles. White pastors of multiracial churches along with their congregations are already embedded in white Christianity. There is never a moment along their journeys toward a racially diverse religious space that white people, clergy or congregants, have to leave white Western Christendom.

The reason this can happen so consistently is because in the United States, white Western Christianity is the broader institution in which most religious organizations are embedded or deeply connected, regardless of their racial composition. This institution does not just include congregations and denominations. It also includes seminaries, Bible colleges and divinity schools, missions agencies, parachurch organizations, Christian publishing houses, college campus ministries, summer camp retreat centers, and more. The expanse of white Western Christianity is broad. There is only one other ethnoracial group that has a religious structure that exists independent of contemporary white Western Christianity, and that is African Americans.[6] That structure has formed over centuries into what we call the Black church and includes several Black-controlled denominations: the African Methodist Episcopal Zion Church; the Christian Methodist Episcopal Church; the Church of God in Christ; and three National Baptist Conventions, which include the National Baptist Convention of America, the National Baptist Convention, USA, Inc., and the Progressive National Baptist Convention, Inc. There are also Black-controlled seminaries and divinity schools, such as the Payne Theological Seminary, the Interdenominational Theological Center, and the Samuel DeWitt Proctor School of Theology at Virginia Union University, among others.

To say racial diversity in churches is a project of white Western Christianity is to say it is rooted in the theologies, cultures, and structures of white Western

Christianity. That is where it begins. That is where it resides, including its rewards. The rewards of racial diversity in white Western Christianity are bestowed only under certain conditions. It must maintain the centering of whiteness. What this study reveals is that even if we are talking about the head pastor, this is the bargain that has been struck to do religious racial diversity. Whiteness must be sustained. For sure, there are pastors pushing back against this. Those in our study who were most inclined to push back were older, established, tenured social justice–oriented Catholic priests. (Yes, that is a lot of preconditions.) The reality is, they could do this because they had the least to lose. Catholicism is suffering a shortage of priests. Heading urban parishes, which is where racially diverse churches usually are, is not a desirable post. Even so, these pastors often had to seek resources for their congregations from white Christians or white Christian circles within their religious affiliations. Therefore, they can push against whiteness only so hard before they and their congregations pay a price.

The 4 Ps: Passion, Potential, Pressure, Practice

Given this, how do pastors who head multiracial congregations lead in these spaces? We propose that there are three factors that impact how they lead: *passion, potential*, and *pressure*. These three factors affect how they will *practice* pastoring a multiracial church.

Passion

When I (Little Edwards) talk to my students about developing a research agenda, one of my main recommendations is to pursue a research question they are passionate about. When you are passionate about something, you will be more driven to follow through on doing the work to answer that question well.

Passion matters in any work one does. It is an important quality for scholars. It is also an important quality for pastors of multiracial churches. The passion for doing the work of building a racially diverse religious community varies among the pastors in the RLDP. Some of the pastors are simply doing their job, and that happens to be in a racially diverse church. They are committed to their job as pastors. And they deal with the peculiar challenges that come with heading a racially diverse congregation. However, they are not emotionally invested in the work of cultivating a racially diverse community. They are not personally committed to the idea of racial diversity. Nor are they invested in fostering community among their congregants across racial lines. A minority of pastors in the study would fall in this classification.

Other pastors have a moderate level of commitment to a racially diverse religious community. By this, we mean they believe that it is important for their congregation to minister to the people in their local community, which may have changed from racially homogeneous to racially diverse. It is important for them that their congregants grow together as a community across racial lines. They will do what they can to gain the training to do this work well. They do believe it is appropriate and important for their congregation. However, they do not necessarily believe this is a general value congregations or pastors should have. These pastors are generally a part of denominations with episcopal or presbyterian polities. They tend to be minorities in some capacity or another, either women or people of color or both.

The last category includes pastors who have a stated passion for or a divine call to build a racially diverse religious community. They are emotionally or spiritually invested in congregations being racially diverse, so much so that they will put a good deal of their resources at risk to make it happen. It also means that their sense of who they are can be intertwined with how well their church is doing at being a racially diverse religious community. These pastors are disproportionately people of color and conservative Protestant. The majority of pastors of color, notably Black and Asian American pastors, have gone so far as to start churches with the specific intent of creating a racially diverse religious community.

We found that, generally, pastors of color were the ones who expressed greater levels of passion for a racially diverse religious community, though there were pastors of color who were not particularly passionate about it, and white pastors who were more passionate. Passion is an important quality to have for work, as we mentioned. It can drive commitment. It can also foster a sense of deep satisfaction when one is doing work that one is passionate about. However, it was common for passionate multiracial church pastors to have made creating a racially diverse religious community integral to their sense of who they are as pastors. Such passion is disconnected and imbalanced. It does not keep in perspective the broader context in which they as pastors and their congregations are embedded and their own limitations within this broader context. Based upon how these pastors talk about their experiences heading multiracial churches, we see this as an unhealthy approach to pastoring a multiracial church. They do not feel good about themselves when their congregations are not doing well. They tend to express the most stress and sense of isolation. Additionally, these pastors do not have a community that is good for their souls. This is because they do not know how to build this community or where they might find it. Some white pastors express a passion for a racially diverse religious community. It can be stressful for them. They do not have white peers who they can relate to. Yet, as we have already noted, being embedded in white Western Christianity protects them in ways that passionate pastors of color are not protected.

We found that the pastors in our study who were moderately passionate about fostering a racially diverse religious community were less stressed than the most passionate. No doubt, fostering this kind of community was difficult and challenging for them as well. This had to do in part with the polity of their congregation. However, their identity and sense of self was not linked to the success or response of their congregations. Conflicts more easily rolled off their backs. Additionally, they had close, safe relationships with other pastors or religious leaders who thought similarly and who had similar passions and commitments.

Potential

Potential is about having the qualities that will lead to success in the future. It signals the likelihood that one will do well at a particular endeavor and even have opportunities to pursue that endeavor. There are different types of potential that emerge from different sources. That potential can be intrinsic to a person, or it can come from the community or group they are a part of or both. As sociologists, we tend to focus on that potential that is forged from our interactions with and experiences in the social world. We gain certain qualities and knowledge as a result of those interactions and experiences.

When we talk about the potential of pastors of multiracial churches, we are talking about qualities that facilitate their success at leading a multiracial church. We define a *successful racially diverse religious space in the United States as one that is a structurally and culturally equitable, just community of mutuality that has decentered whiteness and white supremacy*. Admittedly, this is a tall order, and success will need to be measured along a continuum. Nevertheless, we wanted to provide a working definition.

Pastors have different types of potential that can facilitate success in leading in racially diverse religious spaces, and our study shows that these types of potential fall along racial lines. Pastors of color have that racialized multicultural competency we discussed. They are familiar with multiple cultures. As racial minorities, they have had to learn how to navigate a society where whites and whiteness are considered normative and superior. Their felt experiences with structural and personal racism and racial discrimination have given them an intimate understanding of how these work and manifest in the world. This sets them up to be better able to lead a racially diverse space that has success as we have defined it. White pastors, though, have greater potential to gain access to the kinds of capital—particularly social and financial capital—that are important for any organization to succeed. Racialized multicultural competence comes from living in the United States as a person of color. The potential white pastors have is an artifact of multiracial churches being embedded in white Western Christianity.

Potential is not the same as the actualization or embodiment of potentialities. Just because leaders have potential, it does not mean they use it as leaders. That leads us to our next P.

Pressure

Human beings are social. We develop in groups and communities. We do life in groups and communities. We navigate life across and within social institutions. This means we are not autonomous individuals in the world. We are impacted by the groups, communities, organizations, and institutions we encounter and to which we belong. All these—the groups, communities, organizations, and institutions—comprise the social structures that people are embedded in.

In other work, I (Little Edwards) talk about the importance of accounting for social structure when aiming to understand people's actions and attitudes. I argue that there are multiple sources that affect how a pastor leads. When it comes to pastors of multiracial churches, I highlight four. Pastors themselves have their own ideas about what it means to be a leader as a multiracial church pastor. These ideas and perspectives are bound by many other sources: their congregations, denominations or religious affiliations, and macro-level understandings about race. Throughout this volume you have heard pastors, particularly pastors of color, share their perspectives on what it means to be a head clergy of a multiracial church and why they came to do this and what they think a pastor who leads in their type of context ought to do and be. You have also heard pastors describe their experiences with congregants. At times, these are rewarding and supportive relationships and interactions. And there are those that are challenging. We have also talked about how they navigate their denominations and religious affiliations. All this is happening within a broader social system that infuses and impacts all other interactions, decisions, opportunities, and potentialities. And that system is race.[7]

What does this mean? At every level, pastors of multiracial churches are experiencing pressures that exist outside of them to lead in particular ways. As we have argued here and elsewhere, that way is one that ultimately reinforces whiteness and white supremacy through white hegemony. We argue that even how pastors think about the role of a multiracial church pastor is significantly influenced by race and white Western Christianity well before they even take their first position as a head clergy in this setting. They may think that how they envision the role is just their ideas or simply biblical. But all people in the United States are thoroughly socialized to affirm white supremacy, even when white superiority is taught in subtle ways, like in the lack of representation of people of color in the media or a lack of materials in schools, colleges, and seminaries that take seriously the experiences and ideas of people who are not white. The absence of ideas renders them invisible and dismissible, or at least not normative.

Pastors of multiracial churches may have all kinds of potential, and we have emphasized racialized multicultural competency as well as social capital and financial capital, resources helpful for building a successful racially diverse religious community. Actualizing that potential is very much contingent upon how they can manage the pressures that come from their congregants, denominations or religious affiliations, and whiteness.

Passion + Potential + Pressure = Practice

We propose that the practice of heading multiracial churches is the result of a combination of a pastor's passion and potential and the pressures that come from the groups and organizations they are embedded in as well as the power of whiteness. By "practice," we simply mean how they do their job as pastor. There are myriad combinations of these factors. Different combinations will affect pastors' pastoral practices differently. To illustrate how we are thinking about the way a combination of these factors can affect the practice of a multiracial church pastor, we provide three hypothetical examples. These examples, while informed by our data, do not represent any one pastor in the RLDP.

Example 1
Reynolds McPherson is a pastor of a conservative Protestant church in Dallas. He is Black and was raised in a predominantly Black Baptist church affiliated with the Southern Baptist Convention, though you wouldn't know it from the religious culture of the church or the church's politics. Pastor McPherson's family has been Baptist for as long as he can remember. In addition, he grew up in a largely Black neighborhood in the city. Though his elementary and middle schools were predominantly Black, most of the teachers and principals were white. The high school he attended was racially diverse, with a pretty even mix of Black, Hispanic, and white students. He was a good student despite the school guidance counselor, Ms. Smith, an older white woman who had been at the school for who knows how long, telling him and his friend Jaheem that they probably couldn't handle calculus. She even suggested that they were drug dealers. A high point in high school for Pastor McPherson, though, was playing on the school's baseball team. That is where he first met friends he has to this day, Manuel, who is Mexican American, and Paul, an Anglo white guy.

After high school, Pastor McPherson went to a college in Texas and majored in business. He joined the college's gospel choir and was involved in a college campus ministry group. After college he went back to Dallas, got a full-time job in sales, and returned to his home church, where his family was still actively involved. Somewhere along the way, he felt a "call" to pastoring. He followed that call and decided to go to a seminary nearby. There, he was introduced to all kinds of scholars and writings addressing Christian theology and practice. Like his professors, almost all the scholars he learned about and read were white men. He got a chance to intern at a church while in seminary, a largely white megachurch in the area. The head pastor invested in and mentored him. Soon, he stopped going to his home church and began attending this largely white megachurch. He actually began to question the biblical knowledge of the pastors and lay leaders of his home church and thought perhaps their faith and embodiment of Christianity through their cultural and religious practices were not consistent with scripture.

When done with seminary, he was hired as the social justice minister at the megachurch. A few years after that, he felt "called" to start a racially diverse church. His pastor, the one heading the megachurch, people in his small group at the church, and friends and professors from seminary concurred with this calling. The megachurch and the denomination of the megachurch combined made a $50,000 commitment over five years in support. Pastor McPherson's church grew to about two hundred attendees by the fifth year. The church was racially diverse, with a slight majority of white attendees. There was little about his church that was reminiscent of his home church, culturally or theologically. In many ways, it felt very much like the megachurch where he worked. Pastor McPherson felt alone and unsupported. He was in contact with the pastor and others at the megachurch. But he didn't feel they were an authentic community for him, where he was emotionally and spiritually supported. They didn't do anything directly to make him feel this way. He just didn't feel he could be fully himself with them. Meanwhile, his home church didn't understand him either. They did not see why he left the Black church in the first place and took his gifts and talents elsewhere.

In this hypothetical example, Pastor McPherson's potential was the racialized multicultural competency that came from his sustained exposure to his own ethnoracial culture, the dominant white culture, as well as that of other people of color, like his friend Manuel. It also was formed as he navigated direct hits with white supremacy. He knew what that felt like and how it manifested. Though he was raised in a predominantly Black church and was an active member of that church as a young adult, he came to have a passion for developing a multiracial church and decided to plant one. It is notable that this call emerged after experiencing the pressures of white Western Christianity. He had attended a white-controlled seminary and interned in a largely white megachurch. Perhaps the seeds of pastoring this kind of church were planted when he participated in a college campus ministry. The groups and organizations Pastor McPherson was embedded in affirmed white Western Christianity. Plus, he no longer held dear or respected his Black Christian roots, at least not as much as he did white Western Christendom. When he planted his church, it looked and felt very much like a white conservative Protestant megachurch. He even hid that he was the pastor for the first year, thinking his race shouldn't matter. His practice as a pastor was to mimic what he learned in the largely white megachurch, and in his practice we see that he also succumbed to the pressure of whiteness, hiding that he, the head pastor, was Black.

Example 2

Pastor Doug Jeong was born in Korea and moved to California with his family when he was five. He grew up in a Korean immigrant church affiliated with a mainline Protestant denomination. His neighborhood and schools, all the way through high school, were predominantly white. He recalls language being a bit of a barrier when he was a small child. Other children made jokes about what he looked like and how he talked. But that didn't last. He had picked up English rather quickly by the time he went to first grade. The children's church activities and youth group at his Korean church were held in English. While his family mostly spoke Korean at home and at church, he knew Korean and English fluently early on. Moreover, he had really gotten the hang of the dominant culture. Most of his friends growing up were white and Korean American. He had white friends from the neighborhood and school. His Korean American friends were from church.

Pastor Jeong went away to college and majored in engineering. While at college, he attended a racially diverse mainline Protestant college church near his campus. It was different from his home church, particularly in how the students interacted with the pastor. It was like the pastor was their peer, though of course he was at least ten years older and, well, the pastor. The pastor of the college campus church was Indian. Pastor Jeong had gotten to know him and his family pretty well. As they developed their relationship, he began speaking with his college pastor about going to seminary. By the time Pastor Jeong finished college, he knew he wanted to go into ministry. Actually, he had wondered about going into ministry as a youth. However, it just didn't seem like the best option; at least that is the impression he got from the advice of adults in his life, both teachers and family members, at the time.

The college pastor recommended one of the more highly regarded seminaries in their denomination. Pastor Jeong decided to go to this seminary and pursue a master's in theology. Once done, the local bishop assigned him to a medium-size, predominantly white church as an associate pastor. His next assignment, four years later, was a diverse but largely white Anglo church with an average attendance of about 150 people. Most of the congregants of color were first-generation professionals. The church was experiencing a change in racial composition as the neighborhood changed.

Pastor Jeong was grateful to be assigned his own church as a head clergy. The congregants of color were also grateful. His being there made them feel validated. And he too felt more at home at this church than the previous one. Still, the older white congregants were not altogether keen on making substantive changes to the church culture. Doing so would take time. The church had been around for a hundred years and had been doing church in much the same way for a very long time. In fact, many of the white members had grown up in the church. The denomination wanted to see the congregation grow, in numbers and financially. The reality is Pastor Jeong needed his white congregants to stay. He found himself having to balance what he wanted, what the congregants of color hoped for in him, and the expectation of the denomination to grow the congregation while also making it more inclusive of the new families moving into the community. Major changes to the culture of the church would have to be taken slowly.

Pastor Jeong's potential was in his racialized multicultural competency, which he developed as a result of his upbringing and exposure to more than one culture, his own ethnoracial culture and the dominant white culture. Moreover, he was bilingual. He understood the challenges that come with navigating a society where your first language isn't the dominant one. He experienced brushes with racism and the pressure to be a model minority. He did not have a passion for racial diversity per se. He felt called to be a pastor. No matter where he would be assigned, he would commit to doing his job well. Yet he did have a desire to see the church become more inclusive of the growing number of congregants of color, many of whom were immigrants. He understood what it was like to grow up in an immigrant family as a 1.5-generation immigrant himself. Still, he had to, at a minimum, maintain the size of the church. The white members were not too excited about any changes. His practice as a pastor was one where he primarily would avoid rocking the boat of the older white congregation while building more intimate relationships with families of color in the church. In the meantime, he planned to add a contemporary worship service, though he was not sure when that would happen.

Example 3
Father Hugo Morales was born and raised in Mexico. He and his family are devout Catholics. One of his father's first cousins is a priest in a small town not too far from where he grew up. He often found himself spending time at his cousin's parish, helping out where he could. While a teenager, he had a succession of dreams and encounters that he believed were divinely guided. He believed he should go into the priesthood. After high school, Father Morales's cousin put him in touch with the diocese in Washington, DC. His cousin had connections with priests there through his religious order.

164 CONCLUSION

Spanish was, of course, Father Morales's first language. But he knew English and understood it very well. Following his cousin's advice, he went to seminary in the United States.

Father Morales joined the same religious order as his cousin, which had a focused commitment to social justice. When he finished seminary, Father Morales was assigned to a staff of priests with a parish in Chicago which was predominantly Hispanic. Many of the parishioners were undocumented. He worked closely with the parish's ministry to help them gain documentation so they could stay in the United States legally. He was there for four years. He was then assigned to a parish in Atlanta as the head priest. The parish was Black, Hispanic, and white, about evenly split. The Hispanic population in the church was growing, as was the Hispanic population in the greater metro area.

When Father Morales arrived, there was considerable conflict over the religious culture of the masses as well as where children should be during services. First-generation Hispanics were comfortable with children in the church service. The other parishioners, including some Black and second-generation Hispanic parishioners, thought the children were distracting. Language was also a big sticking point. The former priest was white and did not know Spanish well at all, so the mass was not relatable for the Hispanic congregants, at least not for those who spoke only Spanish. Father Morales solved the conflict by adding a Spanish mass. Hispanic immigrants and their families went to this mass. The other mass would be in English. Black, white, and most of the second-generation-plus Hispanics went to this mass. Father Morales led both masses. His English was very strong, though he had a noticeable accent. However, several of his white parishioners were not so sure he could lead the English mass. On multiple occasions they wondered in conversation with him if they would be getting another priest who would do the English mass. He let them know that this was not going to happen anytime soon. Father Morales is also in the process of training lay leaders in the church who can run a ministry for undocumented immigrants. He hopes to have it up and running by the end of the year.

We see that Father Morales's potential is his racialized multicultural competency. He is bilingual and bicultural, having navigated seminary and everyday life in the United States. Moreover, he has an understanding of the immigrant experience as a first-generation immigrant himself. He also worked with undocumented Hispanics in his previous post. Father Morales's passions are related to issues of social justice more than racial diversity specifically. It is more that in the United States, racial inequality is a core area where social justice is needed, particularly in urban areas. Spanish-speaking Hispanics are the fastest growing population of the Catholic Church in the United States. As a Spanish-speaking priest, Father Morales is in high demand. Additionally, he is a tenured pastor as a priest in the Catholic Church. Still, the diocese expects the finances of the parish to be in order and that the parish pay their annual tax to the bishop. Some of the diocesan priests, especially those in the suburbs, are not particularly supportive of how he is leading the parish. While Father Morales experiences pressure from the bishop and local diocese on matters related to money, he doesn't feel the pressure related to racial diversity or social justice. Some diocesan priests do not get his leadership. But his community of priests in his religious order affirm his leadership and emphasis on racial equity and social justice.

We offer these examples to show how passion, potential, and pressure matter for the ways in which pastors practice being head clergy. We want to highlight how internal desire is not always the primary factor. Possessing certain skills and opportunities are important. As important as and at times perhaps even more important than passion and potential are the pressures—that is, the broader social structures manifested in their social networks, denominations, and expectations that center whiteness.

* * *

Multiracialism in the United States is a project that sustains whiteness, giving it cover in a world where diversity and inclusivity are increasingly lifted as important values even while it reproduces institutions that center whiteness. Elijah Anderson[8] in *Black in White Space: The Enduring Impact of Color in Everyday Life* highlights how racially diverse public spaces, even in a large multiracial, multicultural metropolis like Philadelphia, are "white spaces." Though formally open to all, these spaces are governed by an unspoken deference to whiteness and are thus experienced and perceived by people of color as dedicated to white people. Multiracial space is de facto white space. What a challenge, especially for leaders of color! Christianity in the United States is by no means an exception. Indeed, several scholars[9] have revealed the active role many white Western Christians, churches, Christian denominations, seminaries, and parachurch organizations have played and continue to play in protecting and developing white supremacy. It could be argued that it is in white Western Christianity where whiteness finds its strongest defenders and producers.

Everyone in the United States, though to varying degrees, is socialized to affirm whiteness and white supremacy. That is because such processes are ubiquitous. White people and people of color are almost constantly socialized into the dominant white culture, either through direct intimate interactions in spaces predominated by white Western culture, such as schools, or indirectly through such institutions as the media. Resisting this socialization is difficult. Changing systems that reproduce it is hard work.

Multiracial church pastors are on the front lines of this work. The assault on diversity, equity, and inclusion programs and policies at universities across the United States and the backlash against being "woke" and critical race theory suggest that these front lines are becoming harder to hold, let alone advance. As of this writing, for example, thirty-four state bills aimed at disrupting or dismantling diversity, equity, and inclusion efforts have been introduced, three of which have been signed into law.[10] Still, even though it is leaders of color who are especially invested in racial diversity and justice work in churches—as is the case in other institutions—it is white pastors and white congregants who often receive the lion's share of the benefits and resources that come with being in multiracial religious spaces. White leaders often receive kudos from their peers for doing something that is against the norm and so difficult. They can more easily exit than colleagues of color if they no longer want to do this work. Similarly, white congregants do not have to sacrifice as much as their peers of color to be in multiracial religious organizations.

This book has focused on pastors of color of multiracial churches because they have the greatest potential and passion. But this work can be particularly burdensome for them. These pastors are in a context where their sense of self as people of color who are Christians and leaders is persistently challenged, in subtle and not so subtle ways. We are agnostic when it comes to multiracial churches; that is, we are neither in support of nor against them. We see them as *a* way to do church, not *the* way. There is much need still for predominantly Asian or Black or Hispanic religious organizations in a society that continues to find ways to reproduce and sustain whiteness and white supremacy. For those who are in the pioneering work of leading in multiracial spaces, however, we hope you will use the space to resist dominant structures and narratives of whiteness and white supremacy. No doubt this will require intentionality and considerable effort and even costs. You will need support. Do all you can to resist going at it alone or being estranged. Find and build community with others, particularly pastors, who are leading as you are and with whom you can do life in safety. Seek and create places that support and reinforce your most authentic self. In this, you will be better equipped to make and be the change you seek.

Appendix
Methods

The data for our book come from the first nationally representative comparative study of multiracial congregations across the United States that examines race and pastoral leadership, the Religious Leadership and Diversity Project (RLDP, 2014–16). RLDP data include over one hundred personal interviews with pastors and denominational leaders, over six hundred surveys of congregations and congregants, three dozen focus groups with 230 congregants, and several follow-up interviews. For this book, we rely primarily on 121 in-depth face-to-face interviews that were conducted with the head clergy of multiracial congregations varying across race, gender, religious affiliation, congregation size, and region.

The head clergy interviews were transcribed and then analyzed for emerging themes and categories using the qualitative data analysis software NVivo. Although we analyzed all of the interviews for comparative purposes, we focused on the interviews with the African American, Asian American, and Hispanic American pastors for this book. Our analysis paid particular attention to their religious and pastoral experiences, especially the advantages and disadvantages the pastors said they experienced heading a multiracial church.

Religious Leadership and Diversity Project

The RLDP is supported by a grant awarded by the Lilly Endowment, which supports research on religion in North America.[1] The aims of the RLDP are consistent with this aim. The theoretical and empirical objectives of the RLDP facilitate an understanding of religious leadership, diversity, and race. It interrogates how particular social structures constrain and shape the role of the multiracial church head clergy in the United States. However, the Lilly Endowment also emphasizes the practical application of scholarship. So while we were focused on the theoretical and empirical contributions of the project, we also paid attention to the practical aims and goals of the Lilly Endowment, which at their core are to improve the quality of life of congregations in North America and train pastors to be effective and faithful leaders.

Research Design

In examining the role of head clergy in leading multiracial congregations, we focused on three social structures as sources of the head clergy role: the congregation of the person occupying the role, the denomination or religious affiliation of the head clergy, and race. And, of course, the expectations of the person occupying the role matter as well. Looking at Figure A.1, we see at the center is the head clergy role. The first concentric circle from there is the person or head clergy who occupies this role. This person has ideas about how

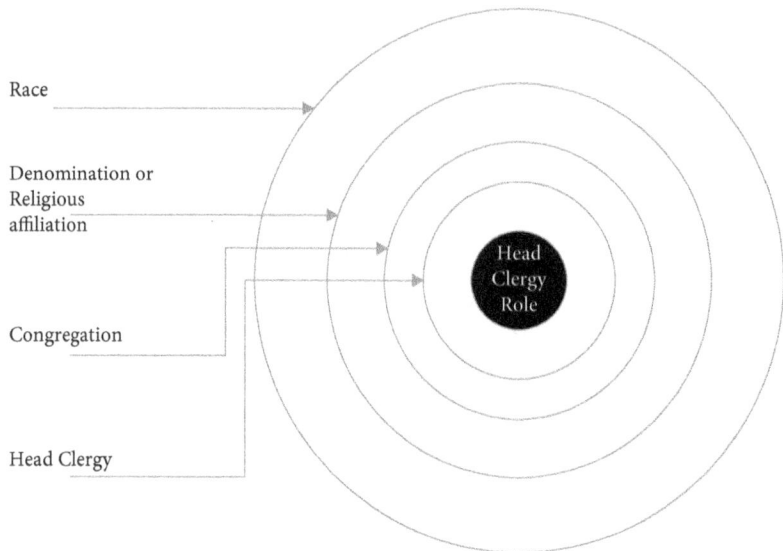

Figure A.1 Multiracial Head Clergy Role in Structure (Edwards 2019).

they are to be in this role. The next concentric circle represents the congregation of the head clergy and its expectations. As congregations exact sanctions, positive or negative, on their head clergy for thinking or behaving in particular ways, the congregation's expectations constrain, modify, or reinforce the beliefs and behaviors of the head clergy. Going further out from the head clergy role are the expectations of the denomination or religious affiliation. Where the expectations of the congregation are specific and particular to that context (e.g., types of social activities, music selections), those of the denomination or religious affiliation are more general, for example, theology or political leanings. These affect what the congregation does or believes or desires to do or believe. They also impact what the head clergy does or believes, or at least aims to. So these too constrain, modify, or reinforce the expectations associated with the head clergy role. The outermost circle represents the structure of race, a hegemonic and all-encompassing social system.[2] As such, it shapes the relationships, resources, identities, opportunities, and cultures of the person occupying the head clergy role as well as every person or organization to which the clergy person is connected. The multiracial church head clergy role is most central to the RLDP. Thus, the research design was organized around understanding the experiences, strategies, beliefs, attitudes, and stories of these head clergy.

Data collection was executed in two phases. The first phase included face-to-face interviews with head clergy and phone interviews with denominational leaders. During the second phase, we focused on the congregants. Interviewing and surveying congregants allow for the triangulation of study results and a fuller, more complex picture of the role and experiences of leaders of racially and ethnically diverse religious organizations. The second phase of the study began a little over a year after the first phase ended. The time between phases gave the RLDP team the opportunity to revisit the congregant research instruments and make revisions to them in view of what was learned from the head clergy and denominational leader interviews.

The RLDP interview team conducted 123 face-to-face interviews with head clergy of racially and ethnically diverse churches in twelve metro areas across the country. Several criteria were considered when selecting recruitment sites. The two main criteria were the racial and ethnic diversity and the population size of the metro areas. We would have the best chance of locating racially diverse churches in large, diverse metro areas. Ease of access was also considered. This meant recruiting in metro areas near where research team members lived. The goal was to get head clergy of churches where no racial group (i.e., Asian, Black, Hispanic, white) was greater than 80% of the congregation. We were largely successful. Congregational survey data (discussed below), which was elicited after interviews, revealed that for 95% of the congregations of head clergy in the study, this is the case. The remaining 5% of churches represented in the sample met a 90% cutoff. The head clergy interviews lasted between one and two and a half hours. They addressed a variety of topics, for example, head clergy's biographies, relationships with their congregants and their denominations or religious affiliations, views on social and political issues, challenges and rewards heading a racially and ethnically diverse congregation, and strategies and resources available for fostering diversity in their congregations. In advance of scheduling the interviews, all potential participants were aware of the expectation that interviews were to be audio-recorded. Still, two participants at the interviews informed interviewers they did not want to be audio-recorded. Interviewers were left to take handwritten notes in these instances. The data from these interviews were relatively thin and less reliable than the data from the remaining interviews, and they were ultimately not included in the analysis. Thus, the final sample size of head clergy interviews is 121.

Head clergy who participated in the study were also asked to complete a brief online survey about their congregations. This survey addressed such matters as congregational demographics, a church's mission statement, leadership characteristics, and material and human resources. One hundred surveys were completed by the head clergy in the study or a knowledgeable staff person. Using the head clergy interview data, we were able to gather information on the congregations of the remaining twenty-one participating head clergy. Research team members then used this information to complete as much of the online survey as possible for each of the congregations of these head clergy. In the end, the RLDP collected quantitative data on 121 of the congregations of the participating head clergy.

Interviewers also took field notes on the interviews. The field notes proved to be highly beneficial. They contextualized the interviews, noting the location of the interviews, describing the setting, and recording who else, besides the interviewer and head clergy being interviewed, was present or near where the interviews took place. While some interviews were conducted at public sites, like cafés, most were done at head clergy's churches. As the field notes address the sites of the interviews, this means that we have descriptions of most participants' churches and, if applicable, other buildings (e.g., school) on church property as well as descriptions of church material culture (e.g., statues, artwork, office furniture, clothing, bulletins), the neighborhoods and communities where the churches are located and, if relevant, church staff. The field notes also provide descriptions of the people being interviewed, insight that is best accessed face to face. For example, the field notes address what people interviewed looked like, how they were dressed, their demeanor or personality, and how they interacted with or treated the interviewer.

Gaining an understanding of the structures of head clergy's denominations or religious affiliations was achieved in two ways: through the interviews with the head clergy and through phone interviews with denominational leaders or persons identified by the head clergy as leaders of their informal religious leader networks. Denominational leaders responsible for or invested in racial and ethnic diversity in their religious communities were targeted. These informal religious leaders were people who actively engaged in promoting racial and ethnic diversity in churches. The aim of these interviews was, in part, to gain perspective on the kinds of resources and support—material, social, cultural, and educational—available to clergy who head or are interested in heading racially and ethnically diverse churches. We conducted interviews with nine denominational leaders or informal leaders of religious leader networks. Four were conservative Protestants; four were mainline Protestants; and one was Catholic.

Congregants' experiences and views were accessed via two methods: focus groups and surveys. The focus groups addressed congregants' views and experiences about attending a racially and ethnically diverse church as well as their thoughts on and experiences with their church's leadership. Focus group interviews were conducted with active congregants. Congregants were considered active if they regularly attended worship services and also participated in church life beyond the weekly worship services. The project restricted focus groups to active congregants for several reasons. These congregants would have the easiest and most direct connection to the head clergy. They are likely the congregants the head clergy rely upon to keep the church going. These people are most familiar with the inner workings of their congregations. And they are also the congregants that head clergy feel the most pressure to please. For the focus groups, we returned to six of the twelve cities we originally went to for the head clergy interviews.

The project was based at The Ohio State University, and only OSU team members conducted focus groups largely because resources could not accommodate another multisite primary data collection endeavor. Additionally, trust, familiarity, and knowledge interviewers gained during the head clergy interview process would facilitate recruitment for the focus groups as well as provide important contextual information for the focus group interviews. So we only returned to cities where OSU research team members had done head clergy interviews. After this, we considered what cities gave us the best chance of getting a diverse sample of focus groups, one that included mainline Protestant, conservative Protestant, and Catholic congregations; those headed by pastors of color as well as white pastors; ones with women head pastors; and congregations of varying sizes and racial compositions. The research team was able to conduct thirty-six focus groups with 230 congregants.

Congregant surveys were conducted online. The topics were broader than those of the focus group interviews. They addressed matters like attendees' level of church involvement, their relationships and friendship networks, and their racial, political, and social attitudes. Anyone who attended the church, not just active attendees, could participate in the survey. All congregations of participating head clergy were asked to facilitate informing congregants about the opportunity to take the survey. Selection into the survey, consequently, depended heavily upon the recruitment efforts of head clergy and their church staff.

The OSU team worked very hard at recruiting churches to help with recruitment into the survey and providing churches with recruitment scripts and materials. It is difficult to know what the response rate is given the recruitment process. While there were very particular protocols we asked churches to follow, we cannot know how they followed them and how many people in the congregation learned about the opportunity to participate in the survey. Ultimately, 684 people participated in the congregant survey. While a larger sample would have been preferred, this N is sufficient to provide another window, in addition to the focus group interviews, into the congregational contexts of multiracial church head clergy.

In the end, the RLDP includes a relatively diverse mix of multiracial church head clergy and congregations. Close to 40% of the head clergy in the final sample identify as people of color. Specifically, 19% are Black, 13% are Asian, 5% are Hispanic, and 2% biracial. The head clergy are affiliated with mainline Protestant (34%), conservative Protestant (48%), and Catholic congregations (18%). Ten percent of the head clergy are women.

Notably, all women head clergy in the study led mainline Protestant congregations. This is not surprising, as both Catholicism and conservative Protestant denominations restrict access to the role of priest or pastor to men.

The locations of the congregations of head clergy in the RLDP were about equally split across the four major U.S. census regions: 27% were located in the South; 25% in the Midwest; 23% in the West; and 25% in the Northeast. The congregations were of varying sizes as well, averaging attendance of 790 and ranging from 35 attendees to 10,000. The breakdown of church size is as follows: 10% mega (2,000+), 17% large (750–1,999), 45% medium (150–749), and 29% small (<150).

Research Team

Thirty-two people worked on the RLDP: four faculty (including the two authors of this book); four graduate students; one pastor of a multiracial church; and twenty-three undergraduate students. Ten of the thirty-two comprised the core members of the RLDP team. Core team members participated in conducting interviews or/and data analysis. They included all the faculty and graduate students on the project as well as the multiracial church pastor and one undergraduate student. Other team members who worked on the RLDP helped with sample development or administrative support. These team members were all undergraduate students. They worked on the project for no more than two semesters, but usually only one.

Since the topic of the RLDP is diversity, team members for the project were recruited with diversity in mind. The members of the team came with varying knowledge, insights, and understandings rooted in various standpoints. The RLDP team was diverse along racial, ethnic, gender, religious, political, vocational, and sexuality lines, among others.

Our Standpoints

Who we are—not who we are as Korie and Rebecca—but who we all are as scholars matters for our scholarship. Our constellation of identities, journeys and experiences inform the questions we ask in our research, how we address those questions theoretically and methodologically, and how we make sense of our findings. As Patricia Hill Collins[3] puts it, our standpoints matter.

I (Little Edwards) intentionally recruited a diverse group for the RLDP research team. We were diverse racially and ethnically, across university rank and class. We were also diverse in terms of our age, gender, sexuality, and region as well as in our religious beliefs and practices. As a team this meant we had the benefit of drawing upon our multiple standpoints in the research.[4] A diverse subgroup of team members contributed to the construction of the interview guide, and the whole team collectively developed the codebook and participated in a first-level analysis of the data, where we organized the data by primary codes. The semi-structured interview guide and training on research protocol and data analysis helped maintain continuity in the data collection and analysis processes across team members while also creating space to hear and draw upon our unique contributions, perspectives, and insights. Even though we were a diverse group, we did not see substantive differences across the interview data and preliminary analysis by team members.

In the end, this book was written by the two of us. We collaboratively conducted an in-depth analysis of the data and worked together throughout the process, though we took responsibility for writing certain chapters. We are both women of color studying and writing about a man-dominated field: pastoring. Yet women often make up the majority of church attendees, across religious traditions. We thus had to manage intergender interactions in nearly all of the interviews and interracial interactions for about half of them. At times, the ways pastors interacted with us made it clear they were cognizant of the intergender nature of the interactions (evidenced by them, for example, going out of the way to communicate why they were keeping the door open during the interview in a way that made the whole scene conspicuous). Generally speaking, however, we felt comfortable with and were able to develop sufficient rapport with the pastors, regardless of gender. Sharing ethnoracial identities with pastors made developing rapport all the more easy. Cultural familiarity seemed to make everyone involved a little more comfortable.

We are also both middle-aged women who are tenured professors. We were around the ages (give or take ten years) of most of the pastors we interviewed. Being a professor carries a certain prestige. Our age and profession, in some respects, helped us to connect and gain rapport with the men we interviewed. Both of our religious backgrounds in monoracial as well as multiracial congregations and familiarity with Christian religious beliefs and practices also no doubt facilitated our interviews with pastors, regardless of their gender. Thus, while we often had to manage intergender relations during the interviews as women interviewing mostly men in a man-dominated profession, the core essence of what we found in the interviews was not different from what our colleagues who are men found in the research team.

Notes

Preface

1. U.S. Census Bureau (1961).
2. Jones et al. (2021).
3. Vespa et al. (2020).
4. Liubchenkova (2020).
5. Sumagaysay (2021).
6. For example, Becker (1998); Christerson, Edwards, and Emerson (2005); DeYoung et al. (2003); Dougherty and Huyser (2008); Ganiel (2008); Garces-Foley (2007); Marti (2005, 2012).

Introduction

1. For a review of critical race theory, see Delgado and Stefancic (2023).
2. See Southern Baptist Convention (2019).
3. Kim (2023).
4. Okuwobi (2019); Okuwobi, Faulk, and Roscigno (2021).
5. Beji et al. (2021).
6. Singha and Sivarethinamohan (2021); Wang and McLean (2016).
7. Dias, Zhu, and Samaratunge (2020).
8. Lorenzo (2010).
9. For example, Logan (2019); Pugh et al. (2008); Sewell (2003).
10. Dougherty et al. (2019).
11. Head clergy is a gendered job. Like many other positions of leadership in the world that are overwhelmingly occupied by men, head clergy are no different. For instance, in 2021, 8.2% of Fortune 500 CEOs were women, and less than 1% were women of color. See Women Business Collaborative (2021). Thirty percent of college and university presidents are women. See American Council on Education (2017). Of all head clergy in the United States, statistics suggest that 90% are men and 85% are white men. See Thumma (2021).
12. For consistency, we use Hispanic to refer to people or persons of Latin American descent because our respondents of Latin American descent primarily self-identified as Hispanic rather than Latino/a/x/e. There were moments when respondents referred to themselves or others of Latin American descent as Latino/a. However, this was less common. One instance that struck us is when a Hispanic pastor did not use the

identifier of Latino/a in the interview until after Little Edwards did so. This was noticeable. Though we did not do a systematic analysis of this, it suggested that perhaps respondents adopted the identifier Latino/a because of social desirability bias—a desire to appear knowledgeable to interviewers.

13. By "ethnoracial group," we mean the group is made up of people who share the same race as well as the same ethnicity.
14. Jones et al. (2021).
15. Gramlich (2021).
16. Logan and Stults (2021).
17. Fiel (2015); Orfield and Lee (2005).
18. Blau, Blum, and Schwartz (1982).
19. Alba and Nee (1997); Allport (1954); Gordon (1964).
20. McPherson, Smith-Lovin, and Cook (2001).
21. Massey and Denton (1993); Wilson (2012).
22. Du Bois (1903).
23. Krogstad (2020). https://www.pewresearch.org/short-reads/2020/07/10/hispanics-have-accounted-for-more-than-half-of-total-u-s-population-growth-since-2010/.
24. Burke (2012); Mayorga-Gallo (2014).
25. Hughey (2010).
26. Douds (2021); Mueller (2020); Underhill (2019).
27. Hughey (2010).
28. Rabii (2021).
29. Hughey (2010); Mueller (2020); Rabii (2021).
30. Trepagnier (2010).
31. Hughey and Byrd (2013).
32. Edwards (2008b); Mayorga-Gallo (2019).
33. Edwards (2008b).
34. Bonilla-Silva (2003).
35. Edwards (2008b).
36. Edwards (2008b:122).
37. Bonilla-Silva (2003:104).
38. Bonilla-Silva and Embrick (2007).
39. Bell and Hartmann (2007).
40. Bonilla-Silva (2003); Burke (2012); Hartmann, Gerteis, and Croll (2009); Kim (2023); Mehta, Schneider, and Ecklund (2022).
41. Bonilla-Silva and Embrick (2007).
42. Barron (2016); Edwards (2008b); Kim (2015, 2016a).
43. Okuwobi, Faulk, and Roscigno (2021).
44. Emerson, Korver-Glenn, and Douds (2015:349).
45. Emerson and Smith (2000).
46. Tranby and Hartmann (2008).
47. Barron (2016).
48. Mehta et al. (2022).
49. Marti (2008).

50. Oyakawa (2019).
51. Alumkal (2004).
52. Metha et al. (2022).
53. Brewer (2007); Gaertner and Dovidio (2012); Mullen, Brown, and Smith (1992).
54. Christerson, Edwards, and Flory (2010); Edwards (2008a, 2008b).
55. Acker (2000); Alexander (2012); Bonilla-Silva (1997); Muller (2012); Omi and Winant (2014); Reskin (2012); Smith (2002); Tomaskovic-Devey et al. (2006); Wacquant (2014).
56. Most of the work that addresses multiracial church leadership actually attempts to understand the congregation, not their leaders. It is the leaders, however, that emerged as an important factor.
57. Edwards (2019).
58. Becker (1998); Christerson et al. (2005); DeYoung et al. (2003); Dougherty and Huyser (2008); Ganiel (2008); Garces-Foley (2007); Marti (2005, 2012).
59. Jenkins (2003); Marti (2005); Stanczak (2006).
60. Edwards (2008b); Emerson and Woo (2006); Marti (2005).
61. Christerson et al. (2005); Dougherty and Huyser (2008); Edwards (2008b); Ganiel (2008); Garces-Foley (2007); Marti (2012); Priest and Priest (2007); Yancey and Emerson (2003).
62. Dougherty, Martinez, and Marti (2016).
63. Edwards (2008b); Emerson and Woo (2006); Priest and Priest (2007).
64. Edwards (2019:417).
65. Barron (2016); Christerson et al. (2005); Cobb, Perry, and Dougherty (2015); Edwards (2008b); Kim (2023); Kim and Murdock (2023); Marti and Emerson (2014); Martinez and Dougherty (2013); Munn (2018); Priest and Priest (2007).
66. Durkheim (1912); Kim (2006); Kim and Murdock (2023); Warner and Wittner (1998).
67. Bonilla-Silva (1997); Bourdieu (1984); Collins (1986); Durkheim ([1895] 1982); Goffman (1959); Lamont and Lareau (1988); Putnam (2000).

Chapter 1

1. There are only two women pastors of color in our study, and they are both Black. While we would have preferred to include a story of the women pastors of color in this chapter, due to concerns about maintaining anonymity, we decided not to. There are too few Black women head clergy generally in the United States, and sharing any information about them beyond what we already have in their biographies would increase the chance of compromising their identity.
2. Okuwobi (2019).
3. Okuwobi (2019).
4. Okuwobi (2019).
5. For the sake of our conversation here, we see the pastor role as a profession if the person in it receives pay and benefits. We see the pastor role as a vocation when they

receive less than full salary and benefits. Not all pastors get paid or receive a full-time salary with benefits. Some have to have another job to financially support themselves and their families. Most pastors in our study had pastoral jobs, but several did not.
6. All of the women head clergy in our study were affiliated with Episcopal Protestant denominations. None was Catholic or conservative Protestant. This is consistent with other research. For example, the Faith Communities Study, which includes data on more than eleven thousand congregations, finds, "Within Mainline Protestant congregations female clergy account for 32% of leaders compared to just 4% in the Evangelical tradition, none in Catholic and Orthodox, but 10% in other faith traditions. Female leaders are also overrepresented in the smallest congregations and under-represented in those with more than 100 attendees. They are also slightly more likely to be in part-time positions than male leaders" (Thumma 2021:8).
7. Pitt (2021).
8. Pitt (2021).
9. Pitt (2021).
10. Portes and Zhou (1993).
11. Takaki (1998).
12. Kim (2004, 2006, 2023); Kim and Murdock (2023). Commonly, campuses have gospel choirs, which are often the only Christian social spaces for Black students.
13. Kim (2004, 2006, 2019, 2022, 2023); Kim and Murdock (2023).
14. Kim (2015).
15. Finke and Dougherty (2002).
16. Finke and Dougherty (2002:106).
17. Finke and Dougherty (2002); Iannaccone (1990).
18. Ammerman (1990).
19. Pitt (2021).

Chapter 2

1. Edwards, Christerson, and Emerson (2013) note that in 2010, 13.7% of churches were racially diverse. Put another way, about 86% were racially homogeneous. Thus, about 86% of head clergy led racially homogeneous congregations in 2010.
2. Ferrara (1998); Guignon (2004).
3. Ferrara (1998).
4. Taylor (1991:40).
5. Pierce (2015).
6. Pierce (2015:454).
7. Eisenstadt and Giesen (1995); Lamont and Molnár (2002); Taylor and Whittier (1992).
8. Eisenstadt and Giesen (1995); Lamont and Molnár (2002).
9. Eisenstadt and Giesen (1995).
10. Lamont and Molnár (2002).
11. Bourdieu (1984).

12. Lamont and Lareau (1988).
13. Although Joane Nagel (1994) does not discuss how subordinate ethnic or racial groups exclude potential group members, she emphasizes the role of the dominant group in establishing criteria for exclusion and inclusion in her discussion of ethnic identity.
14. Our data suggest this is particularly true for African Americans native to the United States, as opposed to the four head clergy in our sample who are Black immigrants.
15. Chou and Feagin (2008); Kim (2022); Portes and Zhou (1993); Takaki (1998); Tuan (1999); Zhou (2004).
16. Park (1928).
17. Park (1928:892).
18. Stonequist (1935).
19. Kim (2016b); Lee (2010); Matsuoka and Fernandez (2003); Phan and Lee (1999); Yong (2014).
20. Kim (2014, 2022); Kim and Kim (2012).
21. Ebaugh and Chafetz (2000); Kim (2014, 2022); Min and Kim (2002); Warner and Wittner (1998); Yang (1999).
22. The U.S. Census Bureau lists "Hispanic" as an ethnicity. However, research suggests that Hispanic and Latino/a /e are treated as racialized identities in everyday life. When we talk of Hispanic people's ethnicity, we are talking about their country of origin, such as Mexican, Puerto Rican, Cuban, Venezuelan, and so on (Rumbaut 2009).
23. U.S. Department of Health & Human Services (2019).
24. Mora (2014).
25. Gonzalez (2011).
26. Flores and Schachter (2018).
27. Portes and Zhou (1993).
28. Portes and Zhou (1993).
29. Tienda and Fuentes (2014).
30. Lee and Edmonston (2006).
31. Golash-Boza (2006).
32. Lichter, Parisi, and Taquino (2015).
33. Lichter, Carmalt, and Qian (2011).
34. For example, Christerson et al. (2010); Giuntella (2016); Wadsworth and Kubrin (2007).
35. Christerson et al. (2010).
36. Wadsworth and Kubrin (2007). Higher socioeconomic status as well as embeddedness in an immigrant Hispanic community may mitigate some of these negative effects of assimilation (Christerson et al. 2010).
37. Portes and Zhou (1993).
38. Durkheim and Halls (1982).
39. Edwards (2009); Nelson (1996).
40. Edwards (2008b).
41. Marti (2010) and Edwards (2008b) similarly reveal the importance of African American religious culture for African American attendees of multiracial churches.

42. One exception is an African immigrant pastor of a mainline church whose ethnic African identity may have absolved him from expectations associated with being a Black (American) religious leader. Another is a Black Catholic priest very embedded in a community of Black Catholic priests and actively engaged in vocally challenging white supremacy. He may not have been policed because he was behaving "authentically."
43. On August 9, 2014, an unarmed eighteen year old black teenager, Michael Brown, was shot multiple times and killed by a white police officer in Ferguson, Missouri. Mass protests aligned with the Black Lives Matter movement erupted across the country in response.
44. Timothy Keller (1950–2023) was a popular white evangelical pastor who planted Redeemer Presbyterian Church in New York City in 1989. The church grew to over 5,000 attendees. Keller authored thirty-one books on Christian life and theology and started a ministry that mentored and supported other pastors on church planting. See Redeemer City to City (2023).
45. Andy Stanley (full name Charles Andrew Stanley) is a white evangelical pastor and author on Christianity and theology. He planted the non-denominational church North Point Community Church in Alpharetta, Georgia, and founded North Point ministries, which plants affiliated churches in Georgia. Andy Stanley is the son of Charles Stanley (full name Charles Frazier Stanley) (1932–2023), a popular 20th century Southern Baptist pastor, preacher, and author.
46. Roberts, Bell, and Murphy (2008).
47. Hylton (2018).
48. While it was relatively easy to find Hispanic pastors who served as associate or assistant pastors of multiracial churches as part of the Spanish-speaking ministry, it was difficult to find Hispanic pastors who served as the head clergy of multiracial congregations.
49. United States Conference of Catholic Bishops (2019).
50. Munn (2019).

Chapter 3

1. Kim (2015). See also Kim (2016a).
2. Given the book's focus on racial diversity and leadership of multiracial congregations, we are not able to elaborate on the various ways that gender and patriarchy affect leadership of multiracial congregations. There can be no doubt, however, that they are a major influence. First and foremost, no women were heads of any of the conservative Protestant and Catholic congregations in our study. As already noted, they were present only as leaders of a small minority of mainline congregations, which tend to be more open to women in leadership. (See Thumma (2021)). And even in such congregations, women encounter real challenges in their role as clergy on account of their gender. Not only are they far more likely to be assigned to small, less resourced

congregations; a primary challenge that women clergy in our study shared, particularly those who are women of color, was simply being seen as a leader of a church, as a pastor. In addition to a racial tax, there is a hefty gender tax in a religious system that is not only white-dominant but thoroughly patriarchal.
3. Du Bois ([1903] 1989:3).
4. Hall (1986); Pyke (2010).
5. Pyke (2010:553).
6. Kim (2015); Lee (2006); Yu (2004).
7. R. Kim (2006); S. Kim (2010); S. Kim and Kim (2012).

Chapter 4

1. Emerson and Smith (2000:145).
2. Christerson et al. (2005); Emerson and Smith (2000); Emerson and Woo (2006); Kim (2015); Martinez and Dougherty (2013).
3. Barron (2016); Christerson and Emerson (2003); Edwards (2008a, 2008b); Garces-Foley (2007); Kim (2015, 2016a, 2023); Kim and Murdock 2023; Marti (2012).
4. Edwards and Kim (2019); Munn (2019).
5. Collins (1986).
6. Collins (1986).
7. Garces-Foley and Jeung (2013).
8. Garces-Foley and Jeung (2013:206).
9. Garces-Foley and Jeung (2013:206).
10. Garces-Foley and Jeung (2013).
11. Bourdieu and Passeron (1977); Bourdieu (1985).
12. Aldrich (2012); Gittell and Vidal (1998); Putnam (2000).
13. Aldrich (2012); Gittell and Vidal (1998); Putnam (2000).
14. Stovel and Shaw (2012:141).
15. Diani and McAdam (2003); Padgett and Ansell (1993); Stovel and Shaw (2012).

Chapter 5

1. McIntosh (1989).
2. Du Bois (1935); hooks (1995); Roediger (2007); Rothenberg (2002).
3. McIntosh (1989).
4. Feagin (2013); hooks (1995); McIntosh (1989); Rothenberg (2002); Tatum (2003).
5. Emerson and Smith (2000); Munn (2018, 2019); Perry (2012).
6. Munn (2019).
7. Goffman (1959).
8. Kim (2023).

Conclusion

1. Joyce Bell encouraged this line of thinking in her discussion of diversity as a racial project of whiteness. See Bell and Hartmann (2007).
2. Edwards (2008b).
3. Barron (2016); Christerson et al. (2005); Cobb et al. (2015); Kim (2023); Kim and Murdock (2023); Marti and Emerson (2014); Priest and Priest (2007).
4. Omi and Winant (2014).
5. Omi and Winant (2014:125).
6. Edwards and Oyakawa (2022).
7. Gender assuredly matters too, and a lot. Though tempted, we cannot address this adequately in this volume. Future research ought to focus on how the pastoral role is situated in a gendered understanding of the divine and divine roles in religious organizations.
8. Anderson (2022).
9. Butler (2021); Du Mez (2020); Jennings (2020); Jones (2020); Jun et al. (2018); Kim (2023); Kim and Murdock (2023); Tisby (2020).
10. Chronicle of Higher Education (2023).

Appendix

1. We are very grateful to the Lilly Endowment for funding the Religious Leadership and Diversity Project.
2. Bonilla-Silva (1997); Omi and Winant (2014); Reskin (2012).
3. Collins (1986, 1999).
4. See Edward (2019) for more.

Bibliography

Acker, Joan. 2000. "Gendered Contradictions in Organizational Equity Projects." *Organization* 7(4):625–32.
Ahmed, Sara. 2012. *On Being Included: Racism and Diversity in Institutional Life*. Durham, NC: Duke University Press.
Alba, Richard, and Victor Nee. 1997. "Rethinking Assimilation Theory for a New Era of Immigration." *International Migration Review* 31(4):826–75.
Aldrich, Daniel P. 2012. *Building Resilience: Social Capital in Post-Disaster Recovery*. Chicago: University of Chicago Press.
Alexander, Michelle. 2012. *The New Jim Crow: Mass Incarceration in the Age of Colorblindness*. New York: New Press.
Allport, Gordon W. 1954. *The Nature of Prejudice*. Cambridge, MA: Perseus Books.
Alumkal, Antony W. 2004. "American Evangelicalism in the Post–Civil Rights Era: A Racial Formation Theory Analysis." *Sociology of Religion* 65(3):195–213.
American Council on Education. 2017. "Summary Profile: Demographics." Accessed August 25, 2022. https://www.aceacps.org/summary-profile/#demographics.
Ammerman, Nancy. 1990. *Baptist Battles: Social Change and Religious Conflict in the Southern Baptist Convention*. New Brunswick, NJ: Rutgers University Press.
Andersen, Margaret L. 2003. "Whitewashing Race: A Critical Perspective on Whiteness." In *White Out: The Continuing Significance of Racism*, edited by Ashley W. Doane and Eduardo Bonilla-Silva, 21–34. New York: Routledge.
Anderson, Elijah. 2022. *Black in White Space: The Enduring Impact of Color in Everyday Life*. Chicago: University of Chicago Press.
Barnes, Sandra L., and Oluchi Nwosu. 2014. "Black Church Electoral and Protest Politics from 2002 to 2012: A Social Media Analysis of the Resistance versus Accommodation Dialectic." *Journal of African American Studies* 18(2):209–35.
Barron, Jessica M. 2016. "Managed Diversity: Race, Place and an Urban Church." *Sociology of Religion* 77(1):18–36.
Becker, Penny Edgell. 1998. "Making Inclusive Communities: Congregations and the 'Problem' of Race." *Social Problems* 45(4):451–72.
Beji, Rania, Ouidad Yousfi, Nadia Loukil, and Abdelwahed Omri. 2021. "Board Diversity and Corporate Social Responsibility: Empirical Evidence from France." *Journal of Business Ethics* 173(1):133–55.
Bell, Derrick. 1992. *Faces at the Bottom of the Well: The Permanence of Racism*. New York: Basic Books.
Bell, Joyce M., and Douglas Hartmann. 2007. "Diversity in Everyday Discourse: The Cultural Ambiguities and Consequences of 'Happy Talk.'" *American Sociological Review* 72(6):895–914.
Berrey, Ellen C. 2011. "Why Diversity Became Orthodox in Higher Education, and How It Changed the Meaning of Race on Campus." *Critical Sociology* 37(5):573–96.

Berrey, Ellen C. 2015. *The Enigma of Diversity: The Language of Race and the Limits of Racial Justice*. Chicago: University of Chicago Press.

Blau, Peter Michael. 1977. *Inequality and Heterogeneity: A Primitive Theory of Social Structure*. New York: Free Press.

Blau, Peter M., Terry C. Blum, and Joseph E. Schwartz. 1982. "Heterogeneity and Intermarriage." *American Sociological Review* 47(1):45–62.

Bonilla-Silva, Eduardo. 1997. "Rethinking Racism: Toward a Structural Interpretation." *American Sociological Review* 62(3):465–80.

Bonilla-Silva, Eduardo. 2003. *Racism without Racists: Color-blind Racism and the Persistence of Racial Inequality in the United States*. Lanham, MD: Rowman & Littlefield.

Bonilla-Silva, Eduardo, and David G. Embrick. 2007. "'Every Place Has a Ghetto . . .': The Significance of Whites' Social and Residential Segregation." *Symbolic Interaction* 30(3):323–45.

Bonilla-Silva, Eduardo, and Tyrone A. Forman. 2000. "'I Am Not a Racist but . . .': Mapping White College Students' Racial Ideology in the USA." *Discourse & Society* 11(1):50–85.

Bourdieu, Pierre. 1984. *Distinction: A Social Critique of the Judgment of Taste*. Cambridge, MA: Harvard University Press.

Bourdieu, Pierre. 1985. "The Social Space and the Genesis of Groups." *Theory and Society* 14(6):723–44.

Bourdieu, Pierre, and Jean Claude Passeron. 1977. *Reproduction in Education, Society, and Culture*. London: Sage Publications.

Bracey, Glenn E. 2015. "Toward a Critical Race Theory of State." *Critical Sociology* 41(3):553–72.

Brewer, Marilyn B. 2007. "The Social Psychology of Intergroup Relations: Social Categorization, Ingroup Bias, and Outgroup Prejudice." In *Social Psychology: Handbook of Basic Principles*, edited by Arie W. Kruglanski and E. Tory Higgins, 695–715. New York: Guilford Press.

Burke, Meghan A. 2012. "Discursive Fault Lines: Reproducing White Habitus in a Racially Diverse Community." *Critical Sociology* 38(5):645–68.

Butler, Anthea. 2021. *White Evangelical Racism: The Politics of Morality in America*. Chapel Hill: University of North Carolina Press.

Chou, Rosalind S., and Joe R. Feagin. 2008. *The Myth of the Model Minority: Asian Americans Facing Racism*. Boulder, CO: Paradigm.

Christerson, Brad, Korie L. Edwards, and Michael O. Emerson. 2005. *Against All Odds: The Struggle for Racial Integration in Religious Organizations*. New York: New York University Press.

Christerson, Brad, Korie L. Edwards, and Richard W. Flory. 2010. *Growing Up in America: The Power of Race in the Lives of Lives of Teens*. Stanford, CA: Stanford University Press.

Christenson, Brad, and Michael O. Emerson. 2003. "The Costs of Diversity in Religious Organizations: An In-Depth Case Study." *Sociology of Religion* 62(2):163–81.

Chronicle of Higher Education. 2023. "DEI Legislation Tracker: Explore Where College Diversity, Equity and Inclusion Efforts Are under Attack." *The Chronicle of Higher Education. Politics and Race*. May 25, 2023. Accessed June 9, 2023. https://www.chronicle.com/article/here-are-the-states-where-lawmakers-are-seeking-to-ban-colleges-dei-efforts

Cobb, Ryon J., Samuel L. Perry, and Kevin D. Dougherty. 2015. "United by Faith? Race/Ethnicity, Congregational Diversity, and Explanations of Racial Inequality." *Sociology of Religion* 76(2):177–98.

Collins, Patricia Hill. 1986. "Learning from the Outsider Within: The Sociological Significance of Black Feminist Thought." *Social Problems* 33(6):14–32.

Collins, Patricia Hill. 1999. "Reflections on the Outsider Within." *Journal of Career Development* 26(1):85–88.

Collins, Sharon M. 2011. "From Affirmative Action to Diversity: Erasing Inequality from Organizational Responsibility." *Critical Sociology* 37(5):517–20.

Cornell, Stephen E., and Douglas Hartmann. 2007. *Ethnicity and Race: Making Identities in a Changing World*. 2nd ed. Thousand Oaks, CA: Pine Forge Press.

Delgado, Richard, and Jean Stefancic. 2023. *Critical Race Theory, Fourth Edition: An Introduction*. New York: New York University Press.

DeYoung, Curtiss Paul, Michael O. Emerson, George Yancey, and Karen Chai Kim. 2003. *United by Faith: The Multiracial Congregation as an Answer to the Race Problem*. New York: Oxford University Press.

Diani, Mario, and Doug McAdam. 2003. *Social Movements and Networks: Relational Approaches to Collective Action*. Oxford: Oxford University Press.

Dias, Davina, Cherrie Jiuhua Zhu, and Ramanie Samaratunge. 2020. "Examining the Role of Cultural Exposure in Improving Intercultural Competence: Implications for HRM Practices in Multicultural Organizations." *International Journal of Human Resource Management* 31(11):1359–78.

Doane, Ashley W. 1997. "Dominant Group Ethnic Identity in the United States." *Sociological Quarterly* 38(3):375–97.

Doane, Ashley W. 2003. "Rethinking Whiteness Studies." In *White Out: The Continuing Significance of Racism*, edited by Ashley W. Doane and Eduardo Bonilla-Silva, 3–18. New York: Routledge.

Douds, Kiara Wyndham. 2021. "The Diversity Contract: Constructing Racial Harmony in a Diverse American Suburb." *American Journal of Sociology* 126(6):1347–88.

Dougherty, Kevin D., Mark Chaves, and Michael O. Emerson. 2020. "Racial Diversity in U.S. Congregations, 1998–2019." *Journal for the Scientific Study of Religion* 59(4):651–62.

Dougherty, Kevin D. and Kimberly R. Huyser. 2008. "Racially Diverse Congregations: Organizational Identity and the Accommodation of Differences." *Journal for the Scientific Study of Religion* 47(1):23–43.

Dougherty, Kevin D., Brandon C. Martinez, and Martí Gerardo. 2016. "Congregational Diversity and Attendance in a Mainline Protestant Denomination." *Journal for the Scientific Study of Religion* 54(4):668–83.

Drake, St. Clair, and Horace R. Cayton. 1945. *Black Metropolis: A Study of Negro Life in a Northern City*. New York: Harcourt, Brace.

Du Bois, W. E. B. (1903) 1989. *The Souls of Black Folk*. Chicago: A. C. McClurg.

Du Bois, W. E. B. 1935. *Black Reconstruction in America: An Essay toward a History of the Part Which Black Folk Played in the Attempt to Reconstruct Democracy in America, 1860–1880*. London: Cass.

Du Mez, Kristin Kobes. 2020. *Jesus and John Wayne: How White Evangelicals Corrupted a Faith and Fractured a Nation*. New York: Liveright.

Durkheim Émile. (1895) 1982. *The Rules of Sociological Method*. First American ed. Edited by S. Lukes. New York: Free Press.

Durkheim Émile. 1915. *The Elementary Forms of the Religious Life: A Study in Religious Sociology*. London: G. Allen & Unwin.

Ebaugh, Helen Rose, and Janet Saltzman Chafetz. 2000. *Religion and the New Immigrants: Continuities and Adaptations in Immigrant Congregations*. Walnut Creek, CA: Altamira Press.

Edwards, Korie L. 2008a. "Bring Race to the Center: The Importance of Race in Racially Diverse Religious Organizations." *Journal for the Scientific Study of Religion* 47(1):5–9.

Edwards, Korie L. 2008b. *The Elusive Dream: The Power of Race in Interracial Churches*. New York: Oxford University Press.

Edwards, Korie L. 2009. "Race, Religion and Worship: Are Contemporary African American Worship Practices Distinct?" *Journal for the Scientific Study of Religion* 48(1):30–52.

Edwards, Korie L. 2016. "The Space Between: Exploring How Religious Leaders Reconcile Religion and Politics." *Journal for the Scientific Study of Religion* 55(2):271–87.

Edwards, Korie L. 2019. "Deconstructing a Research Journey: Methods and Lessons of the Religious Leadership and Diversity Project." *Sociology of Religion* 80(4):415–34.

Edwards, Korie L. 2021. "The Multiethnic Church Movement Hasn't Lived Up to Its Promise." *Christianity Today*, February 16.

Edwards, Korie, Brad Christerson, and Michael O. Emerson. 2005. *Against All Odds: The Struggle for Racial Integration in Religious Organizations*. New York: New York University Press.

Edwards, Korie, Brad Christerson, and Michael O. Emerson. 2013. "Race, Religious Organizations, and Integration." *Annual Review of Sociology* 39:211–28.

Edwards, Korie L., and Rebecca Y. Kim. 2019. "Estranged Pioneers: The Case of African American and Asian American Multiracial Church Pastors." *Sociology of Religion* 80(4):456–77.

Edwards, Korie Little, and Michelle Oyakawa. 2022. *Smart Suits, Tattered Boots: Black Ministers Mobilizing the Black Church in the Twenty-First Century*. New York: New York University Press.

Eisenstadt, Shmuel Noah, and Bernhard Giesen. 1995. "The Construction of Collective Identity." *European Journal of Sociology* 36(1):72–102.

Embrick, David G. 2006. "The Making and Selling of an Illusion: An Examination of Racial and Gender Diversity in Post–Civil Rights U.S. Corporations." PhD dissertation, Department of Sociology, Texas A&M University.

Embrick, David G. 2011. "The Diversity Ideology in the Business World: A New Oppression for a New Age." *Critical Sociology* 37(5):541–56.

Emerson, Michael O., Elizabeth Korver-Glenn, and Kiara W. Douds. 2015. "Studying Race and Religion: A Critical Assessment." *Sociology of Race and Ethnicity* 1(3):349–59.

Emerson, Michael O., and Christian Smith. 2000. *Divided by Faith: Evangelical Religion and the Problem of Race in America*. Oxford: Oxford University Press.

Emerson, Michael O., with Rodney M. Woo. 2006. *People of the Dream: Multiracial Congregations in the United States*. Princeton, NJ: Princeton University Press.

Feagin, Joe R. 2001. *Racist America: Roots, Current Realities, and Future Reparations*. New York: Routledge.

Feagin, Joe R. 2013. *The White Racial Frame: Centuries of Racial Framing and Counter-Framing*. 2nd ed. Hoboken, NJ: Taylor and Francis.

Feagin, Joe R. 2014. *Racist America*, 3rd ed. New York: Routledge.

Ferrara, Alessandro. 1998. *Reflective Authenticity: Rethinking the Project of Modernity*. New York: Routledge.

Fiel, Jeremy. 2015. "Closing Ranks: Closure, Status, Competition, and School Segregation." *American Journal of Sociology* 121(1):126–70.
Finke, Roger, and Kevin D. Dougherty. 2002. "The Effects of Professional Training: The Social and Religious Capital Acquired in Seminaries." *Journal for the Scientific Study of Religion* 41(1):103–20.
Flores, René D., and Ariela Schachter. 2018. "Who Are the 'Illegals'? The Social Construction of Illegality in the United States." *American Sociological Review* 83(5):839–68.
Foucault, Michel. 1980. *Power/Knowledge: Selected Interviews and Other Writings, 1972–1977*. Edited by C. Gordon. New York: Vintage.
Frankenberg, Ruth. 1993. *White Women, Race Matters: The Social Construction of Whiteness*. Minneapolis: University of Minnesota Press.
Frazier, E. Franklin. 1964. *The Negro Church in America*. Liverpool: Liverpool University Press.
Gaertner, Samuel L., and John F. Dovidio. 2012. *Reducing Intergroup Bias: The Common Ingroup Identity Model*. New York: Routledge.
Ganiel, Gladys. 2008. "Is the Multiracial Congregation an Answer to the Problem of Race? Comparative Perspectives from South Africa and the USA." *Journal of Religion in Africa* 38(3):263–83.
Garces-Foley, Kathleen. 2007. *Crossing the Ethnic Divide: The Multiethnic Church on a Mission*. New York: Oxford University Press.
Garces-Foley, Kathleen, and Russell Jeung. 2013. "Asian American Evangelicals in Multiracial Church Ministry." *Religions* 4(2):190–208.
Gittell, Ross J., and Avis Vidal. 1998. *Community Organizing: Building Social Capital as a Development Strategy*. Thousand Oaks, CA: Sage.
Giuntella, Osea. 2016. "Assimilation and Health: Evidence from Linked Birth Records of Second- and Third-Generation Hispanics." *Demography* 53(6):1979–2004.
Goffman, Ervin. 1959. *The Presentation of Self in Everyday Life*. New York: Doubleday Anchor Books.
Golash-Boza, Tanya. 2006. "Dropping the Hyphen? Becoming Latino(a)-American through Racialized Assimilation." *Social Forces* 85(1):27–55.
Gonzalez, Juan. 2011. *Harvest of Empire: A History of Latinos in America*. New York: Penguin Books.
Gordon, Milton M. 1964. *Assimilation in American Life: The Role of Race, Religion, and National Origins*. New York: Oxford University Press.
Gramlich, John. 2021. "Under Trump, the federal prison population continued its recent decline." Pew Research Center. Accessed February 18, 2022. https://www.pewresearch.org/short-reads/2021/02/17/under-trump-the-federal-prison-population-continued-its-recent-decline/.
Gramsci, Antonio. (1971) 1989. *Selections from the Prison Notebooks*. Edited by Q. Hoare and G. N. Smith. New York: International Publishers.
Greenwood, Nan, Theresa Ellmers, and Jess Holley. 2014. "The Influence of Ethnic Group Composition on Focus Group Discussions." *BMC Medical Research Methodology* 14:107.
Guignon, Charles. 2004. *On Being Authentic*. New York: Routledge.
Hagerman, Margaret Ann. 2014. "White Families and Race: Colour-Blind and Colour-Conscious Approaches to White Racial Socialization." *Ethnic and Racial Studies* 37(14):2598–614.

Hall, Stuart. 1986. "Gramsci's Relevance for the Study of Race and Ethnicity." *Journal of Communication Inquiry* 10(2):5–27.

Hartmann, Douglas, Joseph Gerteis, and Paul R. Croll. 2009. "An Empirical Assessment of Whiteness Theory: Hidden from How Many?" *Social Problems* 56(3):403–24.

hooks, bell. 1995. *Killing Rage: Ending Racism*. New York: H. Holt.

hooks, bell. 2015. *Black Looks: Race and Representation*. 2nd ed. New York: Routledge.

Hughey, Matthew W. 2010. "The (Dis)Similarities of White Racial Identities: The Conceptual Framework of 'Hegemonic Whiteness.'" *Ethnic and Racial Studies* 33(8):1289–309.

Hughey, Matthew W. 2012. "Color Capital, White Debt, and the Paradox of Strong White Racial Identities." *Du Bois Review: Social Science Research on Race* 9(1):169–200.

Hughey, Matthew W., and W. Carson Byrd. 2013. "The Souls of White Folk beyond Formation and Structure: Bound to Identity." *Ethnic and Racial Studies* 36(6):974–81.

Hylton, Kevin. 2018. "I'm Not Joking! The Strategic Use of Humour in Stories of Racism." *Ethnicities* 18(3):327–43.

Iannaccone, Laurence R. 1990. "Religious Practice: A Human Capital Approach." *Journal for the Scientific Study of Religion* 29(3):297–314.

Jenkins, Kathleen E. 2003. "Intimate Diversity: The Presentation of Multiculturalism and Multiracialism in a High-Boundary Religious Movement." *Journal for the Scientific Study of Religion* 42(3):393–409.

Jennings, Willie James. 2020. *After Whiteness: An Education in Belonging*. Grand Rapids, MI: William B. Eerdmans.

Jones, Nicholas, Rachel Marks, Roberto Ramirez, and Merarys Rios-Vargas. 2021. "2020 Census Illuminates Racial and Ethnic Composition of the Country," U.S. Census Bureau. Accessed September 6, 2022. https://www.census.gov/library/stories/2021/08/improved-race-ethnicity-measures-reveal-united-states-population-much-more-multiracial.html.

Jones, Robert P. 2020. *The Legacy of White Supremacy in American Christianity*. New York: Simon & Schuster.

Jun, Alexander, Tabatha L. Jones Jolivet, Allison N. Ash, and Christopher S. Collins. 2018. *White Jesus: The Architecture of Racism in Religion and Education*. New York: Peter Lang.

Kim, Rebecca Y. 2004. "Second-Generation Korean American Evangelicals: Ethnic, Multiethnic, or White Campus Ministries?" *Sociology of Religion* 65(1):19–34.

Kim, Rebecca Y. 2006. *God's New Whiz Kids? Korean American Evangelicals on Campus*. New York: New York University Press.

Kim, Rebecca Y. 2014. "Migration and Conversion: The Korean American Christian Experience." In *Oxford Handbook of Religious Conversion*, edited by Lewis R. Rambo and Charles E. Farhadian, 190–208. New York: Oxford University Press.

Kim, Rebecca Y. 2015. *The Spirit Moves West: Korean Missionaries in America*. New York: Oxford University Press.

Kim, Rebecca Y. 2016a. "Evangelizing White Americans: Race, Sacrifice, and a Korean Mission Movement in America." *Open Theology* 2:668–80.

Kim, Rebecca Y. 2016b. "Liminality." In *Encyclopedia of Christianity in the United States*, edited by George Thomas Kurian and Mark A. Lamport, 1350–51. Lanham, MD: Rowman & Littlefield.

Kim, Rebecca Y. 2019. "Toward an Asian American Evangelical Christianity." *Christianity Next* 3:10–34.

Kim, Rebecca Y. 2022. "Making Their Mark: Asian Americans and the Californian 'Christian' Landscape." In *Migration, Transnationalism, and Faith in Missiological Perspective: Los Angeles as a Global Crossroads*, edited by Kirsteen Kim, 93–112. Lanham, MD: Lexington Books.

Kim, Rebecca Y. 2023. "Evangelical Civil War on the College Campus: White Evangelical Right Framing Resistance to Racial Justice in 2020s America." *Journal for the Society for the Scientific Study of Religion*. https://doi.org/10.1111/jssr.12852.

Kim, Rebecca Y., and Sharon Kim. 2012. "Revival and Renewal: Korean American Evangelicals beyond Immigrant Enclaves." *Studies in World Christianity* 18(3):291–312.

Kim, Rebecca Y., and Rachael Murdock. 2023. "To Be Safe and Seen: BIPOC Gen Z Engagement in Evangelical Campus Ministries." *Religions* 14(8):963. https://doi.org/10.3390/rel14080963.

Kim, Sharon. 2010. *A Faith of Our Own: Second-Generation Spirituality in Korean American Churches*. New Brunswick, NJ: Rutgers University Press.

Kim, Sharon, and Rebecca Y. Kim 2012. "Second-Generation Korean American Christians' Communities: Congregational Hybridity." In *Sustaining Faith Traditions: Race, Ethnicity and Religion among the Latino and Asian American Second Generation*, edited by Carolyn Chen and Russell Jeung, 176–97. New York: New York University Press.

Krogstad, Jens Manuel. 2020. "Hispanics have accounted for more than half of total U.S. population growth since 2010." Pew Research Center. Accessed August 9, 2023. https://www.pewresearch.org/short-reads/2020/07/10/hispanics-have-accounted-for-more-than-half-of-total-u-s-population-growth-since-2010/.

Lamont, Michèle, and Annette Lareau. 1988. "Cultural Capital: Allusions, Gaps and Glissandos in Recent Theoretical Developments." *Sociological Theory* 6(2):153–68.

Lamont, Michèle, and Virág Molnár. 2002. "The Study of Boundaries in the Social Sciences."*Annual Review of Sociology* 28:167–95.

Lavelle, Kristen M. 2014. *Whitewashing the South: White Memories of Segregation and Civil Rights*. Lanham, MD: Rowman & Littlefield.

Lee, Jennifer, and Frank D. Bean. 2003. "Beyond Black and White: Remaking Race in America." *Contexts* 2(3):26–33.

Lee, Sang Hyun. 2010. *From a Liminal Place: An Asian American Theology*. Minneapolis, MN: Fortress Press.

Lee, Sharon M., and Barry Edmonston. 2006. "Hispanic Intermarriage, Identification, and U.S. Latino Population Change." *Social Science Quarterly* 87(5):1263–79.

Lee, Shayne. 2003. "The Church of Faith and Freedom: African-American Baptists and Social Action." *Journal for the Scientific Study of Religion* 42(1):31–42.

Lee, Timothy S. 2006. "Beleaguered Success: Korean Evangelicalism in the Last Decade of the Twentieth Century." In *Christianity in Korea*, edited by Robert E. Buswell Jr. and Timothy S. Lee, 330–50. Honolulu: University of Hawai'i Press.

Lewis, Amanda E. 2004. "'What Group?' Studying Whites and Whiteness in the Era of 'Color-Blindness.'" *Sociological Theory* 22(4):623–46.

Lichter, Daniel T., Julie H. Carmalt, and Zhenchao Qian. 2011. "Immigration and Intermarriage among Hispanics: Crossing Racial and Generational Boundaries." *Sociological Forum* (26)2:241–64.

Lichter, Daniel T., Domenico Parisi, and Michael C. Taquino. 2015. "Toward a New Macro-Segregation? Decomposing Segregation within and between Metropolitan Cities and Suburbs." *American Sociological Review* 80(4):843–73.

Lincoln, C. Eric, and Lawrence H. Mamiya. 1990. *The Black Church in the African American Experience*. Durham, NC: Duke University Press.

Liubchenkova, Natalia. 2020. "In Pictures: Black Lives Matter Protests Taking on the World." euronews. Accessed January 22, 2022. https://www.euronews.com/2020/06/15/in-pictures-black-lives-matter-protests-taking-on-the-world.

Logan, John R., and Brian J. Stults. 2021. "Metropolitan Segregation: No Breakthrough in Sight." Accessed February 15, 2022.
https://s4.ad.brown.edu/Projects/Diversity/Data/Report/report08122021.pdf.

Logan, Nneka. 2019. "Corporate Personhood and the Corporate Responsibility to Race." *Journal of Business Ethics* 154(4):977–88.

Lorenzo, Rocío Alonso. 2010. "Untangling the 'Transnational Social': Soft Affirmative Action, Human Rights, and Corporate Social Responsibility in Brazil." *Focaal* (56):49–61.

Marti, Gerardo. 2005. *A Mosaic of Believers: Diversity and Religious Innovation in a Multiethnic Church*. Bloomington: Indiana University Press.

Marti, Gerardo. 2008. "Fluid Ethnicity and Ethnic Transcendence in Multiracial Churches." *Journal for the Scientific Study of Religion* 47(1):11–16.

Marti, Gerardo. 2010. "The Religious Racial Integration of African Americans into Diverse Churches." *Journal for the Scientific Study of Religion* 49(2):201–17.

Marti, Gerardo. 2012. *Worship across the Racial Divide: Religious Music and the Multiracial Congregation*. Oxford: Oxford University Press.

Marti, Gerardo, and Michael O. Emerson. 2014. "The Rise of the Diversity Expert: How Evangelicals Simultaneously Accentuate and Ignore Race." In *The New Evangelical Social Engagement*, edited by Brian Steensland and Philip Goff, 179–99. New York: Oxford University Press.

Martinez, Brandon C., and Kevin D. Dougherty. 2013. "Race, Belonging and Participation in Religious Organizations." *Journal for the Scientific Study of Religion* 52(4):713–32.

Massey, Douglas S., and Nancy A. Denton. 1993. *American Apartheid: Segregation and the Making of the Underclass*. Cambridge, MA: Harvard University Press.

Matsuoka, Fumitaka, and Eleazar S. Fernandez. 2003. *Realizing the America of Our Hearts: Theological Voices of Asian Americans*. St. Louis, MO: Chalice Press.

Mayorga-Gallo, Sarah. 2014. *Behind the White Picket Fence: Power and Privilege in a Multiethnic Neighborhood*. Chapel Hill: University of North Carolina Press.

Mayorga-Gallo, Sarah. 2019. "The White-Centering Logic of Diversity Ideology." *American Behavioral Scientist* 63(13):1789–809.

Mays, Benjamin E., and Joseph W. Nicholson. 1933. *The Negro's Church*. New York: Institute of Social and Religious Research.

McDaniel, Eric L. 2003. "Black Clergy in the 2000 Elections." *Journal for the Scientific Study of Religion* 42(4):533–46.

McGlathery, Marla Frederick, and Traci Griffin. 2007. "Becoming Conservative, Becoming White? Black Evangelicals and the Para-Church Movement." In *This Side of Heaven: Race, Ethnicity, and Christian Faith*, edited by Robert J. Priest and Alvaro L. Nieves, 145–61. New York: Oxford University Press.

McIntosh, Peggy. 1989. "White Privilege: Unpacking the Invisible Knapsack." *Peace and Freedom*. Accessed December 22, 2020. https://psychology.umbc.edu/wp-content/uploads/sites/57/2016/10/White-Privilege_McIntosh-1989.pdf.

McPherson, J. Miller, and Lynn Smith-Lovin. 1987. "Homophily in Voluntary Organizations: Status Distance and the Composition of Face-to-Face Groups." *American Sociological Review* 52(3):370–79.

McPherson, J. Miller, Lynn Smith-Lovin, and James M. Cook. 2001. "Birds of a Feather: Homophily in Social Networks." *Annual Review of Sociology* 27:415–44.

McRoberts, Omar M. 1999. "Understanding the 'New' Black Pentecostal Activism: Lessons from Ecumenical Urban Ministries in Boston." *Sociology of Religion* 60(1):47–70.

McRoberts, Omar M. 2003. *Streets of Glory: Church and Community in a Black Urban Neighborhood*. Chicago: University of Chicago Press.

Mehta, Sharan Kaur, Rachel C. Schneider, and Elaine Howard Ecklund. 2022. "'God Sees No Color' So Why Should I? How White Christians Produce Divinized Colorblindness." *Sociological Inquiry* 92(2):623–46.

Mills, Charles W. 2003. "White Supremacy as Sociopolitical System: A Philosophical Perspective." In *White Out: The Continuing Significance of Racism*, edited by Ashley W. Doane and Eduardo Bonilla-Silva, 35–48. New York: Routledge.

Mills, Charles W. 2017. *Black Rights/White Wrongs: The Critique of Racial Liberalism*. New York: Oxford University Press.

Min, Pyong Gap, and Jung Ha Kim. 2002. *Religions in Asian America: Building Faith Communities*. Walnut Creek, CA: Altamira Press.

Mora, G. Cristina. 2014. "Cross-Field Effects and Ethnic Classification: The Institutionalization of Hispanic Panethnicity, 1965 to 1990." *American Sociological Review* 79(2):183–210.

Morris, Aldon. 1984. *The Origins of the Civil Rights Movement: Black Communities Organizing for Change*. New York: Free Press.

Mueller, Jennifer C. 2017. "Producing Colorblindness: Everyday Mechanisms of White Ignorance." *Social Problems* 64(2):219–38.

Mueller, Jennifer C. 2020. "Racial Ideology or Racial Ignorance? An Alternative Theory of Racial Cognition." *Sociological Theory* 38(2):142–69.

Mueller, Jennifer C., and Joe Feagin. 2014. "Pulling Back the 'Post-Racial' Curtain: Critical Pedagogical Lessons from Both Sides of the Desk." In *Teaching Race and Anti-Racism in Contemporary America: Adding Context to Colorblindness*, edited by Kristin Haltinner, 11–24. Dordrecht: Springer Netherlands.

Mueller, Jennifer C., and DyAnna K. Washington. 2022. "Anticipating White Futures: The Ends-Based Orientation of White Thinking." *Symbolic Interaction* 45(1):3–26.

Mullen, Brian, Rupert Brown, and Colleen Smith. 1992. "Ingroup Bias as a Function of Salience, Relevance, and Status: An Integration." *European Journal of Social Psychology* 22(2):103–22.

Muller, Christopher. 2012. "Northward Migration and the Rise of Racial Disparity in American Incarceration, 1880–1950." *American Journal of Sociology* 118(2):281–326.

Munn, Christopher W. 2018. "The One Friend Rule: Race and Social Capital in an Interracial Network." *Social Problems* 65(4):473–90.

Munn, Christopher W. 2019. "Finding a Seat at the Table: How Race Shapes Access to Social Capital." *Sociology of Religion* 80(4):435–55.

Nagel, Joane. 1994. "Constructing Ethnicity: Creating and Recreating Ethnic Identity and Culture." *Social Problems* 41(1):152–76.

Nelson, Timothy J. 1996. "Sacrifice of Praise: Emotion and Collective Participation in an African-American Worship Service." *Sociology of Religion* 57(4):379–96.

Okuwobi, Oneya Fennell. 2019. "'Everything That I've Done Has Always Been Multiethnic': Biographical Work among Leaders of Multiracial Churches." *Sociology of Religion* 80(4):478–95.

Okuwobi, Oneya, Deborwah Faulk, and Vincent J. Roscigno. 2021. "Diversity Displays and Organizational Messaging: The Case of Historically Black Colleges and Universities." *Sociology of Race and Ethnicity* 7(3):384–400.

Omi, Michael, and Howard Winant. 2014. *Racial Formation in the United States: From the 1960s to 1990s*. New York: Routledge.

Orfield, Gary, and Chungmei Lee. 2005. "Why Segregation Matters: Poverty and Educational Inequality." T*he Civil Rights Project, Harvard University*. Accessed February 18, 2022. https://files.eric.ed.gov/fulltext/ED489186.pdf.

Oyakawa, Michelle. 2019. "Racial Reconciliation as a Suppressive Frame in Evangelical Multiracial Churches." *Sociology of Religion* 80(4):496–517.

Padgett, John F., and Christopher K. Ansell. 1993. "Robust Action and the Rise of the Medici, 1400–1434." *American Journal of Sociology* 98(6):1259–319.

Park, Robert E. 1928. "Human Migration and the Marginal Man." *American Journal of Sociology* 33(6):881–93.

Pattillo-McCoy, Mary. 1998. "Church Culture as a Strategy of Action in the Black Community." *American Sociological Review* 63(6):767–84.

Perry, Samuel L. 2012. "Diversity, Donations, and Disadvantage: The Implications of Personal Fundraising for Racial Diversity in Evangelical Outreach Ministries." *Review of Religious Research* 54(4):397–418.

Phan, Peter C., and Jung Young Lee. 1999. *Journeys at the Margin: Toward an Autobiographical Theology in American-Asian Perspective*. Collegeville, MN: Order of St. Benedict, Inc.

Pierce, Andrew J. 2015. "Authentic Identities." *Social Theory and Practice* 41(3):435–57.

Pitt, Richard N. 2010. "Fear of a Black Pulpit? Real Racial Transcendence versus Cultural Assimilation in Multiracial Churches." *Journal for the Scientific Study of Religion* 49(2):218–23.

Pitt, Richard N. 2021. *Church Planters: Inside the World of Religion Entrepreneurs*. New York: Oxford University Press.

Portes, Alejandro, and Min Zhou. 1993. "The New Second Generation: Segmented Assimilation and Its Variants." *Annals of the American Academy of Political and Social Science* 530(1):74–96.

Posey-Maddox, Linn. 2014. *When Middle-Class Parents Choose Urban Schools: Class, Race, and the Challenge of Equity in Public Education*. Chicago: University of Chicago Press.

Priest, Kersten Bayt, and Korie L. Edwards. 2019. "Doing Identity: Power and the Reproduction of Collective Identity in Racially Diverse Congregations." *Sociology of Religion* 80(4):518–41.

Priest, Robert J., and Kersten Bayt Priest. 2007. "Divergent Worship Practices in the Sunday Morning Hour: Analysis of an 'Interracial' Church Merger." In *This Side of Heaven: Race, Ethnicity, and Christian Faith*, edited by Robert J. Priest and Alvaro L. Nieves, 275–91. New York: Oxford University Press.

Pugh, S. Douglas, Joerg Dietz, Arthur P. Brief, and Jack W. Wiley. 2008. "Looking Inside and Out." *Journal of Applied Psychology* 93(6):1422–28.

Putnam, Robert D. 2000. *Bowling Alone: The Collapse and Revival of American Community*. New York: Simon & Schuster.

Pyke, Karen D. 2010. "What Is Internalized Racial Oppression and Why Don't We Study It? Acknowledging Racism's Hidden Injuries." *Sociological Perspectives* 53(4):551–72.

Rabii, Watoii. 2021. "One of the Good Ones: Rhetorical Maneuvers of Whiteness." *Critical Sociology* 48(7–8):1275–91.

Ray, Victor. 2019. "A Theory of Racialized Organizations." *American Sociological Review* 84(1):26–53.

Ray, Victor Erik, Antonia Randolph, Megan Underhill, and David Luke. 2017. "Critical Race Theory, Afro-Pessimism, and Racial Progress Narratives." *Sociology of Race and Ethnicity* 3(2):147–58.

Reay, Diane, Sumi Hollingworth, Katya Williams, Gill Crozier, Fiona Jamieson, David James, and Phoebe Beedell. 2007. "'A Darker Shade of Pale?' Whiteness, the Middle Classes and Multi-Ethnic Inner City Schooling." *Sociology* 41(6):1041–60.

Redeemer City to City. 2023. "Timothy Keller." *Memoriam*. Accessed August 9, 2023. https://timothykeller.com/memoriam.

Reskin, Barbara. 2012. "The Race Discrimination System." *Annual Review of Sociology* 38:17–35.

Roberts, Rosemarie A., Lee A. Bell, and Brett Murphy. 2008. "Flipping the Script: Analyzing Youth Talk about Race and Racism." *Anthropology & Education Quarterly* 39(3):334–54.

Roediger, David R. 2007. *The Wages of Whiteness: Race and the Making of the American Working Class*. Rev. ed. London: Verso.

Rothenberg, Paula S. 2002. *White Privilege: Essential Readings on the Other Side of Racism*. New York: Worth.

Rumbaut, Ruben G. 2009. "Pigments of Our Imagination: On the Racialization and Racial Identities of 'Hispanics' and 'Latinos.'" In *How the U.S. Racializes Latinos: White Hegemony and Its Consequences*, edited by José A. Cobas, Jorge Duany, and Joe R. Feagin, 15–36. Boulder, CO: Paradigm.

Sewell, Stacy Kinlock. 2003. "'The Best Man for the Job': Corporate Responsibility and Racial Integration in the Workplace, 1945–1960." *Historian* 65(5):1125–46.

Singha, Surjit, and Sivarethinamohan R. 2021. "Diversity Climate of Organization: A Sustainable Way in India." *Ilkogretim Online* 20(4):2563–68.

Smith, Candis Watts, and Sarah Mayorga-Gallo. 2017. "The New Principle-Policy Gap: How Diversity Ideology Subverts Diversity Initiatives." *Sociological Perspectives* 60(5):889–911.

Smith, Ryan A. 2002. "Race, Gender, and Authority in the Workplace: Theory and Research." *Annual Review of Sociology* 28:509–42.

Southern Baptist Convention. 2019. "On Critical Race Theory And Intersectionality." *Resolution*. Accessed May 24, 2023. https://www.sbc.net/resource-library/resolutions/on-critical-race-theory-and-intersectionality/.

Stanczak, Gregory. 2006. "Strategic Ethnicity: The Construction of Multi-racial/Multi-ethnic Religious Community." *Ethnic and Racial Studies* 29(5):856–81.

Stonequist, Everett V. 1935. "The Problem of the Marginal Man." *American Journal of Sociology* 41(1):1–12.

Stovel, Katherine, and Lynette Shaw. 2012. "Brokerage." *Annual Review of Sociology* 38:139–58.

Sumagaysay, Levi. 2021. "Companies Declared 'Black Lives Matter' Last Year, and Now They're Being Asked to Prove It." MarketWatch. Accessed June 22, 2022. https://www.marketwatch.com/story/companies-declared-black-lives-matter-last-year-and-now-theyre-being-asked-to-prove-it-11614972986.

Takaki, Ronald T. 1998. *Strangers from a Different Shore: A History of Asian Americans*. Boston: Little, Brown.

Tatum, Beverly Daniel. 2003. *"Why Are All the Black Kids Sitting Together in the Cafeteria?" And Other Conversations about Race*. New York: Basic Books.
Taylor, Charles. 1991. *The Ethics of Authenticity*. Cambridge, MA: Harvard University Press.
Taylor, Verta, and Nancy Whittier. 1992. "Collective Identity in Social Communities: Lesbian Feminist Mobilization." In *Frontiers in Social Movement Theory*, edited by Alon D.Morris and Carol M. Mueller, 104–30. New Haven, CT: Yale University Press.
Thumma, Scott. 2021. "Twenty Years of Congregational Change: The 2020 Faith Communities Today Overview." The Faith Communities Today Partnership Project. Accessed October 22, 2022. https://faithcommunitiestoday.org/wp-content/uploads/2021/10/Faith-Communities-Today-2020-Summary-Report.pdf.
Tienda, Marta, and Norma Fuentes. 2014. "Hispanics in Metropolitan America: New Realities and Old Debates," *Annual Review of Sociology* 40:499–520.
Tisby, Jemar. 2020. *Color of Compromise: The Truth about the American Church's Complicity in Racism*. Grand Rapids, MI: Zondervan.
Tissot, Sylvie. 2015. *Good Neighbors: Gentrifying Diversity in Boston's South End*. Brooklyn, NY: Verso.
Tomaskovic-Devey, Donald, Catherine Zimmer, Kevin Stainback, Corre Robinson, Tiffany Taylor, and Tricia McTague. 2006. "Documenting Desegregation: Segregation in American Workplaces by Race, Ethnicity, and Sex, 1966–2003." *American Sociological Review* 71(4):565–88.
Tranby, Eric, and Douglas Hartmann. 2008. "Critical Whiteness Theories and the Evangelical 'Race Problem': Extending Emerson and Smith's 'Divided by Faith.'" *Journal for the Scientific Study of Religion* 47(3):341–59.
Trepagnier, Barbara. 2010. *Silent Racism: How Well-Meaning White People Perpetuate the Racial Divide*. 2nd ed. Boulder, CO: Paradigm.
Tuan, Mia. 1999. *Forever Foreigners or Honorary Whites? The Asian American Experience Today*. New Brunswick, NJ: Rutgers University Press.
Underhill, Megan R. 2019. "'Diversity Is Important to Me': White Parents and Exposure-to-Diversity Parenting Practices." *Sociology of Race and Ethnicity* 5(4):486–99.
U.S. Census Bureau. 1961. "1960 Census of the Population: Supplementary Reports: Race of the Population of the United States, by States: 1960." Accessed September 6, 2022. https://www.census.gov/library/publications/1961/dec/pc-s1-10.html#:~:text=The%20white%20population%20of%20the,and%2089.3%20percent%20in%201950.
United States Conference of Catholic Bishops. 2019. "V Encuentro National Statistical Summary." V Encuentro of Hispanic/Latino Ministry. Accessed September 6, 2022. (https://vencuentro.org/wp-content/uploads/2019/10/Regional-Stats-EnglishRD-1.pdf).
U.S. Department of Health & Human Services. 2019. "Profile: Hispanic/Latino Americans." U.S. Department of Health and Human Services Office of Minority Health. Accessed September 6, 2022. (https://minorityhealth.hhs.gov/omh/browse.aspx?lvl=3&lvlid=64#:~:text=According%20to%20the%202019%20U.S.,the%20largest%20at%2061.4%20percent).
Vespa, Jonathan, Lauren Medina, and David M. Armstrong. 2020. "Demographic Turning Points for the United States: Population Projections for 2020 to 2060." U.S. Census Bureau. Accessed September 6, 2022.
(https://www.census.gov/content/dam/Census/library/publications/2020/demo/p25-1144.pdf).

Wacquant, Loïc. 2014. "Class, Race and Hyperincarceration in Revanchist America." *Socialism and Democracy* 28(3):35–56.
Wadsworth, Nancy. 2010. "Bridging Racial Change: Political Orientations in the United States Evangelical Multiracial Church Movement." *Politics and Religion* 3(3):439–68.
Wadsworth, Tim, and Charles E. Kubrin. 2007. "Hispanic Suicide in U.S. Metropolitan Areas: Examining the Effects of Immigration, Assimilation, Affluence, and Disadvantage." *American Journal of Sociology* 112(6):1848–85.
Wang, Jia, and Gary N. McLean. 2016. "Promoting Diversity in India: Where Do We Go from Here?" *Advances in Developing Human Resources* 1(1):102–13.
Warikoo, Natasha. 2016. *The Diversity Bargain: And Other Dilemmas of Race, Admissions, and Meritocracy at Elite Universities*. Chicago: University of Chicago Press.
Warner, R. Stephen, and Judith G. Wittner. 1998. *Gatherings in Diaspora: Religious Communities and the New Immigration*. Philadelphia, PA: Temple University Press.
Wellman, David T. 1993. *Portraits of White Racism*. 2nd ed. Cambridge: Cambridge University Press.
Wilson, William Julius. 2012. *Truly Disadvantaged: The Inner City, the Underclass, and Public Policy*. Chicago: University of Chicago Press.
Women Business Collaborative. 2021. "Women CEOs in America: Changing the Face of Business." Accessed August 25, 2022. https://www.wbcollaborative.org/wp-content/uploads/2021/10/Women-CEOS-in-America_2021_1013-2.pdf.
Yancey, George. 2003. *Who Is White? Latinos, Asians, and the New Black/Nonblack Divide*. Boulder, CO: Lynne Rienner.
Yancey, George. 2007. *Interracial Contact and Social Change*. Boulder, CO: Lynne Rienner.
Yancey, George, and Michael Emerson. 2003. "Integrated Sundays: An Exploratory Study into the Formation of Multiracial Churches." *Sociological Focus* 36(2):111–27.
Yang, Fenggang. 1999. *Chinese Christians in America: Conversion, Assimilation, and Adhesive Identities*. University Park: Pennsylvania State University Press.
Yong, Amos. 2014. *The Future of Evangelical Theology: Soundings from the Asian American Diaspora*. Downers Grove, IL: InterVarsity Press.
Yu, Chai-Shin. 2004. *Korea and Christianity*. Freemont, CA: Asian Humanities Press.
Yukich, Grace, and Penny Edgell. 2020. *Religion Is Raced: Understanding American Religion in the Twenty-First Century*. New York: New York University Press.
Zhou, Min. 2004. "Are Asian Americans Becoming 'White?'" *Contexts* 3(1):29–37.

Index

For the benefit of digital users, indexed terms that span two pages (e.g., 52–53) may, on occasion, appear on only one of those pages.

Figures are indicated by *f* following the page number

advantages to leading as pastors of color
  Asian Americans and, 102–4, 108–10
  assimilation and, 98
  bilingual services and, 99–100, 110–11
  Black Americans and, 97–102, 106–8
  bonding capital and, 113
  broker role and, 113–14
  code-switching and, 97, 101–2
  estranged pioneers and, 115
  future potential of, 111–15
  Hispanic Americans and, 104–6, 110–11
  homophily and, 95
  keys to the imagined multiracial future and, 111–15
  main advantages of, 96
  multiculturalism and, 97–106
  outsiders within and, 111–12
  overview of, 95–96
  potential bridges and, 106–11
  racialized multicultural competency and, 112–13, 114
  racial segregation and, 95
  school of life and, 97, 99
  valued credential and, 97–106
  white pastors and, 96
African Americans. *See* Black/African Americans
alienation
  Asian Americans and, 43, 54–57
  Black Americans and, 43, 49–51
  estranged pioneers experiencing, 42–43, 49–62, 152
  Hispanic Americans and, 43, 57–62
ambiguity, 45–46, 48–49, 55–57

Angelo, Father, 69, 91, 103, 120
antiracism, 117–18, 143, 145–47
Asian Americans
  advantages to leading as pastors of color and, 102–4, 108–10
  alienation experience by, 43, 54–57
  ambiguity experienced by, 43, 45–46, 48–49, 55–57
  assimilation and, 66
  estranged pioneers and, 43, 45–46, 48–49, 54–57, 65–66
  harassment and violence toward, 1
  immigrant experience of, 45–46
  leadership and, 54–56, 77–78, 80–81, 109, 124
  marginal man theory and, 45–46
  model minority perception of, 56–57, 109, 163
  multiculturalism and, 102–4
  as potential bridges, 108–10
  racial segregation and, 6–7
  success of, 55–57
  white mainstream's relation to, 55–57
  work ethic associated with, 56–57
Asian church, 18, 26, 74–75, 122, 150–51
assimilation
  advantages to leading as pastors of color and, 98
  Asian Americans and, 66
  estranged pioneers and, 46–49
  Hispanic Americans and, 43, 46–49, 60–62
  managing challenges of leading multiracial churches and, 87–88
  whiteness and, 47, 56–57, 64, 66, 93–94

INDEX

authenticity
  Black Americans and, 44–45, 48–49, 51–53
  checkpoints for, 51–53
  cultural capital and, 44–45
  estranged pioneers and, 44–45, 48–49, 51–53
  external standard required for, 44
  journeys to leading multiracial churches and, 31
  legitimate culture and, 44–45
  racial authenticity, 44–45

background of leaders of multiracial churches. *See* journeys to leading multiracial churches
Barnes, Pastor, 50
Bell, Joyce, 9
bilingual services, 23, 99–100, 110–11
Black/African Americans
  advantages to leading as pastors of color and, 97–102, 106–8
  alienation and, 43, 49–51
  authenticity and, 44–45, 48–49, 51–53
  estranged pioneers and, 43–45, 48–53
  Hispanic Americans and, relations between, 4
  incarceration of, 6–7
  journeys to leading multiracial churches and, 18, 20, 24–26, 29, 30, 34–37
  leadership and, 45, 51, 53, 78, 86, 92, 122–23
  multiculturalism and, 97–102
  police killings of, 1, 141–42, 146–47
  as potential bridges, 106–8
  preaching style and, 124–25
  racial segregation and, 6–7, 33
  regional concentration of, 7–8
  sociopsychological damage of, 7
Black church
  estranged pioneers and, 50–51, 53
  as independent of white Western Christianity, 154
  journeys to leading multiracial churches and, 24–25, 34, 35–37
  leadership and, 78, 86, 92, 122–23
  managing challenges of leading multiracial churches and, 78–79, 80, 82–88
  preaching style and, 78, 125, 130

Black in White Space (Anderson), 165–66
Black Lives Matter, 2, 32–33, 79–80, 86, 141–42, 146–47
bonding capital, 113, 115
Bonilla-Silva, Eduardo, 8–9
Bourdieu, Pierre, 44–45
Bradley, Pastor, 35–37
bridge role of pastors of color, 106–11
broker role of pastors of color, 6–7, 113–14
Brown, Michael, 79–80
Burke, Meghan, 8–9
Burke, Pastor, 138

Carry, Father, 141–42, 144–45
Carter, Pastor, 25, 35
Categorically Unequal (Massey), 3–4
Catholic church
  diversity and, 10–11
  estranged pioneers and, 64–65
  journeys to leading multiracial churches and, 17, 19, 20
  multiracial churches and, 10–11
  social justice and, 17
  Vatican II, 17
  white pastors and, 148
challenges of leading multiracial churches. *See* managing challenges of leading multiracial churches
Chandler, Matt, 69
Charles, Pastor, 83, 92, 101, 107, 129–31
Cho, Pastor, 37–38
Christerson, Brad, 178n.1
Christianity. *See* Black church; Catholic church; Protestantism; white Western Christianity
churches. *See* Black church; Catholic church; home churches; multiracial churches; Protestantism
clergy. *See* pastors of color; white pastors
code-switching, 97, 101–2
Collins, Patricia Hill, 111–12
Committee for Racial Justice, 146
congregational denominations, 21–30, 40
conservative Protestantism, 3, 10, 13, 19, 21, 30, 36, 40
Critical Race Theory (CRT), 1

Daniels, Pastor, 136–37
Dillon, Pastor, 145–46
diversity. *See also* multiculturalism

antiracism and, 9
appearance of moral superiority gained through focus on, 8
benefits of, 7
blueprint for doing, 42
Catholic church and, 10–11
color-blindness and, 9
conservative responses to, 10
curious time for, 1–2
discourse of, 9
effectiveness of, 2
estranged pioneers and, 42, 58
happy talk version of, 9
history of, 7–8
importance of, 1–2, 7
inclusion and, 2
increase in, 10–11, 42
journeys to leading multiracial churches and, 23, 40–41
literature review of, 2
meaning of, 7–10
multiracial churches and, 8–9, 10, 12–13, 14, 153–55
overview of, 153–55
as product of white Western Christianity, 153–55
racial division, strife, and injustice and, 1–2
racial segregation and, 2, 7–9
regional variation in, 7–8
religious and educational emphasis on, 1–2
scholarship on, 2, 7–10
systemic dimensions of, 9
white comfort and, 8–9
white habitus and, 8–9
whiteness and, 8–9, 154–55
Dougherty, Kevin, 39
Driscoll, Mark, 69, 125
Du Bois, W. E. B., 7, 73
Durkheim, Émile, 49

Edwards, Korie, 8–9, 178n.1, 179n.36
Embrick, David, 8–9
Emerson, Michael, 10, 95, 178n.1
estranged pioneers. *See also* alienation
advantages to leading as pastors of color and, 115
alienation experienced by, 42–43, 49–62, 152

ambiguity and, 45–46, 48–49
Asian Americans and, 43, 45–46, 48–49, 54–57, 65–66
assimilation and, 46–49
authenticity and, 44–45, 48–49, 51–53
becoming comfortable with, 115
Black Americans and, 43–45, 48–53
Black church and, 50–51, 53
Catholic church and, 64–65
definition of, 5–6, 43
differences across groups of, 43
diversity and, 42, 58
emotional burden of, 65–66, 152
exclusion from white hegemonic structure of, 62–66
Hispanic Americans and, 43, 46–49, 57–62, 64
home churches and, 48–50, 51, 54–56, 66
leadership and, 53, 54, 56
mental health challenges of, 42–43
overview of, 42–43, 150–53
racialized multicultural competency and, 152
recruitment process and, 63–64
resource access and, 64
white comfort and, 62
white pastors contrasted with, 42–43
experience of immigrants. *See* immigrant experience

Feltner, Pastor, 139–40
female pastors, 71–73, 99, 121, 141
finding their own tribe, pastors of color as, 90–93
Finke, Roger, 39
free to be, white pastors as, 137–43
future potential of pastors of color leading multiracial churches, 111–15

Garces-Foley, Kathleen, 112–13
Garcia, Pastor, 104–6
Gates, Pastor, 107–8
George, Father, 20
get more, do more, 68–69
Goffman, Erving, 137
good white people, 143–45

Hart, Pastor, 97–98, 99
Hart-Cellar Immigration and Nationality Act (1965), 10–11

200   INDEX

Hartmann, Douglas, 9
Hispanic Americans
    advantages to leading as pastors of color and, 104–6, 110–11
    alienation and, 43, 57–62
    assimilation and, 43, 46–49, 60–62
    diversity of, 46
    estranged pioneers and, 43, 46–49, 57–62, 64
    immigrant experience and, 30–34
    incarceration of, 6–7
    journeys to leading multiracial churches and, 18, 20, 23, 29–34
    leadership and, 87–88
    managing challenges of leading multiracial churches and, 87–88
    multiculturalism and, 104–6
    otherness and, 60–62
    as potential bridges, 110–11
    racial identity of, 46–47, 61
    racial segregation and, 6–7, 33, 46–47
    regional concentration of, 7–8
    tensions from mixed paths of assimilation experienced by, 43, 46–49
    US census classification of, 46–47
Hispanic church, 18, 48, 150–51
home churches
    dissing of, 73–84
    estranged pioneers and, 48–50, 51, 54–56, 66
    journeys to leading multiracial churches and, 5–6, 25, 28, 36, 46
    leadership and, 54, 76–77, 92
    managing challenges of leading multiracial churches and, 73–94
    recharging from, 84–93
    shortcomings of, 81–83
homophily, 11–12, 14, 84, 95
Hong, Pastor, 63, 65–66, 89–90, 109
housing segregation. See racial segregation
Hurh, Pastor, 28, 88, 92

immigrant church, 18, 24, 26, 27–28, 34, 37–38, 54–55, 78, 80–81, 82, 87–88, 90, 91, 102, 125, 162
immigrant experience
    Asian Americans and, 45–46
    Hispanic Americans and, 30–34
    journeys to leading multiracial churches and, 30–34
    managing challenges of leading multiracial churches and, 87–88
internalized racism, 73–74

Jackson, Pastor, 70–71, 75–76, 78–80, 101
Jacobs, Pastor, 135
James, Father, 99, 120
Jeung, Russell, 112–13
Johns, Pastor, 69, 83–84, 128
Johnson, Pastor, 121–22, 123, 124–25
Jones, Pastor, 106–7, 119
journeys to leading multiracial churches
    Asian Americans and, 18, 20, 24–29, 30, 37–38
    authenticity and, 31
    bilingual services and, 23
    Black Americans and, 18, 20, 24–26, 29, 30, 34–37
    Black church and, 24–25, 34, 35–37
    calling to service experience and, 19
    Catholic church and, 17, 19, 20
    college campus ministries and, 35–36
    common "dots" in, 16–17, 38–41, 150–51
    common themes in, 18, 27–28, 150
    congregational denominations and, 21–30, 40
    conservative Protestantism and, 21–30
    discernment process and, 28
    diversity and, 23, 40–41
    growth of multiracial churches and, 16
    Hispanic Americans and, 18, 20, 23, 29–34
    home churches and, 25, 28, 36
    immigrant experience and, 30–34
    multiculturalism and, 22–23
    options and, 19–23
    overview of, 16–17, 38–41
    pastors of color and, 16, 17–18, 21–22, 24–30, 34–38
    polity of religious affiliation and, 18, 19–21, 40
    racial injustice as prompting for, 17–18
    racial segregation and, 16, 18, 33
    seminary education and, 39
    social justice and, 17

telling stories and, 17–18
unplanned nature of, 16
variation in, 17
white pastors and, 18, 20, 22–24
white Western Christianity and, 16, 18, 34–41
justice, social, 3–4, 17, 34, 147–48, 154–55, 161, 164–65

Kay, Pastor, 73, 100–1
Korean church, 56–57, 77, 81, 88, 124
Korver-Glenn, Elizabeth, 10

Latino Americans. *See* Hispanic Americans
leadership
    Asian Americans and, 54–56, 77–78, 80–81, 109, 122, 124
    Black Americans and, 45, 51, 53, 78, 86, 92, 122–23
    Black church and, 78, 86, 92, 122–23
    definition of success in, 157
    estranged pioneers and, 53, 54, 56
    examples of, 160–65
    4 Ps for, 155–65
    Hispanic Americans and, 87–88
    home churches and, 54, 76–77, 92
    managing challenges of leading multiracial churches and, 68–69, 70–72, 76–81, 86, 92
    multiracial churches and, 13, 155–65
    overview of, 13–15, 155–65
    passion and, 155–57
    people of color perceived as less capable for, 68–69
    potential and, 157–58
    practice and, 159–65
    pressure and, 158–59
    white pastors and, 116, 119–37, 139–40, 152–53
    why study leaders, 10–12
    women pastors and, 71
Lee, Pastor, 103–4, 109–10

MacArthur, John, 147
managing challenges of leading multiracial churches
    Asian Americans and, 87–89, 92
    assimilation and, 87–88
    background as source of shame and, 76–84
    Black Americans and, 83–87, 92–93
    Black church and, 78–79, 80, 82–88
    dissing of self and, 73–84
    finding their own tribe and, 90–93
    get more, do more and, 68–69
    home churches and, 73–94
    immigrant experience and, 87–88
    internalized racism and, 73–74
    issues of multiethnicity and, 92
    lack of support and, 83, 90
    leadership and, 68–69, 70–72, 76–81, 86, 92
    looking ahead and, 93–94
    overview of, 67–68, 93–94
    parking lot politics and, 81
    preaching style and music and, 78–81
    racial tax and, 68–73
    recharging from home and, 84–93
    sheep or goat and, 70–76
    shortcomings of ethnic church and, 81–83
    white pastors and, 78–81
    woman pastors and, 71–73
    women pastors of color and, 71–73
marginal man theory, 45–46
Marti, Gerardo, 179n.36
Martin, Pastor, 110
McIntosh, Peggy, 118, 143
methodology of present volume, 169–74
    our standpoints, 173–74
    Religious Leadership and Diversity Project, 169
    research design, 169–73, 170f
    research team, 173
Michaels, Pastor, 132–33
Mike, Father, 3–5, 13, 20
Mill, C. Wright, 15
Mills, Dennis, Pastor, 49–51, 62, 63, 71, 85
Montoya, Luis, Pastor, 29, 30–32, 60, 61–62, 104
Morales, Pastor, 111
multiculturalism. *See also* diversity; racialized multicultural competency

multiculturalism (cont.)
  advantages to leading as pastors of color and, 97–106
  Asian Americans and, 102–4
  Black Americans and, 97–102
  Hispanic Americans and, 104–6
  journeys to leading multiracial churches and, 22–23
  as response to racial division, 2
  valued credential of, 97–111
  white pastors and, 144–45
multiracial churches. *See also* journeys to leading multiracial churches; managing challenges of leading multiracial churches
  barriers to leaders of, 14
  bridges between congregants in, 4
  Catholic church and, 10–11
  challenges of, 3, 14
  civil rights legislation and, 2
  data for study on, 2–3
  definition of success at leading, 157
  demographic changes and, 10–11
  distinctive contributions of present volume on, 15
  diversity and, 8–9, 10, 12–13, 14, 153–55
  divinized colorblindness and, 10
  establishment of, 14
  examples of leadership for, 160–65
  growth of, 2, 6–7, 10–11
  head clergy of, 13–14
  homophily and, 11–12
  inequality downplayed in, 10
  leadership and, 13–14, 155–65
  overview of, 2–7, 15, 150–53, 165–67
  passion and, 155–57
  potential and, 157–58
  practice and, 159–65
  pressure and, 158–59
  as product of white Western Christianity, 153–54
  racialized multicultural competency and, 6, 7, 152, 158, 159, 161, 163, 164–65
  racial projects and, 153
  reconciliation frame and, 10
  scholarship on, 13–14
  social role of religion and, 12
  sociological imagination approach and, 15
  as still the exception, 2
  surface-level success of, 14
  total share of, 2
  white comfort and, 8–9, 153–54
  white habitus and, 8–9
  white hegemony and, 11–12
  whiteness and, 153–55, 165–67
  white pastors and, 3–5, 13
  white privilege and, 10
  why study leaders of, 10–12
multiracialism, 5, 165–66

Nagel, Joane, 179n.13
New Jim Crow, The (Alexander), 3–4, 146–47
"99 Problems" (Jay-Z), 116

Okuwobi, Oneya, 17–18, 19
Omi, Michael, 153
overviews
  advantages to leading as pastors of color, 95–96
  diversity, 153–55
  estranged pioneers, 42–43, 150–53
  journeys to leading multiracial churches, 16–17, 38–41
  leadership, 13–14, 155–65
  managing challenges of leading multiracial churches, 67–68, 93–94
  multiracial churches, 2–7, 15, 150–53, 165–67
  white pastors, 116–17

Park, Pastor, 27–28, 74–76, 77–78
Park, Robert E., 45
parking lot politics, 81
pastors, white. *See* white pastors
pastors of color. *See also* advantages to leading as pastors of color; Asian Americans; Black/African Americans; estranged pioneers; Hispanic Americans; journeys to leading multiracial churches; managing challenges of leading multiracial churches

challenges for, 3, 5
demographics of US and, 6–7
emphasis on, 5
exposure to white Anglo Western Christianity of, 16
increase in, 2, 5
as indispensable brokers, 6–7
inequality and, 6–7
journeys to leading multiracial churches and, 16, 17–18, 21–22, 24–30, 34–38
racial segregation and, 6–7
stress and strain associated with, 5
white pastors contrasted with, 5
why study, 10–12
woman pastors of color, 71–73, 99, 121
Perry, Pastor, 122–23, 125
Pierce, Andrew, 44
pioneers. *See* estranged pioneers
Pitt, Richard, 21–22, 24–25, 40–41
polity of religious affiliation, 18, 19–21, 40
Portes, Alejandro, 31
potential bridges built by pastors of color, 106–11
practical concerns. *See* managing challenges of leading multiracial churches
preaching styles, 77–81, 124–25, 130
privilege. *See* white privilege
Protestantism
  conservative Protestantism, 3, 10, 13, 19, 21–30, 36, 40
  mainline Protestantism, 3, 10–11, 13, 36–38

race and ethnicity. *See* Asian Americans; Black/African Americans; Hispanic Americans; white pastors
racialized multicultural competency
  advantages to leading as pastors of color and, 6, 7, 112–13, 114
  broker role and, 7
  definition of, 6
  multiracial churches and, 6, 7, 152, 158, 159, 161, 163, 164–65
  white pastors and, 116, 117, 119, 131–32
racial segregation
  advantages to leading as pastors of color and, 95

Asian Americans and, 6–7
Black Americans and, 6–7, 33
civil rights movement against, 2
diversity reinforcing, 2, 7–9
Hispanic Americans and, 6–7, 33, 46–47
Jim Crow south and, 7–8, 33
journeys to leading multiracial churches and, 16, 18, 33
pastors of color and, 6–7
persistence of, 6–7
sociopsychological damage caused by, 7
racial tax, 68–73
racism, 1, 116–17, 119, 143, 145–49
religion. *See* Catholic church; multiracial churches; Protestantism
rewards of leading as pastors of color. *See* advantages to leading as pastors of color
Roberts, Pastor, 117–18, 120, 146–47
Rodriguez, Ricardo, 32–34, 64–65
Ron, Pastor, 25–26
Russo, Father, 128–29

Santiago, Manuel, Pastor, 57–60, 61, 63
school of life, 97, 99
segregation. *See* racial segregation
Shaw, Lynette, 114
sheep or goat, 70–76
Smith, Christian, 10, 95
social justice, 3–4, 17, 34, 147–48, 154–55, 161, 164–65
Song, John, Pastor, 54–57, 80–82, 102–3, 124
Souls of Black Folks, The (Du Bois), 73
Southern Baptist Convention, 1
Spirit Moves West (Kim), 68–69
Stovel, Katherine, 114
systemic racism, 1, 116–17, 119, 143, 145–49

Taylor, Charles, 44
Taylor, Pastor, 71–72, 99
telling stories, 17–18
tensions from mixed paths of assimilation, 43, 46–49

white comfort, 8–9, 62, 153–54
white habitus, 8–9

white hegemony, 8–9, 11–12, 153, 159
white space, 86, 107, 165–66
whiteness
  assimilation and, 47, 56–57, 64, 66, 93–94
  diversity and, 8–9, 154–55
  good white people and, 143–45
  multiracial churches and, 153–55, 165–67
  privileging of, 5
  systemic nature of, 9
white pastors
  accusations of racism against, 145
  advantages to leading as pastors of color and, 96
  antiracism and, 145–47
  bilingual services and, 135–36
  Black Lives Matter and, 141–42
  Catholic church and, 148
  challenges for, 3–5, 22, 116
  estranged pioneers contrasted with, 42–43
  free to be and, 137–43
  good white people and, 143–45
  journeys to leading multiracial churches and, 18, 20, 22–24
  leadership and, 116, 119–37, 139–40, 152–53
  limited perspective of, 138–39
  managing challenges of leading multiracial churches and, 78–81
  as most normative leaders, 121–25
  as most preferred leaders, 119–21
  as most resourced leaders, 131–37
  as most respected leaders, 125–31
  multiculturalism and, 144–45
  overview of, 3–5, 13, 116–17
  pastors of colors relied on as bridges for, 134–36
  police killings and, 141–42
  preaching style and, 124–25
  privilege of, 117–18
  racialized multicultural competency and, 116, 117, 119, 131–32
  racism and, 116–17, 119, 143, 145–49
  self-enhanced racial identity and, 143–45
  unraveling privilege of, 119–31
  what to do with privilege of, 145–49
  "white is right" associated with, 128
  witch hunt against liberal "evangelicals" and, 147
  "woke" white pastors, 144–45
  women and, 121, 126–27, 141
white privilege
  definition of, 117
  as never-ending fountain, 143
  unraveling of, 119–31
  what to do with, 145–49
  of white pastors, 117–18
white supremacy, 1, 116, 118, 148–49, 152–53, 157, 159, 161, 165–67
white Western Christianity, 16, 18, 34–41, 151, 153–55, 156–57, 158, 159, 161, 165–66
Williams, Pastor, 133
Wilson, Pastor, 37
Winant, Howard, 153
woman pastors, 71–73, 99, 121, 141

Zhou, Min, 31